Guillermo Bartelt / Bärbel Treichel (eds.)
Don Decker's Apache Odyssey

Guillermo Bartelt/Bärbel Treichel (eds.)

Don Decker's Apache Odyssey

Approaches to Autobiography, Narrative, and the Developing Self

Frank & Timme

Verlag für wissenschaftliche Literatur

Cover: *Apache Sunrise Ceremony,* Don Decker

ISBN 978-3-86596-253-9

© Frank & Timme GmbH Verlag für wissenschaftliche Literatur
Berlin 2012. Alle Rechte vorbehalten.

Das Werk einschließlich aller Teile ist urheberrechtlich geschützt.
Jede Verwertung außerhalb der engen Grenzen des Urheberrechtsgesetzes ist ohne Zustimmung des Verlags unzulässig und strafbar.
Das gilt insbesondere für Vervielfältigungen, Übersetzungen,
Mikroverfilmungen und die Einspeicherung und Verarbeitung in
elektronischen Systemen.

Herstellung durch das atelier eilenberger, Taucha bei Leipzig.
Printed in Germany.
Gedruckt auf säurefreiem, alterungsbeständigem Papier.

www.frank-timme.de

Contents

GUILLERMO BARTELT
Foreword 7

DON DECKER
APACHE ODYSSEY A Modern Journey of an Apache 11

GUILLERMO BARTELT
Negotiating the Traditional and Modern Self 101

ERIKA GERICKE
Discourses as Identities: Applying Critical Discourse Analysis 123

BÄRBEL TREICHEL
Identity Work, Narrative Analysis, and Biographical Processes. A
Sociolinguistic Approach to Identity Constructions in an Apache
Autobiography 133

FRITZ SCHÜTZE
Biographical Process Structures and Biographical Work in a Life of
Cultural Marginality and Hybridity: Don Decker's Autobiographical
Account 159

GUILLERMO BARTELT

Foreword

Meeting Don Decker for the first time in the fall of 1974, during a conference for college counselors in the beautiful northern Arizona mountain community of Prescott, remains one of the more memorable events of my life. At our respective institutions, Eastern Arizona College in Thatcher and Yavapai College in Prescott, both of which have always served large numbers of Native students, we held the position of "Indian Counselor". As a courtesy to his counterpart at the Prescott campus, Don dropped by my office, introducing himself with such a vigorous handshake and verbal enthusiasm that he instantly deflated any of my assumptions of encountering the usual Indian reserve. Many indigenous people of the Southwest do, in fact, display what appears to be a kind of reticent greeting behavior when approaching strangers, which is, unfortunately, often misinterpreted by Anglos as a lack of personal warmth or, worse yet, as a passive-aggressive posture. Ironically, the light handclasp in conjunction with the avoidance of a direct eye gaze represent a Native gestural convention expressing a sentiment of politeness. This communicative strategy appeals to a sensibility of caution and respect for the dignity and integrity of the interlocutor, who may not necessarily be comfortable with as quick of an intrusion into his personal space as is tolerated, or, perhaps, even encouraged, by mainstream American culture. The fact that Don did not approach me in the expected Indian mode of restrained interaction was a tip-off for me that he had accommodated a highly syncretistic way of dealing with the world, a result, no doubt, of the bi-cultural "odyssey" remembered in his autobiography. We became friends immediately, and over the years he has not only been a patient informant for my scholarly forays into Apache language and culture but also a loyal fictive kinsman to my immediate family. Thus it has indeed been an honor and a privilege for me to be involved in this project, which is solely dedicated to the narrative analysis of his life story.

Interpretive approaches to the narrative analysis of life histories, whether spoken or written, have clearly revealed that autobiographical recollections are largely guided by the reconstruction of those past experiences. What the narrator tends to engage in when attempting to create a coherent sequence of significant life events is a selective memory process which focuses on the presentation of the "self" acceptable to others and, perhaps, more importantly, to oneself. This process becomes especially crucial in dealing with painful or disturbing events which have left an indelible mark on one's mental or physical composition. The protagonist must somehow rationalize those hostile environments to himself as having been ultimately beneficial in some way. In other words, retrospectively, the building of one's character necessarily involves a certain amount of requisite suffering in order to reach one's present level of maturity. Selective experiences are, therefore, not only considered valuable but also self-validating.

Don's recollections also involve a number of painful and disturbing events whose reconstruction reflects not only their historical contextualizing but also their rationalization to himself and to others. In this way, he comes to terms with past life-threatening situations, enabling him to pave his way for healing. By extension, he implicitly offers the same rationalizations to his home reservation community of San Carlos, Arizona, where others have also been haunted by the debilitating effects of violence, family dysfunction, and alcoholism. In a sense, the empowering act of writing his autobiography has made available a prescription for healing not only for himself but also for his entire community.

If there are recollections of pain, there are also recollections of triumph. In his contemplation of the seemingly random phenomenon of serendipity, whose logical justification can be just as perplexing as that of misfortune, Don infers the intervention by a supernatural agency. For example, the meeting of his adoptive Anglo parents, who offered him a new life in the Midwest, is viewed as the cornerstone of a grand design guided by a higher power. This acknowledged religious faith, Don derives from fundamentalist Christian and traditional Apache beliefs, whose seemingly conflicting moral codes he perceives, ironically enough, as complementary.

As a collaborator, I have resisted excessive intrusion into Don's particular sense of written English, which, without a doubt, pushes the boundaries of standard conventions but which also reveals a marvelously genuine voice, especially in its impromptu humor reflective of an extemporaneous mode. Respectfully left alone and spared the obstructions of heavy-handed editing, his narrative provides, I believe, unique insights into the American Indian condition, and I felt that his voice needed to be heard. Thus I contacted Bärbel

Treichel, a sociolinguist at the University of Magdeburg, who, for a number of years, has been collaborating with the sociologist Fritz Schütze on interpretive approaches to autobiographical narratives, with a particular focus on identity work. To my delight, my Magdeburger colleague was sufficiently impressed with the potentials of Don's manuscript to organize a symposium at the 2008 AILA World Congress of Applied Linguistics, held that year on the attractive campus of the University of Essen, for further exploration of the relevant narrative issues this particular autobiography raises. The present volume, to which the title of the symposium has been extended, captures the revised versions of some of those discussions.

Don now lives on the Yavapai Apache Reservation in Camp Verde, Arizona, where his ancestors in 1875 had to endure the humiliation and physical suffering of being forced to walk 180 miles under military escort to the infamous San Carlos Agency, a much detested facility set up specifically for the detention and surveillance of all Arizona Apaches and their close allies, the Yavapai. At the dawn of the twentieth century, some Yavapai and Apache families began to drift back to small parcels of land still unoccupied by Anglos in the Verde Valley, and in time they managed to re-establish their separate status as a federally recognized tribe. Others, such as Don's extended family, stayed behind in San Carlos but periodically were offered the option of rejoining their kinsmen in Camp Verde. As a mature adult, Don was among the last individuals who were invited to transfer their tribal enrollment from San Carlos to Camp Verde. By accepting the call, he completed not only his own "odyssey" but also, in a spiritual sense, he took part in the historic peregrination of his people.

Don Decker

APACHE ODYSSEY
A Modern Journey of an Apache

Introduction

The pinpointing of specific people by name on the San Carlos Apache Reservation had to be done in this book. Without them, the writing of this book would have been impossible. I have taken the liberty to take this chance that my people will take this writing in stride and give me some latitude in bringing about a good story.

This book is dedicated to the people of the San Carlos Apache Nation, who have persevered at all possible odds!

Don (Denny) Decker, March, 1997
Flagstaff, Arizona

SPECIAL DEDICATION TO THE LATE ABRAHAM LOGAN, HUSBAND OF MY AUNT CLEORA RANDALL-LOGAN OF SAN CARLOS. ABRAHAM, TRADITIONAL DOCTOR AND SPIRITUAL COUNSELOR WHO THROUGH *USEN* OR *GOD*, MADE IT POSSIBLE FOR ALL APACHES TO SURVIVE.

AND ... TO MY CHILDREN, GERON, CHARLES, JENNIFER AND HER SONS, TAYLOR AND MIKAL; AND TO MY FORMER WIFE, CHRISTY BOWER, FOR CONTINUING AN APACHE LINEAGE INTO THE 21ST CENTURY.

In the northeastern edge of the great Arizona Sonoran desert lies the San Carlos Apache Indian Reservation, 130 miles east of Phoenix. Outsiders might even consider Apache country as forbidden land where the summer temperatures reach above 113 degrees. It is a place where the western diamond rattlesnake makes his home and the evening doves sing their songs.

San Carlos has a distinguished history, which has included a place for some of the greatest Apache leaders such as Geronimo, Cochise and individuals such as the late Clarence Wesley, a noted Apache tribal chairman who started the National Congress of American Indians. The Apaches were the last Indian nations to confront the U.S. Calvary face to face as the boundaries were drawn up for the United States and Mexico. To this day, the Apaches have never surrendered to the U.S. government even though some books claim of a surrender. Warfare against the Apaches was intense and their removal from the geographical areas of southeastern Arizona and western New Mexico was a top priority for the government in the mid-1800s. The government's relationship with the Apaches has been a sad history and great many books have documented this relationship.

Geronimo was imprisoned in old San Carlos at the bottom of what is now known as Coolidge Lake. (In the summer of 1997, Coolidge Dam met its fate by dropping its water level, exposing the old buildings of old San Carlos, which were buried by water in 1912 when Coolidge Dam was built.) Other Apaches were rounded up from the Verde Valley in northern Arizona and brought to San Carlos. The long march decimated many and military records mention Apaches being killed in the Verde Valley as if they had been prairie dogs. The roundup of the Apaches was a futile attempt by the government to bring them to their knees and wipe out a culture that stood in the way of the western expansion of America. Apaches were regarded as a source of problems, and history books still tell of their bloodshed. But they were never annihilated. After the late 1800s, many of the imprisoned Apaches moved back to their traditional lands in the Verde Valley, the White Mountains of northeastern Arizona, and central New Mexico at present day Mescalero.

Old San Carlos was relocated due to the building of the Coolidge Dam in the early 1900s. Seventeen miles north of the old San Carlos, present day San Carlos is accentuated with the typical Arizona Sahuaro cactus, century plants, mesquite trees, yucca plants, cholle cactus, wild berries and sheets of tempered volcanic rock. In the high country, pine trees and clear running streams and rivers provide a backdrop for Apache country.

Originally, new San Carlos was named 'Rice' but the name was never accepted and the old name 'San Carlos' stuck with the new settlement. In Spanish, San Carlos means 'St. Charles', and the community might have been named after this Catholic saint. No one knows for sure to this day.

Today, San Carlos is home for 12,000 Apaches with the remainder relocated 60 miles north in the White Mountains. Geronimo's relatives live in the Ft. Sill, Oklahoma area. Each early fall, around September, Apaches from across the country travel to a huge celebration in Ft. Sill, Oklahoma.

Growing up on the San Carlos Apache Reservation was definitely an experience. No Hollywood movie script writer could interpret the sights, sounds and smells of Apache land. Standing or lying down inside of a traditional willow arbor brings back many memories for me.

These brush arbors, called wickiups, are made from the various assorted trees which line the San Carlos river. In the 40s and 50s, San Carlos was still only forty five years old and I can recall the primitiveness of this Apache world as it presented itself during my childhood years. I was raised by my grandparents Johnson and Ivy Irving. My grandfather, Johnson, was a Camp Verde Apache who had been born along the Verde Valley river in northern Arizona. In the early 40s, he migrated to eastern Arizona after having spent many of his formative years building all of the roadways between Wickenburg, Prescott, Payson, Jerome to Ashfork. These old roads, which are now abandoned in favor of the new interstate and state highways, are to his credit. Johnson was the son of Henry Irving, a scout for the U.S. Army in the Verde Valley during the mid-1800s. My grandfather was born in the 1890s, which would have made him around 70 years old when he died in 1961. His stomping grounds were Payson, Camp Verde, Sunflower, Gisela, Tonto Basin, Prescott, Seligman and Jerome. It was at one of these road camps that he assisted with the birth of my mother, Grace or 'Es'sahn'choo (Big Woman) as she was to become known. Grandfather, finding it too hard to care for all his children, placed three sons and two daughters at the government boarding school known as Phoenix Indian School in the late 30s and early 40s. On July 26, 1944, I was born at the Phoenix Indian Hospital not far from the school my mother attended. She was only 15 years old at the time. Shortly after my birth, I was placed in the care of a German family for two years in Phoenix. My mother was too young to care for me and she was still in school at the time. My grandparents then took custody of me. My late grandmother, Ivy, told me that I was standing in front of a doughnut shop in Phoenix with my German teenaged babysitter. I supposedly cried all the way back to Globe, Arizona when my grandparents came to take me. At that time, my grandfather was still working in the copper mines in Miami, where his labor supported the efforts of World War II. It was my grandfather's mined copper which supplied the metal tips for bullets fired in Germany and the South Pacific. Sometime around 1948, we moved to the San Carlos Apache Reservation 21 miles east of Globe.

The primitiveness of Apache land was a continuation of our old ways. The Apache world was laden with the mysteries of the spirit world, which was held in place by the ancient prayers and the cattail pollen from the San Carlos River's edge and the eagle plumes which provided the medium for the Apache medicine men to say their prayers. Some of the well-known medicine men and singers like the late Charlie Hoffman, Philip Cassadore, Abraham Logan and Murphy Cassa kept our Apache culture on a continuum. From early spring until late fall, the sacred ceremonies of the Changing Woman or Na'I'ase allowed the Apache songs to be sung and the prayers solidified the unity of the Apache world. To this day, the songs are still there and are being carried through by the new Apache medicine men who have learned the prayers. The Changing Woman is one of the few last sacred ceremonies which is still being carried on in San Carlos today. The late Abraham Logan, who went to the spirit world in late fall of 1997, kept the Apache prayers and maintained the Holy Grounds of San Carlos. Logan took care of the last of the sacred Apache hoops and wooden crosses which have the prayers of the Apache painted on them. Through the years as a medicine man, Abraham has carried the burdens of his people.

Apaches were a nomadic people who were hunters and gatherers. Modern Apaches have become less nomadic and now live in cull-de-sacs and modern apartments and low-rent housing areas. Moving in closer together negated the nomadic lifestyle of the primitive Apache world. Quickly, Apaches in the 40s became dependent on the government through welfare. The rapid change in the living arrangements created hardships and hostility among tribal members in the 50s. One has to remember that there were no large communities in Apache land prior to the arrival of the Europeans. It was only at the instance of the white world that fences took hold and territorial boundaries became known. Soon, the value system changed and Apaches began to acquire large herds of cattle on the reservation. In the old Apache society, only 15–20 people lived or traveled together and were always on the move for protection from other warring tribes and soldiers. Home was anywhere in the deep canyons of the Dragoons in southern Arizona to the high mountains of eastern Arizona or western New Mexico. These were the places that provided plenty of deer, acorns, wild berries and run-offs from the mountain snow. The modern Apache became an enigma due to the confines of the reservation. However, to this day, there is a strong social system which binds the San Carlos Apaches together. It is the geography of the Apache world which has sustained the modern Apache world as well.

I was raised by my grandparents. My grandmother, Ivy Randall-Irving, who was really my step-grandmother, cared for me as well as my grandfather. There were others in my family like Cleora Randall-Logan who cared for me when I was a mere baby. I learned some of the Apache songs from my step-uncle, Abraham, husband of Cleora. As I got older, I took matters into my own hands by improvising bailing wire for fish-hooks, which caught some of the biggest catfish in the history of San Carlos and chasing desert rats at night under the glaring lights of pickup trucks. I became independent at an early age.

In San Carlos, there was a strong social control and there wasn't much of a chance to deviate from the norm. Sure, you could sneak in a Lucky Strike or slug down a cold beer, but the overall penalties outweighed the persistence in bad behavior. My grandparents were pretty strict. The fact that my grandmother was a Bible thumper must have had something to do with it. Old Apache adults were pretty adamant about how one behaved in most situations. Doing something unacceptable was kept in check by these old folks. Screw up once and you could rest assured that some adult would pull on your ears or give you a stare and embarrass the holy hell out of you.

In 1952 I met my great-grandmother in Grover Canyon near Miami, Arizona. Some say she was 117 years old. This would mean that I had the opportunity to meet someone who was around during the administration of Abraham Lincoln. I can still recall the peculiar smell she carried with her during that time. I was told that she was from Camp Verde, Arizona. She stayed for a while and during this time, she usually talked to herself and hallucinated continually. One morning I discovered several policemen on our front steps in Grover Canyon. Apparently, my great-grandmother has misplaced a large roll of cash and someone had found the money. This was a big event for me and the neighborhood. Of course, my grandmother just sat there completely oblivious to what had happened.

Being an Apache meant you had to live by the precepts of those who had come along earlier on the trail. I don't believe there was any question what one had to do to assure the survival of a family member. No one would stop to question your motives for your actions. These actions were instantaneous and your behaviors didn't require much 'backup documentation' government people would have you believe today. Supporting the survival of your immediate family meant making sure they had enough to eat on the table (or on the ground if you were a traditional Apache) and waking up to a pleasant next day. It was an unconscious behavior which characterized the true Apache of the 40s and 50s. In some ways, growing up as an Apache wasn't any different from anyone else's upbringing. However, one difference was understanding your language, your songs, and prayers. Sometime in 1954, we moved back to the reservation right after my grandfather was laid off from the copper mines in nearby Miami, Arizona. Grandfather lost an eye due to an acid spill at the plant where he worked. There were no legal settlements with this incident.

The Apache blood line reaches considerable distances across the Apacheria. Sometimes, bloodlines are undetectable until someone reminds you of how you are related to one another. On my step-grandmother's side there were the Martins, Randalls, Talgos and the Bonds, and on my grandfather's side there were the Evans, the Campbells, Irvings, Bleechers and so forth. There wasn't a day that would go by without some old folk telling you how you were related to all the people in the Apache world. What made it difficult was if you fell in love with someone within your own circle of relations, such as a distant cousin who was considered still too close. Apaches knew about genetics and social control, and having an affair with a close or distant cousin was and is still considered a taboo in Apache country. Even some of the hardcore traditionalists of today still insist on honoring these traditions through the clans. As one can see, being related by a small blood quantum was and is an essential aspect of the social organization of the Apache world today. I often thought that this biological revelation was an alien idea to many Apache people, but I grew to know the truth. One of the very first questions asked when meeting new friends in Apache is, "Who are you related to?". This question usually saves a lot of problems later on. It is as if the right answer makes it safe to pursue a member of the opposite sex who is not related to you. Apaches, to this day, have a lot of interdependence among the clans for survival. Nobody likes a loner and Apaches who rely on this strong kinship system make it a point to make sure that you are cared for. At gatherings, people are introduced and relationships are identified quickly. These constant reminders and reassurances let us know that we live as one—in unity.

Social class awareness was operating in San Carlos. You could tell who had some or all of the cattle. Some of the Apaches had good jobs, such as working for the government or in the mines. People who had large herds of cattle usually were held in high esteem by the people in the community. If there was death, these large cattle owners were usually asked to donate a cow for feeding of the masses. Even at public events, these people donated to feeding the people at these functions. In this aspect, social status was established. Obviously, if you didn't have any cattle, you couldn't live in a high profile status in the Apache world. I came from a very poor family. Other people who usually got respect were the spiritual leaders. Gaining respect was contingent upon how you cared for people and supported those less fortunate than you.

Growing up in poverty in San Carlos in my formative years had its benefits in later years. I can still appreciate the value of money today and my values haven't changed since leaving the reservation. Somehow, our family managed to get by even with the meager offerings of Social Security and government commodity food (Please pass the canned ham). Relatives, friends and church people would drop by occasionally to give us food. These donations consisted of potatoes, sugar and coffee. Grandfather Irving could make excellent corn bread with the government commodities. For the rest, Charlie Higgins' Trading Post provided the pork chops and beef dumplings known as 'Tamale'choo' or big tamale, which was a popular item in traditional Apache cooking. Sprinkled in the dumplings packed with dried meat and soup were acorns from the high mountains of Ash Creek. When someone butchered a cow, the word would spread very quickly and if you were lucky, you would receive some of the best parts of the cow, such as the intestines and hooves for cooking. I recall old Apache ladies boiling cow hooves for additional flavoring in soups. If you've ever seen cow hooves sticking out of a metal cooking can on an open fire, you're in for a real treat. Intestines and stomachs of cows were also favorites of reservation cooks. One part I didn't mind was the portion of the cow's stomach called the "bible". In fact, if you flipped through this piece of a cow's tummy, you could easily see the pages of the Big Book. With a slight dash of salt, the bible became a delicacy for me.

Typical day at home on the rez.

One interesting event that occurred each year on the reservation was the annual cattle sale by the tribal cattle ranches. Near what used to be my former Bureau of Indian Affairs school grounds in San Carlos was a huge barn complex that served as temporary holding pens for hundreds of cattle that were brought in from the cattle cooperatives in the high country. This cattle sale was a big-to-do for the social scene as well as the business world of the Apaches. The Apache cooks working for the ranches cooked up a first-class meal which usually consisted of Dutch oven biscuits, roast beef, salads and stew. You name it, it was usually all there for the local folks, who came out by the hundreds, to eat. Of course, it was free as well. Promptly, at noon, you could find many people lined up for the big feed. The amusing part of this noon meal was when some of the old ladies would bring their large empty coffee cans with makeshift handles made from bailing wire from home to be used as food containers. I recall seeing these old ladies throwing in a piece of cake, a dash of gravy, some potatoes, some beans, sugar and salt and bread—all into the coffee can. Wherever there was food in San Carlos, you could always count on seeing lots of folks there.

A typical Apache diet consisted mainly of acorns, potatoes, beef jerky, beans, flour, sugar and coffee. For many years, grandfather did all the cooking in our home except for times when we had company or when I had to crack open one of the cans of pork and beans. One of grandpa's favorite small breads was called "Squaw bread". With a little bit of baking powder, water, salt and flour, he could bake some bread that could astound any bread lover today. Much of the recipe came from grandpa's northern Arizona road camps experiences in his formative years as a road worker. Each evening when I'd come home from school, he always had a skillet full of potatoes, pork and beans ready. In the early mornings somewhere around 4:30 he would also build a nice warm fire in the cast iron stove that we used for cooking and heating the wooden shack that we lived in for years.

When a small band of Camp Verde Apaches moved to upper San Carlos on present day Gilson Wash, most of the other Apache called us 'Camboodie' which approximates 'Camp Verde'. I called myself 'Camboodie' because my grandfather was originally from Camp Verde, Arizona. When we moved to Camboodie, grandpa bought a one room frame house that he dragged with a tractor 3 miles away. It was a one room shack and by today's standards, this structure would be considered third-world substandard housing. It is hard to comprehend that my living space was limited to an area roughly equal to 114 square feet of living space for almost fourteen years of my life. This would be comparable to a room in a modern hospital. On the floor of this house you could see the tiny nail holes from the corrugated metal roof casting the sun's image on the wooden floor. There were two-sided windows, one which had one window pane and the other had wooden boards that were nailed together and covered with canvas and tar paper. In hindsight, this would be considered a not-so-attractive house. In the summer, the window would be propped open with a stick. As a young boy, I remember spending lots of time preparing this shed for living quarters for us in the early 50s. As I got older, the house became somewhat of an embarrassment for me. When I would go and catch the school bus, I usually made it a habit to walk a considerable distance from the house just so no one would know that I lived in that one particular house. Of course, everyone knew. The reason why I felt this way about my house was because my personal values were slowly changing as I was growing older. I always wanted a nice home but I never could have one. Some of the children I grew up with had good homes. To this day, I wondered what other Apache children thought of that old wooden shack that I grew up in. When I look back to that house and compare it with today's lumber market prices, I would estimate that the total value of the lumber in the house was about $150. I remember when grandpa bought the first roll of tar papers from the tribal store, we papered the house with it. It was a major event. Grandpa was the all-around handyman. One of the things I clearly remember today is, when he told me not to chop mesquite wood next to ironwood. Mesquite is one of the hardest woods to be found in the southwest. To chop this wood required constant sharpening of the ax. One of the hazards of chopping wood was the sudden breaking of chopped pieces. Since grandfather had one eye, he was really afraid that I was going to lose an eye to wood chopping. Every chance I got for chopping wood, I would do it because I didn't want my grandfather to lose his other eye.

Grandpa planted an acre of corn each year for about five years when we lived in Gilson Wash across from the late Johnny Patten's home. Irrigating the fields required the coordination of several people who also farmed along the irrigation ditch. On several occasions, grandfather would walk up the ditch to find out that someone had cut off his water supply to his on-going irrigation project. It was a tough job slogging into the muddy field carrying a shovel and wearing heavy rubber boots. Planting the corn was even harder. The corn was soaked for several days prior to planting. The tractor would arrive on planting day from the tribal offices. It had one plow, enough to turn over the whole acre. On several occasions, a horse plow was brought to the field to turn over the farmland. To plant, you had to carry the bucket full of soaked corn and follow the horse drawn plow and cover up the corn in the plowed rows. This was a tedious process which required lots of time and sweat as well. In late September, the corn was ready for harvest. Carrying a gunny sack, we made our way between the rows snapping off the semi-dried ears of corn. Most of the corn was hand carried to the top of a brush arbor where the corn was spread out to be dried out by the hot Arizona sun. Finally, after the corn was thoroughly dried in October, each kernel was taken off of the cobs with a sharp tool fashioned much like a screwdriver except it was pointed.

In the fourteen years that I knew my grandfather, I listened to many of the stories he told while sitting around the hot cast iron stove in the middle of winter or when we traveled. On one occasion, while traveling in a pickup truck with my relative named Buy Evans, grandfather pointed to the four peaks west of Roosevelt Dam. These peaks can be seen very clearly from Phoenix as well. Grandfather said that the four peaks were a holy place where the Apache deities lived … the birthplace of Mountain Spirit dancers. While we passed the four peaks, he said on numerous occasions, fires could be seen on the mountain sides. The fires are usually lit in a row with five fires spread apart. I recall as he spoke of these fires, that I actually saw them coming down the mountain. These were the night fires of the spirit dancers, the Ghans. In his stories, he also told of a cave with two serpents as guards. To this day, you can see these snake designs painted on the headdresses of the Ghans. Inside these caves and in some subterranean area, the spirits live forever. This story has been told by other Apache elders and although there are several variations of the story, the essence remains the same.

The Ghans play an important role in the spirituality of the Apache people. To this day, you can witness the dances of the Ghans. The spiritual codes forbid the identification of these Ghan impersonators. It is a secret and a sacred group of beings who still perform these ancient rituals. I remember when I was young, we would also make it a point to see these dancers come up from the river's edge in San Carlos. One thing that was strictly forbidden was to see these impersonators get ready for the ceremony. These dancers are the holiest of all Apache and desecrating or making fun of them could cause permanent psychological and physical disfiguration of anyone who dared to question their purpose.

Apache Sunrise Ceremony.

One interesting dancer in the group is the last dancer—the clown 'El-buyyeh', as he is called, usually doesn't follow any of the dance routine of the other four dancers. The clown usually raises a lot of havoc at these traditional Apache ceremonies, such as chasing little kids who seem to be mischievous. Usually tourists who come to these dances stick out like sore thumbs and they become easy targets for the clown. I have also seen Elbuyyeh spank some of the Apache kids. Clowns have a function in our societies and in Apache society by showing us our own egos, which keeps us in check with the real world and, of course keeps us from going off into the abyss of insanity.

Apaches still practice their ancient spiritual ways with the puberty rite ceremony for young females who are about to enter womanhood. This particular event usually consists of a sing by a medicine man from the community who is chosen by the young female's parents. In the 50s and 60s, this ceremony was usually held at one of the traditional dance sites in San Carlos at either a place called the Holy Grounds or Beaver Springs in Peridot near present day Highway 60. The puberty rite ceremony is a unique event which signifies the passing of a female in womanhood marking her first menstrual cycle. This is one of the oldest ceremonies still being conducted today. People who can afford these events are usually the ones sponsoring the ceremony. To assure a female's journey through life as a woman, a family usually decides to bless her with a proper ceremony to ensure happiness and well-being. This ceremony requires many hours of planning on the part of the female's parents and godparents who are sponsors of the event. The godparents are important because they serve as counselors and advisors for the family during the puberty rite ceremony called Na'i'aase. Co-sponsors also have to provide expense money for this ceremony to pay for special gifts, paying the singers in the medicine man's group and other helpers as well. These expenses amount into the thousand of dollars sometimes.

The young girl wears a buckskin dress made especially for her ceremony. An eagle plume which is taken from the under belly of an eagle along with an abalone sea shell is placed on her forehead. A long cane taken from local wood is made for the girl to carry at the end of the ceremony. This cane assures strength and guides her into old age. Throughout the ceremony, which takes four days, the traditional medicine men sing special songs. Pollen extracted from the cattail plants which line the San Carlos river is used exclusively. Pollen is a sacred medium, very much like the holy water used in the Catholic church. I usually made it a point to catch these ceremonies each spring and into early summer because I enjoyed singing with the old men who usually stood up to the early morning sun to the east of San Carlos. To this day, I still remember the songs which were sung. As late as 1988, I was honored to participate in the puberty rite ceremony in nearby Whiteriver, Arizona, where I carried one of the water drums and sang with the singers. Playing this drum brought back many memories of my earlier days in San Carlos. I have continued to reaffirm my Apache beliefs throughout the years since I left the reservation in the early 60s. Singing in these groups can bring some strong feelings to you and it also brings back the past. I have come to understand myself and my people by participating in these ceremonies. Apache culture is distinct, and slowly many of the ceremonies are being lost. Not many of the younger people know the old songs or the prayers. In another generation the Apache culture may very well become a thing of the past. Who will know the songs then? The puberty rite ceremony remains the last most significant ritual in the Apache world. The puberty rite tells of a catastrophic event in Apache history when the world was once covered with water. In anticipation of the destruction of the world, a lone female was sealed with pine pitch on a large log which was to preserve the blood lines. After the floods came and the water receded, the lobe female made her way out of the log and stood before the morning sun. She walked on the sunrays into the sun where she mated with the deity to continue the Apache world. And to this day, you will still see the abalone shell hanging from the forehead of the young girls who are going through their womanhood initiations. The abalone shell was picked up from the edge of the receding waters.

When we settled in our new location in Gilson Wash, my grandmother's brother, Ernest Martin (who went to the spirit world in September of 1997) from nearby Miami, Arizona brought his Model T-Ford truck to the reservation to haul fresh willow tree branches from the San Carlos River. These willow trees and cottonwood branches were used to build a brush arbor that provided shading for us during the hot summer days. These brush arbors are still seen in San Carlos today. One time, I discovered the modern principles of air conditioning by spraying water on the side of the brush arbor. The hot Arizona winds were quickly cooled down as these breezes made their way into the brush arbor where everyone hid from the blazing sun. I finally brought technology to San Carlos.

Apache country can be considered forbidden land since the summer heat rises above 110 degrees in mid-July and August. Waiting for the summer monsoons in July was the highlight of Apache weather forecasting. Each day, threatening thunder heads would roll in from the east. Prior to each storm, 40–50 mile an hour winds would whip the hell out of San Carlos. You had to be fast in shutting the windows and taking things into the house from the brush arbor which held up everyone's laundry.

When it rained, it poured. Living in the one-room frame house with a metal roof did not exactly offer a feeling of security especially if it hailed. Hail made the metal roof sound like frying bacon in a skillet. The sound was too overwhelming and created an eerie feeling. I can still see the flashes of lightening piercing the tiny holes on our corrugated metal roof at night. I always wanted the storm to end.

After hours of rain, you could hear nearby Gilson Wash gurgling and moaning. Kind of like a fast freight train rolling through town. In Seven Mile District 3 miles north, I recall a 100 year flood which knocked out many homes near the San Carlos River and Seven Mile Wash down river near areas of Riverside Park, Farmer's Station and further down. The old wooden bridge which stood near the south side of the tribal headquarters always managed to withstand the tons of water which rushed underneath from Gilson Wash. If you wanted excitement, you could stand on this bridge and watch the brown boiling water which was dragging other debris like mesquite bushes and old rubber tires from upper Gilson Wash. After the summer flash floods would subside, you could hear hundreds of frogs croaking as well. Early morning after the rains, the wash would drop to a mere trickle and finally dry up under the hot August heat wave. The smells of mud and other shrubbery seemed to stand out. Over across Gilson Wash, the Brown's home seemed a likely target for the river. Apaches lived in that area less than 20 feet from the huge mud cliffs which held back the raging river. On one occasion, a car was swept away in upper Gilson Wash where the dirt roads traverse the dry wash. No one was hurt.

The summer rains in the upper mountains usually brought a flash flood to the San Carlos area. The terrain of the dry creek bed changed significantly each year after a hard rain. The little hill that was at a certain place last year would end up somewhere in the bottom of Coolidge Dam 17 miles south of San Carlos.

In Gilson Wash, Jack Patten and the late Roger Stevens (Jack's cousin) and some of the neighborhood friends would test their bravery by jumping into the rushing river and ride the thick milky chocolate river water down to the tribe's cattle pens a half a mile down stream. Without life preservers but with lots of Apache nerves, the soaked river riders with their waterlogged Levis managed to get a decent ride in the flash flood. In the water you could always catch a glimpse of a bobbing tire, tree branches and some live rattlers that were snatched up earlier up stream by the racing river. Riding the waves meant keeping your head above water while facing down river and floating daredevil-style.

Other tests of nerves was jumping the Southern Pacific freight lines which rolled through San Carlos on their way to pick up rolls of copper at nearby mines in Miami and Globe 25 miles west. These trains which traveled at 20–30 miles per hour through San Carlos would sometimes manage to pick up riders who wanted to ride to Globe 21 miles west. With good physical conditioning and an eye for coordination, you could hop one of these freight trains easily. The trick was to ride and jump off before the train picked up more speed out of San Carlos. I remember one summer in '56, Uncle Harvey and his cousin Milford Martin came to visit our family in San Carlos. After their visit, my uncle tried to hop on one of the cars while cousin Milford yelled at him from the car up ahead. Harvey didn't do too well that day as he was flung down a ravine. It was too late for Milford to jump off as the train sped up.

Summers also meant staying out all night long as a teenager. Apache traditional water drums could be heard 10 miles away at night. If you didn't know where a dance was, all you had to do was listen very carefully for the drums. "Goo-chii-tal" or an Apache ceremony attracted many people in San Carlos.

One of the places for scared ceremonies was a place called Holy Grounds across the San Carlos River a half mile east of the government headquarters. The reason I was most familiar with this place was because my aunt Cleora was married to the son of a well-known medicine man who started the Holy Grounds in the early 30s. They were followers of another well-known medicine man named Silas John, a sort of a modern Wovoka. Holy Grounds is still a sacred place for many traditional Apaches, who still come to this place for songs and prayers. In the mid-50s, Holy Ground was also the sight of numerous social dances. One of the favorite pastimes at these dances was jumping on the back of pickup trucks which forded the San Carlos river as they made their way to Holy Grounds. Some of us would wait in the weeds next to the dirt road waiting for pickup trucks and cars that were making their way to the dance. When we'd see one coming down the road, we would run behind the cars and jump on the bumpers. Having taken lots of risks while running through thick clouds of road dust to hop a car, we got a charge from this activity. Sometimes you'd find some smart drivers who would slam on their breaks and start yelling at us as we made our way into the dark San Carlos night. Ambushing these cars tested our nerves and gave us something to do.

Arriving at the ceremony, some of us would manage to scramble into the circle of singing medicine men who were drumming to the Apache songs. The men sat very close together on the makeshift benches which still sit beneath the old Walnut trees at the Holy Grounds. At night there would be a large bonfire which light up the Apache sky. All the trucks and cars would be parked in a semi-circle fashion where you could catch a glimpse of the large fire in the refractory prisms of car headlights.

One of the fun parts about these dances was the passing of cigarette rations to the singers. The cigarettes were placed in traditional Apache woven baskets. Normal customs dictated that the singers get one cigarette per pass. When the plate managed to pass in front of us, we'd always manage a handful of Lucky Strikes or Camels. By early dawn, we'd have enough cigarettes for a week's worth of smokes.

Experimenting with tobacco came about when I was about nine years old. At a place called Higgins Trading Post in San Carlos, many of the older men would gather in front of the store sitting on the benches each morning. Picking up cigarette butts that were tossed by these old guys gave us the nicotine kicks we needed. I never knew the dangers of cigarette smoke then nor did we care whose mouth the cigarettes had been in. We'd just pick up the butts and re-roll them in Bull Durham papers.

Neesto.

Neesto, an old Apache elder who was probably in his 80s in 1956, supplied us with rolled tobacco as well. Each summer afternoon, and right on schedule, Neesto would make his way down to the Higgins Store 2 miles down the railroad tracks. Walking on the railroad ties made a good walkway for him. Neesto probably knew Geronimo because Neesto was about twenty years old in 1890. He looked like a character out of the Kung Fu television series—a

Chinese warlord. He had grey hair, slanted eyes and stained brown teeth. You couldn't miss him. The best part of Neesto was a bag of Buldurham tobacco he always carried in his shirt pocket. It was easily recognizable because there was a yellow string and a paper tag attached to the bag which was used as a draw string. Each afternoon, we'd walk up to Neesto and ask him for tobacco. Also, in his pocket, he carried Day's Work plug tobacco. We would ask Neesto "Naa-tooh-shawn-tee" or "give me a cigarette" in Apache. In the corner of his mouth you could see the tobacco juice slowly seeping out. He always had a smile on his face because he knew we were wet behind the ears. He would ask us if our parents knew we smoked. We'd nod in the affirmative. You could hardly see Neesto's eyeballs but you knew Neesto kept score on all of us. Of course, we'd tell him our parents knew we smoked. He would make a small smile knowing that we were bullshitting him. He would take out his tobacco bag and allow us to start pouring the tobacco on the cigarette papers. At nine or ten years old, rolling tobacco is not easy. First you loosen the string on the bag and carefully dump the tobacco into the folded paper—gently. All this time Neesto is looking us over in amusement. It usually ended up with Neesto taking matters into his own hands by rolling one or two good smokes that looked like they came out of one of the Lucky Strike packs at Higgins' Trading Post. Neesto's spit on the rolled cigarettes didn't make any difference to us since we were all dying for a smoke. We'd light'em up and fill our lungs with some of Neesto's best smokes. We could have taken all of Neesto's tobacco everyday but that would have ended our summer tobacco supply for sure. Kind of like the earlier days when Apache raiders used to steal corn from the Pueblos in New Mexico. The raiders never stole all of the corn. This assured a good return to steal another crop next year. We were abstract thinkers then.

    Carving names on the railroad ties and trestles was another favorite pastime. Everywhere you went in San Carlos you would find names of people from San Carlos on stop signs and bridges. People would carve their names with knives, write with chalk or tapped them out with rocks. Graffiti in San Carlos may have begun long ago before kids in New York ever thought of it. Perhaps they were seen by traditional Apaches on the ancient rock art of cliff dwellers in eastern Arizona and New Mexico where the Mimbres civilization from hundreds of years ago had left their art on the rocks. The best part of the graffiti in San Carlos was to add something mean or nasty to their name, if you didn't like someone's name. It was a good way to get even with someone you didn't like. In a recent visit to San Carlos, I noticed that a different type of graffiti is showing up which is a more gang-related type of street lettering.

At the Southern Pacific water tank near what used to be Osborne's store, you could see names written up high where it was difficult to reach. Put your name where no one could reach it and you would be assured of a permanent notoriety in San Carlos. My name is still there some forty years later. Chopping your name or initials with a railroad spike on a railroad tie meant permanency—for life.

One time I wanted to tie myself to a rope and dangle myself off of the back side of Coolidge Dam and write "Don Denny", the name I had before I was adopted, on the inside of the giant concrete pylon holding back the water. This would have been a first and a fatal one too. Living in San Carlos involved lots of risk-taking. Sometimes the thought of getting killed was not so terrifying at all. Climbing the rock ledges south of the old Higgins' Store was a dangerous activity which was only attempted by Leo Chase's mountain goats, which seemed to have an easy time being glued to the rocky cliffs.

Halloween was a special occasion for most of us in San Carlos. I started trick-or-treating in about the fifth grade. The only place in San Carlos where treats were given out was at the government compound, where the Bureau of Indian Affairs employees lived. These were mostly teachers and medical personnel who ran the local hospital. There were about thirty homes and apartments at the compound. No other family on the reservation practiced the fine art of giving away candy during Halloween. So, each year, we would dress up in outfits just to visit the white folks who awaited our visits during Halloween. There were no cheapskates in the government housing areas.

During the 6th grade we figured out an ingenuous way to double our treats during our forays into the Halloween night. Since most of the houses were lined up suburban style, some of us decided to wear two costumes. One was worn as we made our first pass through the government compound. As we made our last stop to collect our goodies, we would shed our first set of disguise and make our final round back across the homes. We went back to the same houses and doubled our take. It was that simple and no one had ever thought of this routine before. We wore masks so none of the folks knew what was going on. We got a real good laugh after we made our haul. The following year we were discovered because our security system had been breeched by one of the teacher's pets from the school. After that year, some of us had to take our masks off when we made our rounds for trick-or-treating.

Another favorite pastime of San Carlos was going out on a desert rat hunt in the nearby hills of San Carlos. David Boni, his brothers Kenneth, Buddy and Gibson and I would all climb into the truck and look for uranium deposits. I had seen my first Geiger counter traveling with these brothers. While prospecting west of San Carlos near the western border of the reservation, we would take a break and hunt these big fat desert rats. We'd find some pretty nice-sized ones, the right size for the big cast-iron skillets back home. These rats were a delicacy if you knew how to cook them.

Desert rats live in dens usually on top of cactus plants. They build their homes from different pieces of dead desert plants such as yucca and barrel cactus. If you can visualize a beaver den out in the middle of the desert, you will get a good mental picture of what a desert rat home looks like.

David and his brothers would take a long pole about 8 feet long and start poking around the dens. You had to keep a sharp eye because these rascals could come out at any time making a mad dash for their lives. Every once in a while these rodents would escape our attacks but never too often. With big clubs in our hands, we would chase these creatures out of the dens into the open. We would all be laughing while clubbing these critters. With a quick snap we would stun them and finally clobber them out their senses. The quicker the better. Hunting at night was more productive because the rats seemed more confused under the headlights of the truck. Desert rats are like rabbits and you cook them the same way. An evening harvest consisted of 15–20 kills. Back home, wild storied were told about how each of the kills were made. It was rewarding to take two or three of these varmints home to my grandparents. Grandpa would skin them, gut them, bread them with flour and fry them in the skillet. Colonel Sanders would have been mighty proud of my rat escapades in the late 50s.

We used to kill lots of birds in San Carlos. We'd arm ourselves with BB guns and slingshots made from car inner tubes. First you have to find a good mesquite tree with a perfect Y formation which will fit into your hand. Then you whack off the Y with the family butcher knife and peel the bark all the way off. From a good inner tube, cut the catapult bands about 12 inches long by an inch. Get a piece of buckskin or leather from the tongue of the shoe and fashion this into an oval shape about 2 inches by 2 inch. Strap the rubber inner tube to the armature and assemble the rock holder to the bands. The Apaches called this bird killer "bettittushee", a slingshot.

Jack Patton, my neighborhood buddy had a cousin, named Roger Stevens, who was pretty good at dropping sparrows out of the bushes near Gilson Wash. It didn't take much. Plop a nice round rock from the Gilson Wash into the leather pouch of the slingshot, pull back, aim and let got. Smack! Birds falling out of trees laying there with their eyeballs all squashed out from the high velocity of a simple creek rock. Sometimes the birds would only get stunned momentarily, and you had to hit them again with the slingshot and maybe the same rock. It was not a pleasant sight. Snakes were another target for us, especially rattlers that crawled down from the nearby mesas. The deadgiveaway was the tracks left on the dry creek bed of Gilson Wash. These slithery creatures usually spent their time lying underneath the shaded shrubbery near the creek's edge hiding from the hot Arizona afternoon sun. Obviously, these encounters with the birds and snakes were an exercise in cruelty to the wildlife of San Carlos.

We carried these slingshots with us everywhere in San Carlos. They were like silent companions ready to be used at a moment's notice to defend our turfs. (Busting beer bottles and breaking windows out of junked cars was the next favorite pastime in San Carlos.) We destroyed and conquered with these primitive weapons.

Another favorite pastime was gathering acorn nuts in the high country east of San Carlos. Acorns are the traditional foods of the Apaches to this day. The only place you can find these acorns are on the big oak trees up in the mountains near a place called Ash Creek. However, some even closer in nearby Miami in Pinto Creek made for a good harvest field.

One summer I traveled with my Aunt Cleora and her husband, Abraham Logan, up to Ash Creek 40 miles east of San Carlos in the mountains where we gathered acorns by the pounds. We spent several days picking these small acorns. It is not an easy task picking acorns which are about the size of the tip of your smallest finger. You have to bend over or get on your hands and knees when you pick acorns. Quality control consisted of cracking an occasional acorn to check for worms—the yellow larvae which usually indicated that the acorns were spoiled. If you found more yellow worms, this usually meant moving on to a new location for acorn gathering.

In Ash Creek that summer, it rained every July afternoon. The summer monsoons usually drenched our camp frequently. Black thunder heads usually rolled in from the east. At night, lighting flashes could be seen inside of the tent. I was never comfortable sleeping inside of the tents. It was always nice to see the morning light after having listened to the night storms. During the day you had to look out for dangerous rattlers that snoozed under the giant oak trees. In Ash Creek there was little civilization so these rattlers were more visible there than down in San Carlos at the lower elevation.

After a good harvest of acorns, we would come home with about 100 pounds of acorns which would later be used to barter for goods in San Carlos for cash. Since acorns were hard to pick up and find, most Apache bartered for acorns. Acorn is a nice complement for beef stew. Cracked open, the shells are separated by trashing them in the air. Archaeologists still collect grinding stones of the past. These stones called metates were used by prehistoric Indians in the Southwest to grind corn, dried meat and wild fruits. In the early 50s, I recall most Apaches had some kind of grinding stone around the house. With the advent of the modern hand cranked "food processors" of the 50s, my aunt Cleora often resorted to setting up such a contraption that is usually mounted on the edge of the table. After the acorns were shelled, they were ground to a fine powder and placed in glass jars. Having acorn created a feeling of status. Word would quickly spread that my aunt had acorns. Relatives usually came first. In Apache values, you don't turn anyone down, so my aunt was always quick to give away the prized possessions which were collected from the giant oak trees in the mountains. Acorns have a bitter taste to them. With the grinding and evaporation, most of these chemicals dissipated quickly. They do have a lot of vitamins in them. These traditional Apache snack items were a favorite of ours as youngsters. To this day, (the modern) sunflower seeds were no match for the acorns.

Making money by selling Peridot, semi-precious green transparent stone, was also a good way to stay busy and make much of money in San Carlos. A half mile south of San Carlos on top of the mesa, there are large deposits of Peridot stones. Many Apaches still mine them today to sell (those stones) to gem collectors worldwide. In the 50s, if you walked on the mesas near these deposits, you could still find large nuggets of Peridots. Nuggets that weren't mined usually didn't have any cracks in them.

A coffee can full of these Peridots usually brought in a few dollars for buying groceries. In later years, dynamite was used to blast out large chunks of the volcanic rock which had strands of Peridot embedded in the formation.

To acquire a sizable amount required staying on the cliffs and pecking away in the rock formations for hours at a time. There were regular buyers who came to the reservation and who bought several pounds of the rock and took them away for processing in distant cities. Peridot can only be found in very few places on earth. The two main places are in San Carlos and in Hawaii with other deposits in other parts of the world. We actually didn't know what Peridots were used for when white people came to the reservation to buy the stones.

In later years, I found them in jewelry stores, where they were gracefully mounted on exquisite gold settings such as rings and bracelets. My high school class ring catalog even had a picture of a ring with a Peridot on it. Peridot is also a birth stone.

One time we lived off of the reservation in a nearby town called Miami (not to be confused with the Miami, in Florida!). This town, located 30 miles west of San Carlos, had one of the largest copper mines in the world. In the early 50s, the prize for copper was phenomenal. In Miami, copper was mined from the raw rock formations from the open pit and underground mines. Processed copper could be found underneath the electric power lines in the nearby hills. These scrap pieces of copper wires were collected by us and later sold for a small profit. Other Apaches living in Miami had an ingenious idea for quick cash. They climbed the tall tailing hills to pull the heavy copper nails out of the specially constructed wood structures which carried waste water from the copper leaching plants a few miles away. Late night forays up into Inspiration Copper Mine wooden structures was not uncommon, especially on a full moon when one could see very well. Large canvas bags were used to haul large copper nails which were the size of pencils. Over the years, the wooden structures on top of these mine tailings slowly began to crumble thanks to the marauding Apaches who took the nails out for profit. To this day, mine officials probably wondered how these wooden structures met their fate so fast. Finding copper created status for many of the neighborhood residents, which included many Mexicans.

Pollution of the streams near these large tailings was evident in the 50s. Dead insects and other animals was a common sight near these polluted streams in Miami. In addition, the immense discharge of untreated sulfur smoke from the large smelting smoke stacks made life miserable in Miami and in the Globe area. The stench was so bad that it would choke you, give you a raspy throat and make your eyes water for days at a time.

Each year my grandparents and I would go to Thatcher, Arizona 60 miles east of San Carlos, to pick cotton for the Daleys. They were big time white farmers in the Gila valley near Safford. Other Apaches and Navajos came to pick cotton as well.

Picking cotton by hand was a very tedious task which required long hours of stooping over and dragging an 8 foot canvas bag filled with about 200 pounds of cotton at the end of each row which was the size of two football fields—lengthwise. One had to drag the bag between the rows of cotton plants and one had to pick fast and weigh in when the bag became full. I usually had a gunny sack since I wasn't big enough to drag one of these bags. We would pick from daylight to evening for mere pennies. These were really harsh times in the lives of Apaches.

One day my grandfather Irving said he felt something on one of his thighs. He looked around to see who was nearby and seeing that no one was around, he pulled his pants down. Right on his leg was a giant black spider—a tarantula—a woolly spider which appeared deadly. Quickly, he knocked the spider to the ground and pulled his pants back up and continued down the rows picking cotton. I wanted to kill the spider so badly but my grandfather gave me a non-verbal communication which basically said "Leave the spider alone". I never questioned him on this situation, even years after it happened.

In the cotton fields I'd get hungry. Each day an Anglo man would come in an olive colored jeep loaded with goodies. Pumpkin pies were his specialty and it became a ritual for me to get a pie everyday the jeep made its rounds in the cotton fields of Thatcher. If there was a motivation for getting up each morning and going out to the cotton fields, it was because of the pumpkin pies.

My grandparents would get paid each day. They must have made about $15 dollars a day and with me picking hard, an additional dollar perhaps.

Near the cotton fields, we lived in a traditional Apache wickiup which was set up near a canal. In late fall, it was cold in these grass huts. My grandfather managed to cover part of the grass hut with used flour sacks, gunny sacks, cardboard boxes and pieces of canvas. Each evening there was a small fire built in the center of the hut. We kept warm with these fires but eventually, the fire would die down late at night. Sometimes if the frost was very heavy in the morning, grandfather would try to keep the fire going all night. We had our own special spots on the cold ground.

These were truly hard times in my early childhood, living in poverty and fighting the elements. This was different than sitting in a beautiful home on the hillside of the Camelback Mountains of Phoenix where I might have stayed with the German family when I was two years old. I had no concept of the past so I didn't mind what was occurring to me in that grass hut. Also, there was no concept of the future for me at the tender age of ten.

When we returned to the reservation in San Carlos after the picking season, we found our cabin tent had been completely gutted. The front door was nowhere to be found. Inside of the tent, all of our personal belongings were scattered everywhere. Old photographs from the 30s and 40s had been left exposed to the elements. There were pictures of my grandparents when they were younger and other mementoes of my aunts and uncles when they were kids. Everything in the tent was destroyed by the reservation marauders who enjoyed breaking into people's homes. I remember grandfather taking the torn tent which was now in 30 different pieces and tried sewing it back together. Having been gone for over three months, there was no way for him to tell how long it had been left this way. The tent appeared as though it had been hit by a hurricane. I could not understand how anyone could be so mean as to destroy other people's property. Not far from the tent lived two brothers who were later caught breaking into the local government school where they were defecating in the desk drawers of office workers. I knew that these boys had torn our tent also.

Grandfather gathered all of the torn pieces of the tent and proceeded to sew them back together. Not long after this, we took down the cabin tent and the lumber supporting it and moved to Gilson Wash 2 miles southwest. Grandfather said the reason why the tent was torn was because many of the Apaches in the area disliked the Camp Verde Apaches. Our Irving family was part of a small contingent of Verde Valley Apaches left in San Carlos after the great interment of the mid 1800s in old San Carlos.

We were the renegades of Apache land. Camp Verde Apaches had originally migrated from the Cibicue area and then down slowly into the Verde Valley in the late 1800s. Part of Gilson Wash in San Carlos was known as 'Camboodie' slang for Camp Verde. This was a small geographical area where many of the Camp Verde Apaches settled after they were released from the containment in Old San Carlos 17 miles south. Our family was less fortunate than most people and we weren't quick to point that out to people in San Carlos. People just understood we were poor and that was a given.

Grandpa Irving didn't spend any time knocking or scrounging around for food or money. The pride he carried with him was exhibited by his initiative to seek work outside of San Carlos. After he lost his eye, when I was eleven years old, he continued to search for work anywhere. Whether it was picking cotton in Thatcher or cabbage in Tempe, Arizona, we were there with him. If there was work to be done, he could do it, knowing this meant survival for all of us in the family.

One morning sometime in 1954, grandfather and I were hitchhiking from San Carlos to Guadalupe, near Tempe, looking for work. As we proceeded out of San Carlos in upper Gilson Wash, we were picked up by a white man in a big truck. We threw all of our paper box suitcases in the back of the truck and headed out to nearby Cutter 12 miles west. Along the way we stopped at a gravel pit where grandpa was asked to drive the truck while pulling a tractor which had a hard time getting started that morning. I never knew that my grandfather could drive a truck because that was the only time in my life when I had ever seen him drive a motor vehicle of any kind. He surprised me. We helped start the stubborn tractor and walked out to the main highway leading to Globe after this. We didn't have to stick our thumb out to catch a ride—we just walked carrying our paper boxes that once held bananas in a market. We got picked up by an Apache family heading into Globe that day. There was a snot-nosed kid who kept pinching my arm as we sat in the back seat. He had a runny nose and I knew this kid wasn't too disciplined. He kept turning around from the front seat grabbing my finger and twisting it. I looked at my grandfather who was now looking at the window enjoying the fine view of the Pinal Mountains to the south of Globe. While grandpa was looking out the window, I twisted the naughty kid's finger hard—so hard that he let out a wild scream to his mother. I knew that his mother would be unsympathetic to him and I didn't fear the consequences of my actions.

After leaving Globe that day, we arrived in Tempe near Phoenix where my uncle Charlie Irving was on the look out for us near at what is now Broadway and Mill in Tempe. Subsequently, we ended up in Guadalupe 3 miles south of Tempe where many Mexicans and Yaquis lived. My uncle was working at the A.J. Reynolds aluminum company in Phoenix at that time. That fall, after harvest, we went to a company picnic with my uncle who assured us that Santa Claus would arrive. It was a momentous occasion with balloons, food, Santa and lots of entertainment for the children.

We lived in Guadalupe all that fall until close to Christmas. After that it was back to San Carlos. But during that time while in Guadalupe, I got to know my cousins Kenny, Geraldine, and the late Joanne Irving. In addition, my uncle, named Billy Irving, who worked at a crop dusting firm nearby, got to take care of us a lot. Uncle Billy was a spitting image of grandfather. He looked like him but he didn't act like my grandfather in later years as Billy turned into an alcoholic. However, I got to know the other side of Billy in 1980 in a reunion in Prescott, Arizona. Billy later passed away.

In Guadalupe we lived in a tiny shack behind my uncle's house. Since it was so hot in Phoenix, we slept outside most of the time. Uncle Billy had a homemade radio receiver that he had assembled. Everyone had fun with the radio which was able to pick up all sorts of transmissions from around the world.

The following fall, we came back to Guadalupe to live with my uncle again. It was cabbage picking time again.

In Guadalupe, I saw my first Yaqui Deer Dance. Up to present time, this ceremony is still held each year around Easter in the community of Guadalupe. The only difference in the 50s was that there weren't any tourists bumming around spoiling these events with their cameras.

In 1954, there were no buildings south of what is now Broadway in Tempe and Mesa. In Guadalupe I attended the local public school which was filled with nothing but Mexican students. Being the only non-Mexican there, I had no alternative but to learn the Spanish language. There were some natives there like my first cousins, but we all had to learn how to speak Espanola.

Romona, one of my early heartbreakers in Guadalupe gave me a bloody head during recess one day. I can still remember this incident. This light-skinned Mexican girl was very popular at school. Having a crush on her, I managed to confront her one day at recess. After a fellow classmate dared me, I lifted her dress and her response was a swift hit on my head with a rock found on the playground. I knew I had been hit when I reached up to my head to feel the warn liquid on my hands. I saw the palms of my hands which were now soaked with warm blood. I screamed like a wild banshee and knew then that this was the last time I was ever going to test the turfs of females.

Music class at Guadalupe consisted of Mexican songs not to the London Bridge or Hickory Dickory songs. Our assembly hall was a building covered with corrugated metal. Spoken Spanish came very easy within weeks. There was no choice for me. By the time I left for the reservation that late fall I had a good command of Spanish.

Not long after returning to San Carlos in 1954, I encountered traveling Mexican nationals. They were walking through San Carlos on their way to the cotton fields 90 miles to the east in Thatcher. It was plain to see that these illegal aliens were lost and stranded in Apache country. Their attempts to speak English were an exercise in futility. The only thing they would say was, "Where is your seester?" After that, their English was unrecognizable. My neighborhood buddies turned to me and asked if I could speak 'nnakai-ye' or Spanish. It was easy for me to speak Spanish to them. This was probably the greatest surprise of their lives as I began to give directions quickly. Now, 'seesters' was out of the picture and the nationals wanted food and agua. We directed them to a nearby church. It was the last time I saw Mexican nationals on the reservation.

Since I spent some of my time off the reservation, I managed to grasp the English language very well also. I got along with the teachers on the reservation and Mrs. Baggett, who appeared to be about 200 years old, became my guiding light in 4th grade. I learned how to play the harmonica in this class and how to sanitize them with rubbing alcohol using a feather brush as well. This was also the first time I heard of the 'germ' theory. Along with learning to play the harmonica, I grasped the 'hokey-pokey' dance routine in 4th grade while wearing a sailor's uniform under the tuledge of Mrs. Baggett. Each year we traveled to nearby Globe, where we performed for the local women's auxiliary luncheons. Mrs. Baggett, who is now long gone, was a crucial person in my life during my formative years in San Carlos. Another teacher, a black lady named Mrs. Lester, who exposed me to one of the strongest perfumes in the world, helped me see the horizons of the other world, the black men's world. I distinctly remember her cigarette breath also. Then there was Roy Spencer, a full-blooded Navajo, who became the male role model for me. He had a gentle demeanor about him and as an Indian person who taught school, I was reassured daily that I would be safe. Some 40 years later in 1997, I discovered Spencer's photograph in a worn copy of the Navajo Times, a tribal newspaper, which captured Spencer in a rodeo announcer's stand way back when he was probably 25 years old. Spencer is now long deceased as well.

I was quick to learn the concepts of math and the mechanics of English from these teachers. No matter what ridicule these Bureau of Indian Affairs teacher have received from others, I can state unequivocally that I never had a bad experience with any of these teachers. As a matter of fact, credit should be given to them for instilling discipline in all of us and showing us the way to survival in this world.

Part of the reason why I was quick, I believe, was because I had spent part of 2nd through 6th grade in white public schools in Thatcher and Phoenix during harvest seasons.

One of the most curious things that ever occurred on the reservation was when one of my Apache cousins from Miami brought a Texas Armadillo to my grandfather's house in Gilson Wash. He had acquired the creature somewhere and had the animal for a short amount of time. On a hot summer day he let the animal loose on the sand bed of Gilson Wash a few hundred yards from our house. All the kids from the neighborhood went down there to see the weird looking animal dig into the sand bed. If you had never seen one of these animals, you are in for a real surprise. The animal looks like a prehistoric creature, a midget dinosaur perhaps, in armor suit with a long snout and little beady eyes. They are harmless and have a tenacity for burrowing into the ground. During the showing of this animal, my cousin let the animal get a little carried away with his digging. No sooner that he had turned the creature loose to dig, it began digging with its snout for various bugs. The animal actually began throwing sand out with his hands and feet. It was like a machine that had gone amuck. Yes indeed, it was methodical and quick. My cousin stood there very proud of his new 'toy' and not knowing that this creature was on its way to China by way of Gilson Wash! All of the kids just stood there quietly as the animal continued to burrow into the dry creek bed. Soon it was obvious that the prized possession from Texas was getting too carried away with the show. My cousin's expression changed from happiness to sudden fear. By now, the animal had totally disappeared from the top of the ground. You couldn't even hear it anymore or see it kicking the sand out of the hole it had dug. At this point, it was a foregone conclusion that the infamous animal had made a clean break for freedom. We used shovels and our bare hands all that day trying to locate the varmint. No one saw this animal until a week later when up overhead we spotted some crows circling near where the armadillo had disappeared. It was obvious that the eight to ten crows had found themselves a first class dinner. Sure enough, he had turned up not far from the hole where he had last been seen seven days before. Apparently, the animal had keeled over and died from natural causes. He had been dead for some time. The story of the disappearing armadillo circulated San Carlos for some time thereafter. This rare armadillo was the first and the last to be seen in San Carlos. Since then, I have always had a deep respect for animals.

While living in Tuscon with my mother in 1956, I attended public school for a few weeks. On the way to school I always stopped at a feed store where I observed hundreds of baby chicks in cages each morning. As of 1993, the store is still there actively selling animal feed but no chickens. With a sincere interest in raising chickens for pets, I bought two baby chicks. Since we lived in a small apartment, we had to build a small wire cage for my new chicks. I took care of those chicks for a few weeks until it was time for me to move back to San Carlos to live with my grandparents that spring. I had never been able to figure out at the time how the man in the feed store knew which one was the male and female chick.

I went back to San Carlos that spring with my new pets. The chickens began producing eggs almost daily. My grandmother Ivy decided to name them Henny and Penny. They were very unusual chickens because of their unique color and temperament. No one in San Carlos had chickens like mine. Henny would crow early in the morning communicating with other roosters in Gilson Wash. Even when we didn't have any food at home, the chickens always managed to find something to eat around our yard.

One day I came home from the Globe schools and found my grandparents inebriated and passed out. It was pretty quiet around the house and Henny the rooster was nowhere to be seen. I looked around and saw Penny sitting in the shade of the house. "Bock, bock", was all I could hear from Penny as she turned her head sideways as if she was trying to tell me something. Henny was definitely absent.

The rooster had the ability for fooling me on a number of occasions. They had been with me for two years now so I knew both of them pretty well. Out of the middle of the holy ground was Henny. He lay there being real still and I thought he was dead. I went to where he lay and stood over him. His tongue was dangling out and I detected a faint pulse from his tongue.

I couldn't figure out why he was lying out in the hot sun for no apparent reason. He had never done this before. I even noticed that the crows were now circling above our home. I touched him and he made a jerking move. I knew he was still down 'for the count'. He barely moved when I tried to push him. Usually he sprang to his feet and ran as fast as he could when I would try to catch him. What I saw was a chicken with bloodshot eyes, staggering and trying to maintain his balance. I made a quick check inside the brush arbor where my grandparents were asleep. I noticed an empty tin cup on the ground. Inside the tin cup was a small trickle of raising jack—the mighty white lightening of the Apaches. I figured that Henny had been hitting the cup after he had run out of water in his regular dish. I had a drunk rooster on my hand. I picked him up carefully and laid him under the shade of the house where he snoozed for hours into the hot San Carlos evening. He must have had one hell of a hang over the next day because it took him quite awhile to get moving the next morning.

Not long after this incident, Henny kicked the bucket and made his way off to chicken heaven. He probably died of cirrhosis of the liver. I didn't have the nerve to throw him in the pot so I gave him a dignified burial down in Gilson Wash where the Texas armadillo had met his fate earlier.

* * *

The summers in San Carlos were unbearable. Spending time at the river swimming and fishing was an excellent pastime. We would make canoes out of corrugated sheet metal and sail the river all day. Standing in the middle of the tall river plants was a suffocating and itchy experience. It was like a thick jungle and the tall sunflowers like plants dusted us with its polls.

For drinking water all you had to do was dig a hole in the sandbar near the river and wait for the murky water hole to settle. After the hole cleared you could dunk your head in the water and drink it. Unlike the tap water it tasted flat but we never got sick from it. Indeed, this method of getting water from the river was an old technique that had been passed down through generations of the Apache world.

After having spent a hot day out in the river, coming back to the family's brush arbor was a welcome experience. On one of the tables my grandfather made, there was large and tall metal water jug that was filled with water and wrapped in gunny sacks. Throughout the day one of us in the family would pour water on the outside of the jug, which allowed the water to remain cool. It was a huge water jug much like what you would find at a construction site today. In the jug was a community water dipper that everyone used to drink water, including all the neighborhood kids with runny noses.

One day I reached up to get a dip of water and proceeded to drink my heart's content. As I finished a hardy drink and belched, I became curious about the water level in the jug. Letting the jug become empty would be unthinkable especially during the hot summers in San Carlos. I climbed up the table to see how much was left in the jug, and as I looked down inside of the jug I discovered a dead lizard floating around. He was suspended and making turns as if he was in a gravity-free space environment. His mouth was wide open and he sort of had a permanent smile on his face. I just couldn't believe that I drank the whole dipper of water after seeing this lizard in the jug. Apache superstition has it that if you fool with lizards one of them would eventually show up underneath your skin around your neck. Very much like having an implant under the skin. After this horrifying incident with the drowned lizard, I checked my neck daily for stray lizards under my skin in the neck area.

* * *

One of the antitheses of white and Indian relationships came to light when I was 11 years old. Each week full-featured movies were shown at the government school. It was the big social event of the week with hundreds of Apaches filling the gym. John Wayne and Audy Murphy were the top billing for these movies. After seeing the cavalry troops get decimated by marauding Apaches, reinforcement by white troops were usually greeted with cheers, foot stomping, whistling and clapping by the Apache movie aficionados. Somehow we associated ourselves closely with the do-gooder, in this case the white soldiers in the movies. It was as if we had forgotten who we were … the real saviors of the Apache world. Of course, our behavior was completely ironic. I don't recall a movie where the patrons yelled for the Apaches when the white troops were being scalped. Not until later years did I root for Indians in the movie "Little Big Man" with Dustin Hoffman. This was a welcome change after taking sides with the white soldiers in my formative years as a movie-goer in San Carlos.

* * *

Eating in the school cafeteria at the government school in San Carlos was quite an experience. There were approximately 40 oak wood tables in the cafeteria with about 200 high back oak chairs. The cafeteria furniture was definitely for adults. The edge of the tables usually hit you at the chin. Scooting the chairs back under the table was quite a chore because each must have weighed 150 pounds, or so it seemed at that time. The cafeteria was definitely a no-man's land. Spike Kniffin, the head cook, a Shoshone Indian from Nevada, cooked some pretty good meals. Kniffin was married to one of my favorite childhood nurses at the government hospital. The school cafeteria 'manager' was Sarah Reede, an Apache cook. Each day her eyes roamed the whole cafeteria like a radar scanning the skies for spy planes. It was her job to make sure the school kids ate all of their meals on the metal trays. The normal procedure was to have all the students at your table eat fast so we could be excused by Mrs. Reede. You couldn't just leave your table any damn time you pleased. This was a government school cafeteria. To be excused from the table was done in an orderly fashion. Each table was dismissed one at a time. You had to keep an eye on Mrs. Reede—a simple nod of her head meant it was O.K. to leave as a group from the table. Like robots we'd scoot our chairs back and marched our empty trays to the window were they were washed. One day in the cafeteria was like an eternity in hell. The anxieties of eating fast so we could get to the rubber balls and other playground equipment first was nerve-wrecking. One day, I got a large serving of spinach in my tray. No matter how I chewed the stuff, it wouldn't go down the chute. It was oozing out of my ears and nose. It couldn't be swallowed. As I looked around that one particular noon day, I noticed that our table was way ahead of everyone—possibly in line to be the first to leave the cafeteria. All I remember was the school bully named Elmer yelling at me. He said I better eat the spinach pronto fast or else I was going to receive one of his weekly knuckle sandwiches. I did everything in my power to assure our success at leaving the cafeteria first. But to no avail, the spinach overruled that day. There was too much of it on my tray and in my mouth. Seeing that Mrs. Reede had her eyeball out for another table, the ultimate had to be done. With the finesse of a magician, I calmly took all of the spinach off my tray and stuffed it into my pant pocket, including what was left in my mouth. I was positive Mrs. Reede missed the slight-of-hand trick I just pulled. We did it! Our table was the first to finish the daily noon rush sweepstake for the rubber balls. All of a sudden there was a stillness, like the quietness before a storm. A certain sanctimonious aura prevailed, that feeling of accomplishment with pride. However, much to my surprise, another table was dismissed first. Then another table and so forth.

Fifteen minutes later 200 Apache kids had vacated said premises with the exception of our table. We sat there including me with the spinach stuffed in my pocket. There was a sudden realization that the jig was up. We had been had by Mrs. Reede. Slowly, like the guard out of the movie "Cool Hand Luke", Mrs. Reede meandered over to our table with her arms folded into her chest. Good effects. She came over behind my chair and stood there for what seemed like an eternity. The next thing she said was "Eat all of your food". I pretended not to hear her. I had twelve pairs of eyes upon me by now from around the table. Mrs. Reede said, "Now!" The command was quite clear and it was directed to me from behind.

Slowly, I reached into my right pocket and took out the spinach I had hidden earlier. I took it out with my fingers and the juices ran down my crouch and under my butt. It was like a death sentence, the finale of a slow motion TV commercial. I choked and gagged on the spinach as I slowly shoved it into my mouth. Not a word was said. The message from Elmer was clear. He didn't have to say anything. One stupid move would have caused a tidal wave reaction for twelve Apache boys and Mrs. Reede, the kitchen guard. The spinach got caught in my throat and some of the juices spurted out of my nostrils unto the tray. Mrs. Reede stood her ground. The spinach finally hit the bottom of my stomach like a solid rock. I didn't care now it was over with and I wouldn't pull this trick again—ever. Quickly, with a soft voice, Mrs. Reede said, "You're excused". We marched off with our trays. I hate spinach to this very day and I'll skip asparagus and cabbage as well. No reflection of Kniffin's cooking. However, my thanks to the San Carlos School, which provided me with enough vitamins to survive another day in Apache land.

* * *

School was murder. The world's fastest haircuts were given there. We would be seated on wooden boxes 4 feet off the floor, and within 20 seconds, buzz, buzz, twenty to thirty heads at a time would find their hair on the floor. Weekly showers were also required at the school. There was a shower stall west of the school grounds that accommodated all the school children. There was absolutely no privacy for us. It was as if the government was involved with every aspect of our lives.

After stripping down, we would line up under the shower heads. The Navajo barber was there to hand us our homemade soap out of a steel bucket. It was a cake of soap that looked like an oversized brownie. If you weren't looking or paying attention, you would get hit on the head with one of these blocks of soap.

The worst part about these showers was when the man turned on the big wheel at the end of the shower stall, which regulated the amount of water rushing out of the shower heads. Yep, it never failed. Ice cold water shocked you first, followed by hot scalding water prior to fine-tuning the water temperature. This was not a good experience with exception that this was our only shower we would get during the week. After a few minutes, the water was finally adjusted somewhere between hot and cold. The steam was so intense you could hardly see beyond your nose. Every once in a while, the shower man would take out a fresh towel and pop our butts. No one stepped out of the shower stalls until the water was turned off. And if you dropped your soap you had to be aware of other unwanted anatomical intrusions that you may have been warned about before you went to the army forces. The cement floor was very slick. From the west wall, where the wooden benches were located, you had to walk about 8 feet forward and step down about 6 inches into a trough. Where the floor met the drop-off was a crack in the floor that had razor sharp edges. I remember an incident where one of my buddies, Burton, got pushed by one of the school's bullies. He fell hard, knocking his head on the cement floor and cutting his finger severely, which bled like a broken hydraulic line on a bulldozer.

Every effort was made to keep you clean by the school. This was one of the big jobs of the government schools in the 50s. Conversely, the cleaner you were, the more susceptible you were to diseases. Kind of like standing in the middle of a swamp after taking a shower. The cleaner one is in a non-sterile environment was one sure way to get sick. At least that's how traditional Apaches looked at cleanliness.

The government school had a man-made fish pond in front of the school auditorium, which was filled with goldfish. In the middle of the pond was a pedestal fountain, where a trickle of water flowed into the pond. This was definitely an ingenious attraction for the school kids, so intriguing that one night we hooked a few of these stinky goldfish. Try finding a fish pond at a school today.

In the San Carlos river you could catch tons of carp or catfish. But catching a goldfish was different. I never knew that goldfish were slimy and uglier than carps. That was my basic conclusion.

In the 5th grade, I got my first job working at the school's snack bar. Terry Kitcheyan and I ran the store after school for Mr. Leminger, an old Whiteman who worked for the Bureau of Indian Affairs. He had been in San Carlos since the stone age. He always had a lighted cigar in his mouth even as he scooted across the school grounds in front of the school children. He had a flare for doing things. Besides a gardener and a farmer, he was a man with all sorts of knowledge and talent. I used to steal candy from him quite often until one day he confronted me on some missing change in the cigar box that he used as makeshift cash register. I finally confessed and realized how the cash-on-hand transactions were handled. He counted the number of candy in the boxes and the change in the box. Simple mathematics. Old man Leminger nailed me for taking spare change. Dishonesty didn't pay.

Terry and I would cook extra buckets of popcorn just so we could snack on the way home. We'd work all of the basketball tournaments for Leminger, who had developed a trust of us by now. It was a big money operation, and I paid pretty close attention to the cash flow. The accounting system was now refined and the old man never missed a nickel after that.

In the 6th grade, I joined the 4-H Club and learned about basic electronics. Our group traveled to the University of Arizona in Tucson where we kicked butt and ended up placing first in most of the electronics categories. Mr. Owens, my 4-H leader, was a tall, lanky gentleman probably from the Midwest. He wore the same fedora that a 1940s detective would wear. He spent a lot of time helping us to understand polarities as well as negative and positive field forces. To this day I have the certificates for my 4-H accomplishment. I actually learned more about science in 4-H than in the regular classroom.

* * *

Since the advent of time many children from the 'rez' (short for 'reservation') have attended Phoenix Indian School. As of this writing, the Phoenix Indian School buildings have been razed to make room for a show-case community center for the greater metropolitan area. Many of the children attending this school were referrals from the Bureau of Indian Affairs' social adjustment programs. Those who were displaced in home environments such as parental abandonment were first to go. Second, the juvenile offenders who had brushes with reservation laws, and third, children of traditionalists who thought it was the thing to do. This group usually followed the mandates of their parents. In July, the Bureau of Indian Affairs (BIA) always placed a list of eligible students who were to get on school buses at the two stores in San Carlos bound for distant government boarding schools in Nevada, California and Arizona. In mid-August, Apache children as young as ten years old would line up for roll call in front of the school offices in the government school compound in San Carlos.

When I was bound for 7th grade, the BIA had me earmarked for enrollment at Phoenix Indian School. The only chance I would have to see my grandparents would be once in a nine month period—Christmas. Big Christmas present! So, many of the children sent to these types of schools were outcasts in San Carlos. I remember sometime in July of that dreadful year, my grandfather took me down to the local trading post and bought me one of those ugly blue metal suitcases which a fake brass border around the edges that you still see in the bunk rooms of cowboys today. These suitcases had a paper tray in them. At each end were snap latches with a locking devise about mid-way across the case. We went through the whole store and bought Levis, shirts, socks and underwear. They were all too big to fit me ... but what the hell, right? I wasn't gonna be around anyway. Along with my personal belongings, I packed the suitcase in the second week of August in preparation for the much-talked about Phoenix Indian School. I was ready for it.

My grandfather took me down to the school ground that hot August day to catch the bus. There were about ten buses there all heading west to Nevada, California and Arizona. Each bus had a number on it to signify its destination. The school officials took my blue metal suitcase and shoved it underneath the back seats of the school bus. I climbed up the front of the steps finding a seat in the middle of the bus. It was loaded with other Apache kids as well. Everyone was clean and dressed up for the long hot trip. I remember I had on a cowboy shirt with fake pearl buttons and a set of PF Flyers tennis shoes that were by now baking my stinking feet. My Levis were too long and the cuffs were rolled up 3 times, if not more. I sat next to a kid who I may have seen a few years back picking his nose in his dad's car on the way to Globe when I was hitchhiking with my grandfather. He was still licking his runny nose.

It was hot and miserable inside the bus. I looked out the window and I could see my grandfather standing there staring at the bus. He couldn't see me.

He was probably wondering how I was going to make it in the boarding school. The noise in the bus suddenly came to a halt after an adult came on board with a clipboard in his hand. He got everyone's attention in Apache and said he was going to read off names and that we had better pay attention. He began reading the long list on his official-looking clipboard. There was a string tied to the metal clip and the other end had a long pencil tied to it. The names were in alphabetical order and when he came to the D's (Denny was my last name at the time), he didn't call my name at all. I was waiting to him to do so because I kept track of everyone's name on the list. I sat there the whole time wondering what the hell was going on. It must have been an hour before someone came on the bus and said, "Don Denny, off the bus".

I slowly walked off the bus and soon felt the cool breeze hitting me underneath the tamarack trees which shaded the bus I had been sitting on. I must have felt relieved because my heart wasn't really set on leaving San Carlos. I had already heard some horrible stories about these distant schools. My grandfather walked up and spoke to the man with the clipboard. I couldn't hear what they were saying except I heard the man say he didn't know what was going on.

The next thing I know, we were all walking to the back of the bus where one of the older boys tossed my metal suitcase to the ground. It made a large thump and I could visualize my white oversized socks doing somersaults. My grandfather quickly lifted the blue suitcase to his shoulder, and we started walking toward home in Gilson Wash. Grandfather didn't say much, but he got stronger as he carried the huge suitcase without stopping for a rest.

I ended up attending Globe Public School Junior High in 1957, riding the late Fergus Sneezy's daily commuter bus that ran to Globe every day 21 miles away. Fergus was an Apache who lived in San Carlos. His daily mission was to haul 30–40 rowdy Apache kids into the Globe schools. Each morning, the bus ran throughout San Carlos picking up Apache kids including some of the white kids who lived at the government school compound. These white kids were dependents of white employees who worked for the school and other government agencies like the hospital in San Carlos.

The bus made a distinct sound as it made its round up and down the various districts. I'd wait inside of our house and would manage to slug down one of grandpa's fresh cups of coffee each morning. After that, a quick run out to the edge of the road where the bus would finally stop to pick us up. Each time the bus stopped, it would dump a few pounds of reservation dust on us. It was inevitable that we would get very dusty before we set foot in the hallways of Globe Junior High that morning. During this time, hair pomade was very popular. Harry Patterson, a close neighborhood friend of mine, always managed to slick down his hair with it. It actually looked like clean white axle grease, except it was made for hair. Harry had a nice duck tail on the back of his head and a neat little twist which hung down on his forehead. You'd try to look real nice each morning but that old bus would always manage to dust you with fine powdered dust.

The upper classmen would usually sit in the back of the bus. The lower grades sat in the middle or front rows of seats. Baxter, the son of the bus driver and the star running miler and football player for the Globe Tigers, sat in the back with Brian Bunney, who was also known as E-nawsh-keen or white boy. Charlie Stevens, son of the late Jesse Stevens, former tribal chairman of the San Carlos tribe and a star miler and other prominent members of the Globe Tigers lettermen's club, sat in the back as well. If you got too close to these guys, you would usually get thumped on the head with one of their fingers. Riding this bus was a 42 mile round trip of running the gauntlet inside of it. It was light harassment from these guys each day.

I got beaten up one day just as I was arriving home. Yes, beaten up by a girl. I made an off-color remark to a girl who was sitting behind me. Mr. Sneezy, the bus driver, was in front of me driving the bus. I looked in the mirror up above Mr. Sneezy, and I immediately saw the girl leave her seat tromping down the aisle toward me. I sat there momentarily and the next thing I knew, she had a hold of my hair and flung me down the floor. The bus driver quickly stopped the bus after seeing what was happening behind him. The girl did a number on me. I had no chance to respond. It was quick and over within seconds. I had gotten beaten up by a girl. She was fat. I still got beaten up though.

Coming to Globe was always a chore. Once we'd get to Globe, some of us would go to the Cut-Rate Store near the junior high and drink pop, eat doughnuts and maybe smoke a cigarette or two. One morning, several of us decided to ditch school. We started to run back to San Carlos 21 miles east. Jerry, myself and others took off east along the Southern Pacific's rail track which would take us directly back into San Carlos. We trudged for 8 hours straight. Somewhere between Globe and San Carlos the white truant officer, named Max Oliger, would finally catch up with us in his olive drab Chevy tooling down Highway 60 at a slow speed. He would catch a quick glimpse of us but we would zip into the camouflage of mesquite bushes along the dry creek bed. He was a real detective and we dogged him all day long. We ran all day with no water. To avoid Mr. Oliger we took a short cut over the rolling hills of upper Gilson Wash. Near Dripping Springs we saw some wild boars, which were known to attack humans. Some of them carry long fangs on them for easy attack and defense. We avoided these monsters as much as possible. We had heard too many stories about these creatures to feel at ease around them. When we got near our home in Gilson Wash around 4 p.m. that evening we would wait a few extra minutes to coincide our arrival back in San Carlos with the Mr. Sneezy's school bus return from the Globe schools. As soon as the bus dropped off the bookworms we'd simply make a break for the house. I did this routine about three times until we were brought into principal Walter Knox's office at Globe Junior High. That's when we got the best of Globe's board of education.

* * *

Richard Harris, a hot shot entrepreneur of Apache land, was the first to introduce me to good candy bars and all the hazards of tooth decay. He drove an old Chevy truck with a built-in metal cover on the back. It was green with the paint fading away all over and was slowly turning factory grey. In the back were sundries of candy: Butter fingers, Oh Henry, bubble gum, you name it, it was all there. Old man Harris had revolutionized the game of entrepreneurship in San Carlos. He wore a short stubby hat, the kind that Gregory Peck may have worn in To Kill A Mocking Bird. We would wait for him in anticipation each morning. The trick was to hop on the running board right before he even stopped. Quick, slick and clean get-a-ways by the young stealth Apache warriors of twelve years always had the advantage. Reaching under the tarp which protected the merchandise from the desert dust, we managed to get a few waxed Coke bottles filled with flavored drinks. Mr. Harris would finally crawl out of the cab and roll back the tarp. In hindsight, he reminded me of a crap dealer in Vegas. Careful eyes, watching all the tiny hands as they skim over the boxes of candy. You couldn't steal anything when he was looking. He was too quick so you had to beat him to draw by jumping on his truck much earlier than when the wheels would finally stop rolling. In our time with old man Harris, we must have lifted 50 candy bars from his tenure as a candy man of San Carlos. If and when I get to Heaven, I'm sure Mr. Harris will be waiting for me.

* * *

Stealing in San Carlos was a sometime event for most of us youngsters. If the topic of stealing were to be discussed in modern day philosophy classes, I would classify our thefts as minor infractions in the codes of Apache land. After all, historians know us too well with regard to stealing horses and corn from the Pueblos and mescal from the Mexicans. But I never thought of stealing as a serious crime in San Carlos. Now if you stole government trucks or siphoned gas out of people's cars or took money out of Sam Pechuli's cash register at Higgins' Trading Post—that was stealing.

When I mean stealing, I mean an occasional candy bar from old man Harris' candy truck or whacking off a few ears of corn out of Elson Brown's cornfield at night or maybe a nice plumb watermelon out of Mr. Leminger's garden at the government school compound. Just your typical mischievous and ornery kind of stealing. Nothing major. These were minor escapades of mental testing which usually made life more interesting in San Carlos.

Like the many nights we would go over to the school barn and ride Oliver Dean's (Apache Indian) pigs. If you have ever smelled pig shit, you're in for a real surprise. We'd roll our pant legs up, jump off the corals and chase those squealing pigs until they tired. Then we'd mount them and stay on for as long as possible while some of the younger Apache warriors kept an eye out for Oliver Dean. We never took showers except once a week at the school, so I have wondered to this day what I did with all that pig poop which was left between my toes after riding Oliver's pigs.

Another favorite activity was going to the school grounds late at night and have the night watchman chase us around. He was fast and how he could run. I remember him well. He wore his black felt hat, had a thin moustache, a wad of Spearmint to keep him alert at nights, a flashlight in hand and a pass key that dangled from his side. We'd keep an eye on him and them make noises to distract him or draw attention to us. It was as if he was trying to be at several places at one time. We kept him busy all the time. Now, we never broke no school windows or tried to crawl through Spike Kniffin's kitchen pantry window at the government school cafeteria. But we had fun keeping the night watchman busy during the summer months when it was usually dead. We had fun re-charging adrenaline flows in our bodies.

The most serious crime I recall at the school was when two boys broke into an office and defecated in several office desks. My recollection from this incident was that when the office folks arrived Monday morning they had a few 'administrative decisions' to make. The final stop for these boys was Ft. Grand, a notorious reformatory for adolescents near Wilcox, Arizona.

* * *

In 1952 when I was about eight years old, I almost lost a childhood friend. My grandmother had a niece who had a child as old as I was. His name was Marvin. While traveling with him in his uncle's car on Highway 60 between Globe and San Carlos at a place called Cutter, Marvin suddenly flew out the door while the car was traveling approximately 50 miles an hour. I was sitting on my grandmother's lap and Marvin was sitting in his mother's lap. My grandmother's brother Ernest was driving at the time. What happened was that Marvin accidentally had opened the door while his mother Emily wasn't looking. In the 40s, cars had doors that opened toward the front. 'Suicide doors' as they were called, caused Marvin to take a walk out into space. One minute he was sitting there and the next minute he was gone. I looked out the back small oval window of Uncle Ernest's car and saw Marvin tumbling and sliding down the highway. Ernest immediately stopped the car and turned around to go where Marvin was lying. It was a hard landing for him, as evidenced by his head having been split wide open. His face was a bloody mess and his mother was crying and screaming at the sight of Marvin. It was a terrible sight. Uncle Ernest quickly picked him up and transported him to the Indian hospital in San Carlos, where he was kept for many days. He survived that accident with some giant stitches in his head. In the summer of 1988 I saw Marvin again after having not seen him for over 30 years. We chatted about that near fateful day when he almost lost his life on a lonely stretch of a highway west of San Carlos.

* * *

In less than 100 years, Apache land had been transformed from a nomadic lifestyle to one community, San Carlos was divided in 3 districts: Peridot,

Seven Mile and Gilson. And to the east, 16 miles away was Bylas, another community largely forgotten by the central government of the Apaches. My childhood buddies in the 50s were Adam Noline, Fremount Valor, Terry Kitcheyan, Sylvester and Fernando Pechuli, Kenneth and David Boni, Jack Patton, his brother Billy and his cousins Roger and Happy Clark. Some of these guys became victims of the harsh life I have described.

   I never got to know many of the other kids from the various districts. We were pretty much adversaries, very much like covering our own territories in the inner cities of Chicago or LA. Anytime any of the other boys came into the Gilson Wash area, we'd let them have it—a good knuckle sandwich or a swift kick in the ass. One kid used to come to our area on a horse because he knew that if he came on foot, we'd kick the holy hell out of him. We'd throw rocks at him and his horse while he literally tried to run us over with his horse.

   As unbelievable as it sounds, us Apaches were not unified. We pretty much worked against each other … not any different than your average community outside of the reservation. Living in San Carlos had to require constant vigilance to make sure you didn't get knifed by some crazy lunatic staggering around at night. Being out at night always presented many dangers. I always dreaded walking home at night after playing with my neighborhood friends. One person I really feared lived in my district. He was known to carry knives, and threatened and beat up all sorts of people in San Carlos. He had no mercy even for the old folks. He was pretty much of a terror—like the junk yard dog. Twenty years later in the late 70s I saw this same person in San Carlos after my absence of twenty years. Now he was an old fart who had a beer belly. I wanted to knock some sense into him but because of my strong Christian upbringing I let him go. This time he was begging for money and bumming cigarettes. He was truly indicative of the early juvenile delinquents of San Carlos who had a jail record a mile long. I was wondering who had the college degree now, the bank account and a decent car. He was fifty years old sitting on the roof of someone's house in Tarzan Valley in upper Gilson Wash. I can't believe I even wasted a paragraph about him here.

   Another guy I didn't care for was a person who supposedly spent his time in the Army Airborne. His face reminded me of a pit bull: his eyes were at least 10 inches apart with a thick neck. Sure, he was built like Coolidge Dam, stout and strong but he had the intelligence of that pit bull. This guy always wanted to beat people up just for the hell of it. In the late 70s during my yearly forays to San Carlos I saw the pit bull at Pinky's Bar in Globe shooting pool and bullying his way around the bar. He was wearing a Harley Davidson t-shirt and a pack of Luckys tucked up one end of his sleeves. His facial features had changed somewhat. Instead of a pit bull he began to look more like a carp. It made me wonder why the hell the good Lord didn't put this guy away instead of my good friends like Happy Clark, Kenneth Boni and Roger Stevens.

There were truly many fine people in San Carlos. Like the mentally retarded boy who lived in another district. He always dressed clean and his relatives always gave him a cowboy hat to wear. When I was ten years old he must have been in his early 20s. I went to the Assembly of God Church in Gilson Wash with him, and often I ended up playing with him and goofing off with him in church. Sometimes some of us boys would ask him all sorts of stupid questions just to see what answer he would come up with. Present-day psychologists would probably classify him as moderately retarded. And sure enough, he would come up with some gobbledygook answer that was off the wall and totally unrelated to the question we would ask. Of course this would make us totally giggly. Sometimes he would carry lots of change in his pockets and we would trade one or two marbles for two of his quarters that he had. He was totally oblivious to what we were doing. Of course, at the age of ten, anything was fair game in San Carlos. We didn't know any better. Our retarded friend knew how to play because mentally he was our age although he had whiskers and appeared 10 times stronger than us.

This same person would also go to baseball games and hang around at Higgins Trading Post with all the old fuddy-duddies of San Carlos, chewing tobacco and smoking Camel cigarettes. Somehow, this person also had the unique features which allowed him to be an adult some of the time and a kid most of the time. Being around him made life more bearable in San Carlos.

* * *

I had my first 'French kiss' when I was thirteen years old in San Carlos on a hot frustrating summer night in upper Gilson Wash when my testerone level was at an all time high. It was on the Southern Pacific railroad where I witnessed a near derailment one time. This time my emotions were being derailed by a 16 year-old girl. Me and her were sitting there under a full San Carlos moon. It was awkward with me and my arms wrapped around her shoulders. We contemplated the whole scene and proceeded to do what was natural—kissing! It was definitely a new experience for me. Thanks for showing me my first

French kiss, ah, what was your name? This young lady knew what she was doing and I remember the taste of her mouth. It was worse than spoiled cabbage or that wad of spinach I spit out at the school cafeteria earlier.

I tolerated that experience and chalked it up as an introduction to what was to come in future years chasing ladies in Illinois.

No one talked to us about birth control or venereal disease, except those guys who fought in the Korean war. If someone found a 'rubber' it was just one big giant joke. No one knew you had to have it on. In hindsight, whoever was dropping these rubbers had a good handle on not "knocking up the babes" in San Carlos.

One of my close friends finally did contract that dreaded condition that became known to me as "the clap". Most of my uncles who came to visit me from Phoenix usually told me to stay away from sex because "it would make one blind".

* * *

The Southern Pacific train was almost an Apache culture in itself. Everyone had something to do with it although the train only did business in San Carlos once or twice a year shipping cattle from the sales on the reservation. I remember one time a friend of the family attempted to commit suicide in Gilson Wash on the railroad. It was in the afternoon when I heard the unending horn of the train. This always signified disaster on the railroad in San Carlos. Hear that long and lonesome whistle and you could always count on a fatality. The train was stopped. By the time I got there, there was a crowd near the engine. It was a horrific sight: a man had stepped in front of the engine and the wheels of the train had severed his legs and one arm. He was still alive when the hospital officials arrived to retrieve his torso from underneath the locomotive. Perhaps this is where the "loco" originates from.

* * *

While living in Thatcher, Arizona picking cotton with my grandparents, we usually listened to the shortwave radio in the morning before going off to work in the fields. Without notice, Grandma Ivy burst into loud screams one morning after hearing that her sister Molly had been ran over by the S.P.

(Southern Pacific) train in San Carlos. We went to the closed casket funeral not long after that.

A usual occurrence was the storming of the S.P. caboose when it came by the Farmer's Station swimming hole during the summers. The swimming hole was a nice pond of fresh irrigation water. On one end was a huge 16 inch pipe which discharged tons of water hourly. We swam in it during the hot summers. Each afternoon the westbound S.P. freight would come by the swimming hole. When we heard the horn a distance, about 50 Apache youths would gather their favorite stone at the pond's edge to prepare to meet the iron horse of Apache land. Customarily, the engines were never hit. But the caboose, yes. A whole barrage of rocks pounded the wooden car. You could see the steel meshed guard window screen in the caboose. There was no waving caboose man here. The irony of this whole thing was that 2 miles west of Farmer's Station, the returning freight train would always drop off the blocks of ice for thirsty and eager Apache children. During the hot summers, every other day, if you stood near what used to be Osborne's Store, you would be assured of ice compliments of the S.P. Railway. Get a hunk of one of the big pieces and you could cool down a tank of water or some fresh beer from the local bootleggers. The S.P. railroad was inseparable from Apache culture.

One time while attending Thatcher Public Schools in the 4th grade, Larry, a childhood friend, and I were walking home from the school back to our camp where we picked cotton. Larry thought up the idea of setting fire to tumbleweeds, which grew 10 feet high near the S.P. railroad telephone lines and rail line. With no encouragement from me, Larry struck that fateful match which set the large tumbleweeds on fire. If you have never seen blazing tumbleweeds you are in for a real show. Just imaging pouring gasoline on a dead two month-old Christmas tree and setting it on fire and multiply that by ten. What followed was a gigantic fire that could be seen for miles around Thatcher. Coincidently, the S.P. freight train coming down the rail came to a screeching halt near the huge fire that Larry started. Larry and I ran as fast as we could. I looked back and I could see the telephone poles on blaze and the smoke plume could be seen one mile up into the air.

* * *

I didn't learn how to swim in the most pleasant way at Farmer's Station. First I had to experience near death. I had tried to learn when we would go to a swimming hole in Seven Mile Wash when I was younger. Up until twelve years of age, no luck at learning how to swim. Dog paddle, you name it—this body could not float. I was always scared of the water and occasionally I'd get dunked in shallow water on the fishing trips on the river by the Boni brothers, David and Kenneth.

One hot summer day I learned the fine art of swimming in one minute after having been unsuccessful for a few years. It happened when I was hanging around Farmer's Station, an old swimming hole which was holding a pond for irrigation of the nearby alfalfa fields. I have been wading in about three feet of water around the edge of the pool. To the side of the pond a huge pipe pumped out ice cold water into the bottom, 12 feet under. On this day there were many Apache youths there enjoying the cold water to wash off the summer's dust. There was a kind of diving board also. Except this board was a huge beam jutting out into the center of the pond. At the end it was supported by a telephone pole. The swimmers would run along the 16 foot beam and dive into the deep clear water. I had no desire to do that because water had always terrified me.

As I was wading near the pond's edge, a drunk Apache man wandered up to the edge of the pond. Very quickly, he viewed the entire area and his radar immediately put a fix on me. He said, "Do you know how to swim?". I replied with a negative nod. Before I knew it, he was in the water pursuing me. Trying to get out of the water was like trying to push a semi truck. My water-logged pants slowed me down to a stand-still. I ran out of breath and was grabbed from behind by the drunk man. I yelled and screamed asking for mercy from this individual who was about to kill me. With flying arms and legs, maliciously carried me up to the pond's edge and over the large beam which was jutting out into the deep abyss of the pond. As he carried me, we teetered-tottered on the beam while he was careful not to spill me over into the shallow end of the water. I looked into my adversary's eyes and I saw no reprieve. Yes, I was going in. I pleaded to no avail. All I heard was laughter from him and everyone else on the edge of the pond. As I fell out of his arms into the dark deep pond, it was a slow motion descent and I had no time to think nor analyze my predicament. I don't remember hitting the water. I went the whole 12 feet. I touched the bottom of the pond with my hands and next thing I knew, my lungs were straining for oxygen. I could see daylight at the top as I made my way toward this light. Perhaps it was a scene from a near-death experience, that light at the end of the tunnel. It seemed like forever to come to the top. When I came to the top I heard laughter from the drunken idiot who threw me over. He was standing directly above me on the wooden beam. I was kicking and flailing my arms, but in an organized fashion, as I swam toward the edge of the pool. For the first time in my life, I was swimming to save myself. I stood there shivering from what had just happened. My heart continued to pound as I continued to reflect while watching the cold water swirl around my feet. I heard the wino stumbling away, mumbling something under his breath as he made his way to the thick tall Johnson grass which grew outside of the pond's edge. This was just another chapter in my daily near misses with death in San Carlos.

* * *

I spent a lot of time at the Assembly of God Church in Gilson Wash. My grandmother Ivy was arthritic so spent most of her life in pain. Every effort to become well necessitated the attendance of church. It was a church where people spoke in tongues—the Holy Spirit. I remember going into the prayer room at the conclusion of a service and praying with all the men. The women went into their own prayer rooms as well. There was much yelling and shaking in these rooms. Every once in a while I'd take a peek with one eye ball to make sure everything was ok. The end of the world started in the early 50s for me. Each night the preacher pounded the pulpit as he shouted for deliverance. I was almost sure San Carlos would fall straight into hell any moment.

'Holy Rollers' as would call them, had a large following in San Carlos. Samuel Harris, an Apache minister of the Miracle Church in nearby Peridot was the main kingpin of this movement and still is today. Samuel had the flare of a politician when he preached. He had a dynamic voice which would command anyone's attention. There was no snoozing in Harris' church. To see this Apache native preaching energized the local community and it kept everything interesting. Holy rollers were ridiculed because they were so outspoken on issues affecting San Carlos, alcoholism being the top priority.

I spent many hours in Samuel's church sitting there with my grandmother Ivy. Grandpa Irving rarely went to church, preferring to stay home reading magazines through the thick magnifying glasses he received from the Indian Health Service doctors. At many of these rallies by Harris, I saw many of my young friends coming to the altar to accept His word. One individual named Adam had the experience of being energized by Harris. After watching several Apache people dance and wiggle on the floor, Adam was seen jumping up and down dancing like a kangaroo under Harris' tent. He had received the message from above, so I thought. After about 5 minutes of seeing Adam's contortion out on the floor, he suddenly stopped and walked to a water spigot, where he got a mouthful of water. All this time, I had thought he was in some sort of trance. His behavior was unusual and now I knew he wasn't sincere in what he was doing. He saw me and made a smile. He quickly got back to the dance floor and faded into the rest of the holy rollers.

Life in San Carlos was no bowl of cherries. It seemed like the devil himself had cast all of the world's misfortune on that community. Anything you did required ten times more energy both emotionally and physically. Sometimes it was one disappointment after another. Kind of like the old adage "anything San Carlos touches turns to shit". With all good intentions, some people tried to create a good environment for the community. Anything could happen at anytime without notice though.

Like the times we got plastered with ping-pong sized hail at a Canyon Day outdoor church revival on the White Mountain Reservation, 40 miles north of San Carlos. My grandmother and I had gone to that revival under the big circus tent. Each day, numerous individuals were saved through baptism in the river. We stayed overnight and the finale of these revivals was a wholesale baptismal. It was a scene from the movie *The Greatest Story Ever Told*. The late Marvin Mull Sr., an Apache, stood there preparing to baptize other Apaches who had committed themselves after 3 days of prayers. I felt a closeness to God which I had never felt before. While standing in the line to be baptized, I was the first to receive a direct hit on top of my head from what I thought was a rock being thrown from the cliff above me. After looking at the ground, I saw a round white ball about the size of a golf ball. Feeling immediate pain to the top of my head, I could soon hear "plop" in the river. There were more plops, plops and soon I could see Marvin dunking into the river to escape the pounding of the hail. He would go under but he always had to come back up for air, at which time he received one of the white balls from heaven. I grabbed a nearby corrugated sheet metal which was lying nearby. The pounding on the metal was unbearable. People were scattering to whatever cover they could find. Some crawled underneath pickup trucks parked near the river's edge. The whole incident took no more than 5 minutes. I had welts on my head that looked like giant boils. The Lord does work in strange ways, and I believe that my time wasn't right to be baptized. I have continued to be a religious person though.

Ping-pong sized hail.

Another time, danger seemed to seep up everywhere and the holy rollers were probably right when they say the devil himself was creeping around San Carlos. Like the night when an electrical short from a guitar knocked the player and others off of the church's stage. People fell over as if they had been dominoes at an old folk's home. Kind of made me wonder if our prayers were being answered.

Being pursued by marauders into a church was a scary experience. While attending a church function in Seven Mile Wash one night, we built a fire outside of the church. Standing there we heard a voice from one of the nearby cliffs near the church. We didn't know who it was that was shouting at us. After we shouted a wise-ass remark back, the marauder was silenced temporarily. Within 10 minutes, the campfire became the sight of a surprise fighting attack. Six boys being beaten up by one large stocky Apache boy. My closest buddy was beaten badly. We all got up and ran into the church, taking the first two rows of the pews. All I could hear was my ear pounding away. The preacher was glad to see the instantaneous converts from the outside darkness. There was my buddy with his swollen forehead and me with my bruised ear. We could see the marauder peeking through the window pointing to us motioning in such a manner that he wanted our asses. I didn't want church to end that night, and I prayed for immediate salvation. Brian Bunney, son of the Anglo preacher, was there reassuring us we'd be saved. We boarded the church's van which safely took us home that night.

I witnessed the 'backsliding' of a close friend of mine who was a devout Christian. He always carried his Bible with him where ever he traveled. One night I went to his place only to find him in a drunken stupor. He looked pitiful as he stood there with his finest church suit. He was crying and babbling away and trying to rationalize his mistake. He was one of my favorite neighbors, and his parents were well respected in the community as well. Not long after that, he went back to his church, where he continued to be active. Later on in life, he became a policemen as well. In 1974, we met again in Whiteriver, Arizona, where he was a policeman for the White Mountain Apache Tribe. I have always had a lot of respect for the late Buddy Boni.

I continued to attend all of the churches in San Carlos. The benefits of belonging to a church were many: Christmas parties, (the Mormon's basketball court) and the bingo games at the Catholic church. The Mormons had a nice basketball court so some of us joined the church.

I almost lost my life once along with the missionary sons, the Bunney boys. We were all in our teens. Brian, the oldest of the Nebraska boys, knew how to drive his dad's car. They had a Dodge panel truck which they used for church activities. These boys were a welcome addition to our community. They were the only white kids. We didn't treat them differently than any of the other Apache kids. Sure, there were times when we'd fight and argue over candy and other petty things. Growing up we spent lots of time together and developing a natural trust for each other. One evening, we all went on a drive in upper Gilson Wash to gather wood. Brian was at the wheel while I sat next to the right hand door of the panel truck. Brian's brothers Mark and Loren were in the back. Driving along one of the wash board roads is no easy task in San Carlos, especially if you are in a vehicle that is top heavy. The first curves were taken very easily, but in the final curve the van went out of control. As I looked out of the rear view mirror, I could see the dust rolling out from underneath the van. Very quickly I became aware that the van was now bouncing out of control. It tipped over on its side and slid for quite a distance. It was a miracle that my arm was not sticking out of the window because that was the point where the truck landed on my side. There was utter chaos in the van as Brian fell on top of me. The boys in the back were screaming, and you couldn't see anything because of the thick dust which had engulfed us. Within seconds, the back doors were opened by the two brothers, and we made our way out. We were in a state of shock as we began to wander outside. The youngest brother, Mark, began to walk away from the van quickly. Brian yelled at him and brought him to his senses. This was an automatic reaction that most accident victims experience. Soon we were all giggling because we knew that we were alive. Within minutes a white man who had been collecting junk nearby came to the accident scene. We assured him we were alright.

Brian had the unfortunate duty of going back to his house, 3 miles down the road, to tell his father about our accident and how the van got rolled into a tight little ball. From what I remember, when Brian's dad arrived, he was very calm with us. No reprimands or scolding of Brian. Hey, he was the minister, right? It was an accident and we were all alive.

Months after the accident, the van was still seen cruising around the roads in San Carlos with its sides still bashed in. Except Brian had made an attempt to band the dented sides in with a sledge hammer. I joined Brian's church right after that accident. I became a believer.

Brian found me again in 1993 in Flagstaff, Arizona after an 18 year absence. He tried to get me to join Amway this time.

The Bonnys lived across the road from us. Behind their house was a smaller trailer home. This was part of their living quarters. Up in one of the storage compartments in the trailer was a Sears Silverstone guitar that was used by Brian's father for church services. When his dad wasn't around, Brian would drag out the guitar and fire up a few tunes like 'Charlie Brown, he's a clown' or 'Bee-Bopa-Lula' and Buddy Holly's 'That'll be the day'. At night we'd take the guitar out to the S.P. railroad tracks in front of Brian's house and pick out a few rock-n-roll songs. "Teach me this, teach me that" I'd say to Brian. Brian was real patient with me as he taught me the chords which went with songs like 'Amazing Grace'. With this new found talent of playing guitar, in later years at Globe High School I was able to land the lead role of Conrad Birdie in a high school music entitled *Bye, Bye Birdie*. In addition, I made the big coffee house music scene as a folk singer in the Midwest during the 60s. All of this due to Brian Bunney and his missionary work.

One summer night while sitting on the old San Carlos bridge with other Apache boys from our area, we yelled at a passing car which was being driven by a local village hoodlum from near the Holy Ground. He was one of the first bullies who I knew as being generous with his butch hair wax. When he came back from the Army, he always intimidated the little kids. On Thursday nights the government school always showed movies. This same bully always managed to harass us after the movie. He'd chase us all over the school grounds at night beating us up.

That night when we were sitting on the bridge we turned our attention to a bright set of head lights coming our way. Not knowing who it was, we started yelling. Much to our surprise, the village bully appeared. He stomped on his brakes and jammed his car in reverse and wheeled it to where we were sitting. We ran toward the end of the bridge quickly, downhill into the darkness of hell. Gunfire broke out and I heard the bullets flying over our heads. The bullets had a "whiffing" sound to them. I believe to this day that he wanted to kill us. When we ran down into the darkness, we all collided with a barb wire fence which had been waiting for us. If there was an Apache sound of barb wire meeting our flesh it was "geesh".

Near brushes with death were a common experience in my life in San Carlos. To this day, I believe that Apaches who went to fight in Vietnam had a good handle on the meaning of death, because they had prior experience dealing with this type of situations in San Carlos. I also believe that most of us who grew up in San Carlos during these harsh times of the 50s and early 60s experienced some type of post-traumatic stress disorder (PTSD). My alcoholism and eventual loss of my family in later years may have been a result of years of mental warfare in San Carlos. I believe that Indians have unique psychological problems that may be the direct results of the types of social problems I have described. This was not a normal childhood life for most of us who grew up in San Carlos.

When I was about six years old my grandparents went drinking in downtown Globe near where the famous 'Ice Box' used to be parked. It was an abandoned rail car that was permanently parked off to the side in downtown Globe. One of the party folks who was there was a man by the name of Manuel. He was a black man who was accepted by the local Apaches and who frequented the watering holes of Globe. Apaches were always with Manuel. He spoke some Apache too. And since Apaches' had a hard time buying liquor in some of the local bars in Globe, Manuel was the point man for these alcohol parties.

I was on Manuel's lap one day while he was sitting on a concrete retaining wall. Behind him was a 10 foot drop-off. At the bottom were assorted broken liquor bottles from previous alcohol binges. Manuel and I suddenly tumbled over backwards with me still in his lap. As we plunged down the wall I somehow ended up landing underneath him. I lay there for a few moments, crying and screaming while a 200 pound man lay on top of me. I could feel the glass splinters in my back. People from the top of the wall simply stood there in amazement looking at what had just happened. It was indeed another brush with death for me.

The 'Ice Box', as it was called, was a haven for drinkers. Apaches crowded around their cars drinking wine and beer under the large cottonwood trees in the dry creek bed which ran through Globe. On occasion a fight would break out. High stakes poker games were a featured entertainment. At this time, alcohol consumption in public was illegal, so there were massive arrests of Apaches in Globe. Thirty days for public consumption was a hefty price for Apaches. I recall one sign in a bar in Globe which read, "No Indians Allowed". However, I don't recall my grandparents ever setting foot inside of a bar. Usually they relegated themselves to sitting on the white tailings of copper leaching, which dot the lower end of Pinal Creek west of downtown Globe. Attending one of these beer busts was a treat for us youngsters because the adults usually paid us off for keeping quiet and minding our own business. It wasn't unusual to receive several denominations of coins for staying out of the way.

* * *

San Carlos means "St. Charles" in Spanish. I wonder if the Catholic church made a mistake in naming San Carlos after a saint! San Carlos was still primitive in the 50s considering the fact that Geronimo had died only 30 years before my arrival in San Carlos.

I don't recall anyone drinking alcohol responsibly in San Carlos. I don't believe there was such a thing back in those days of massive consumption. It was usually a quick slam. Kinda like dumping gas into the racing cars at the Indy 500. Drinking to enjoy was unheard of. Quart-sized bottles were the most popular size. Beer could also be drunk without icing them down—straight and hot. Some of the Apaches would warm their beer in a frying pan over an open fire. One of the Apaches was overheard saying, "It gets to your head faster". During these drinking binges most of the drinkers got real animated, loud and boisterous. Normal for alcoholics. A popular expression is "Kay-Yay", which would be comparable to "wow" or "cool" or "come on, tell the truth". This Apache saying was and is still being used for statement of disbelief in a joking manner. It is a good expression to use, especially if you are listening to a chronic bullshitter. Depending on the inflection of your voice you can make it into different meanings to fit the situation. I can still hear Apaches throwing this expression around.

Humor has its special place in the Apache culture. The general set up for these jokes and bantering sessions was when one person would make an outrageous and unbelievable remark that was so farfetched that everyone would simultaneously blurt out "Kay-yay" in perfect unison. If you drag out the first part of "Kay-yay" to a "Kaaaaaaay-yay" and raise your voice while doing this you could sure stop a chronic liar dead in his/her tracks. You see, we have our ways to keep people in check.

White people always were the brunt of Apache jokes, especially when Apaches impersonate white people. You may call it role playing which may be patterned after a white person at the local trading post or one of the government offices on the reservation. These English words may be highly exaggerated during their pronunciation. Along with this, if an Apache has very limited English abilities, these expressions can become very comical in their own context. Playing with the English language was a favorite pastime and still is in Apache land. No one wants to learn formal English but poking fun at it makes things more interesting in San Carlos to this day. Part of the poking fun also casts a doubt on the true intentions of white people who may appear to be sincere but deep down don't really mean what they say. It is this juxtaposition of Whiteman's thought patterns which has become a social playground for Apaches.

The hottest home-brew drink in San Carlos was 'rais in 'jack and malt liquor. Both of these concoctions were made from yeast and sugar and of course some tender love and care. No one for sure knows how the Apaches started brewing this hooch. This ingenious booze was usually the main course for Apache alcoholics. The stuff was made from boiling water, yeast, sugar and a quart of malt base with the blue ribbon on it. After two days of brewing, usually in a wooden barrel with grandma's blanket, the final product looked like brown creek water from Gilson Wash right after a blasting rain storm. The drink was usually sold in gallon jugs. This drink was so strong that anyone could get croaked in a very short amount of time. Local bootleggers had a day with this drink because it was so cheap to make with a high profit margin. I have tasted and consumed this drink on several occasions as a teenager. Usually I received a stomach ache from this brew, which would take an award for being a bad-assed beverage only drunk by the bravest. "Beeyasequazee" or ice cold beer, as it was called in Apache, was a delicacy for those who could afford it. Nearby Globe, 21 miles away, was the place to get beer at places like Pinky's Tavern (still there after all these years), the Owl Bar and Connie's Store on Ice Canyon Road.

Bootleggers made a hefty profit by selling iced beer in San Carlos, with a 300% markup. Bootleggers were pretty secretive about their operations, local cops always managed to find out who had the booze. So naturally, they would bust the bootleggers and destroy the home-brew devices.

Traditional Apaches would also brew a drink called tulapai or 'tullipie'. This was a drink brewed with sweet corn and native herbs from the mountains, involving a long drawn-out four-day process. This corn was ground into a fine powder and mixed into water and herbs. After letting it boil for a while, the drink cooled down for consumption. In the old days, this drink was saved for special occasions such as weddings, puberty rite ceremonies and other pleasant events. Never at funerals though. When I was about ten years old, I'd go visit my aunt Cleora near the Holy Ground where her mother-in-law usually had the tulipai brewing. It is a delicate drink that you can get croaked on if you drink enough of it. I remember just getting a slight buzz from it and getting very sleepy. Since it takes a lot of time to make this drink, very few Apaches make it today. The best part is drinking it from a gourd which was made into a dipper. You have to stir the bottom of the container to get the special ingredients floating to the top. When I was young, it was brewed on special homemade basket bottles which were coated on the outside with pine pitch. In my mind I can still taste tulipai today. If your stomach isn't used to the ingredients you can get a bad case of Montezuma's revenge.

* * *

From Globe to San Carlos proper is 21 miles. Globe is called a border town where Apaches keep the town alive economically. Globe also has the distinction of having one of the oldest J.C. Penny stores still in operation in the mid 90s. The 21 mile stretch of road was also the site of many tragic automobile accidents which claimed many Apache lives. A distant cousin of mine was involved in one of these accidents, resulting in the death of his girlfriend. She was beautiful and the cousin had a difficult time dealing with this tragic event for many years after that. The road was definitely a no man's land. It was as if the highway had an appetite for Apaches. Highway 60 continues to enjoy this reputation.

* * *

I witnessed the murder of a policeman one time. I was eating supper with my grandparents one evening when a police paddy wagon stopped to pick up a drunk person. A lone policeman got out of his van and walked up to the young boy who was drunk. A confrontation broke out and the young boy took the pistol out of the policeman's holster and as the physical encounter continued, the policeman was knocked to the ground. The young man pointed the gun directly at the policeman and fired it several times. I could see across Gilson Wash about half a mile away. The policeman lay motionless as the young boy staggered off. Subsequently, the boy was arrested. I was getting ready to run across the dry wash to see what had happened but my grandfather said I better stay put. The next day I walked over to the murder scene where I saw a patch of dried blood. It was sad to witness such a tragedy in the Apache world.

On another occasion a woman was found completely butchered in Gilson Wash. Earlier in the evening I had met this man on the old San Carlos bridge where he had asked me if I had seen his wife. I was only eleven or twelve then. I told him that I had seen her earlier in lower Gilson Wash. The next day, I saw a flock of white men in business suits combing the stockyards. I asked what happened. One Apache policeman said a lady got murdered during the night. I cried because he told me who it is. I somehow felt responsible for this lady's fate at the time.

Apache funerals were always gruesome to me. A lot of people were wailing. The only other time I witnessed such feelings was when I was on a funeral detail in 1965 for the U.S. Army in South Carolina among black people. In San Carlos during these funerals, there is usually an outpouring of personal care of those who are affected by the departed. People come to homes of the survivors to leave gifts of food, sugar coffee, potatoes and other staples to feed the masses who participate in funerals.

Apache traditions require an overnight wake for the deceased at his or her home. The body lies in state all night with the burial the following day at one of the local cemeteries. Inside the room where the body lies is usually decorated with crepe paper. All personal belongings of the deceased are removed from the home. When the body is brought home by the funeral home on the first day, there is usually a lot of uncontrollable crying by family members and friends. Hundreds of community members come to express their condolence. As soon as the body is entered, the next day the body must exit through another opening in the house. The body is never brought back through the same opening as it was brought in. This assures a permanent one-way journey for the departed. At night the family members and special visitors seat themselves near the coffin. Others may sit outside if there isn't enough room inside.

There is usually light bantering and quiet talk by the visitors. However, this solemn occasion and the final second day is usually the worst for the survivors. At night no mention is made of the deceased. Only when the sun is up the deceased is talked about. On the first day, people from the community usually drop by to bring food and to express their condolences to the family. There is usually plenty of food for everyone.

The women sit near the fires at night on the ground while making tortillas, boiling coffee and preparing some type of food for the visitors who will be eating at midnight. The hardest part of the night is about 2 a.m. when one or two of the folks doze off momentarily. Other people usually enter the room to take place of those desiring a break from sitting. Outside several fires are kept lit to assure warmth for the people. Hot coals are carried around on the shovels to people who are huddled under blankets outside. Usually the local jail furnishes a few trustworthy jailbirds to assist with the chores of a funeral detail. Their responsibilities are to do what the immediate family directs them to do. No one ever heard of a jailbird escaping from these wake details when they are on duty. Not that funerals are pleasant occasions but many of these jailbirds find relief from sitting in those cold cells. In addition, since so many of the Apaches were inter-related, these inmates were usually respectful. When my grandmother died in 1977, one of the jailbirds who worked for us got croaked on some brew that was passed to him that night.

The final interment consists of a motorcade to the church where a short service is held and then a short ride to the cemetery. The longer the funeral procession is, the more status for the deceased. My grandmother was buried near my grandfather. On that hot and dusty June day, we stood on a dusty hill finalizing the burial. Mysteriously, a large cloud appeared above us which shaded the whole area for a few moments. Poison Ivy, as my grandmother was called, was known for her mystic powers toward the end of her life. When I lived with her I never noticed that she dabbled in traditional healing methods until I got older. In 1976 she once told me that many Indians from different parts of the state came to visit her for her healing powers. Perhaps on this day the signals were strong enough to warrant temporary shading by the large cloud. When the grave is completely covered with dirt, each visitor and those who shoveled dirt on the grave are encouraged to place a rock around the edge of the grave. It is a tradition carried over from the old days. After the rocks, a bucket of ash is placed at the head of the deceased. Each participant takes a handful of ash and spreads it clockwise around the grave and makes a complete turn with the body upon completing this ritual. The purpose of this is to prevent spirits from leaving the gravesite. People are also encouraged to dust off their pant legs to shake out all of all the dust from the graveyard.

All personal belongings of the deceased have been placed in the grave also. I have seen cameras, rifles, and blankets placed in these graves. On one occasion, several Apaches were arrested for opening up graves and stealing these items. After the burial is completed the family members and participants go back to the home to clean up. At night, a spot of ash is marked on the foreheads of the family members as they turn to sleep for the night. This is always done as a precaution against evil forces of the night. Some of these ashes are spread completely around the house. Anything left belonging to the deceased is either burnt or smashed up. Pots and pans are usually chopped with an ax and thrown away at the dump. If these items are not properly taken care of, they are known to rattle by themselves at night.

Talking about death has always been a taboo for my people. On the other hand, an old story still circulates in San Carlos about an incident which occurred in old San Carlos many moons ago. Apparently an Apache funeral procession had gotten stuck in the bottom of a dry wash. The wagon was up to its' axles in sand. Everyone in the procession proceeded to push the horse drawn wagon to no avail. Suddenly, the lid to the coffin opened up and the deceased assisted with this sudden predicament. The helper jumped back into the coffin and everyone rode off to the cemetery.

In the summer of 1956 I stayed in Chrysatile near the Salt River Canyon about 50 miles north of Globe. Aunt Cleora and her husband Abraham Logan invited me to stay there with them for the summer. It was a good respite from the horrible heat waves of the desert country in San Carlos. There I met another Apache kid, named George, who was staying there with his relatives also. We spent endless days digging around highly carcinogenic asbestos tailings, breathing the fine fibers and pulling long strands of the stuff and blowing it into each other's faces. We made makeshift slides with corrugated metal slides and slid down these tailings. That was 41 years ago and if medical technology proves correct I should be coming down with lung cancer very soon. There wasn't a day that passed when we plunged down those asbestos tailings.

One afternoon while swimming in a dark lagoon in the canyon near these asbestos tailings George and I heard someone yell, "fire in the hole, fire in the hole", three times. We made our way back up the hill toward the company rock houses, and just as we were standing there a thunderous explosion showered hundreds of large chunks of rocks straight into the lagoon where we were swimming a while ago.

Large rocks tore into the big sycamores lining the canyon knocking off several huge branches. You could see the rocks plopping into the lagoon where moments ago George and I were swimming. God was truly merciful when he spared our lives that day. It was indeed a miracle. We stood there shivering from the cold winds which were generated from the blast moments ago. For the longest time George and I stared at the pool below contemplating the huge blast which nearly killed us. How were we supposed to know what "fire in the hole" meant?

After I left George there that summer, he found a blasting cap around the mining camp. Not knowing it was a device you stick into dynamite to detonate the dynamite, George stuck a nail inside the cap which promptly exploded and ripped off some of his fingers, pieces of his ear and part of his eyelid. I never saw George after that.

Uncle Abraham worked in the mines for many years. When he was alive, he suffered from several medical conditions including a form of cancer which may have been attributable to his asbestos mining days.

Aunt Cleora, who washed my uncle's asbestos-laden pants, suffers from a similar type of that medical condition as well. Not much was known about asbestos in the 50s but we know now that asbestos is a known carcinogen. Abraham was a highly respected traditional medicine man among the Apaches in San Carlos. He was also the last of the traditional caretakers of Holy Ground, a sacred landmark where traditional ceremonies are still held today.

* * *

I learned to wash a car when I was twelve years old when I lived across from Tom Faras, a Mexican family in Gilson Wash. The family made the best tamales and tacos north of the U.S. border. They had a daughter, named Margaret, who was much older than I was (Margaret is still happily living in San Carlos today). I got my first job at the Fara's house washing the family car. I got to do it frequently and old man Faras taught me the fine art of washing cars. The trick: rinse the dirt off and soap one section at a time and then rinse off quickly. Take another area and repeat. At first, I'd soap down the whole car and let the soap cake up the windows. Mr. Faras was quick to correct me for this slight mistake that no one made a big deal out of. I still use the same technique I learned from old man Faras. On Sundays it was a big day at the Faras' because that's when Apaches would come from miles around to buy some hot tamales and tacos. I always made it a habit to save money for Sundays because along with my tamales, I would get the cartoon sections of the Sunday paper that came wrapped with the tamales. Steve Canyon and Joe Polooko made my early days in San Carlos. If I was lucky, I'd get the crossword puzzle sections as well. Thanks Margaret Faras wherever you are in San Carlos.

Sometime during the summer of 1958, while sitting on the railroad tracks running through San Carlos, I was determined to change my future. At the young age of thirteen, I began to realize that I had some control of what I wanted of my life—in the distant future.

After experiencing what I have lived through so far, I knew that a change had to take place before the wrath of hell consumed me in San Carlos. Being raised by my grandparents, who had no formal education to speak of, did instill in me some precepts to live by. They were quick to point out the importance for providing for the welfare of everyone, including non-relatives who were a part of this small Indian community. Living by good example was a good measure of well-being and not how much money you had in your pocket. For this reason, even on the bleakest days in San Carlos, there was enough food for everyone. This meant giving up some of our own food for those who had none. Yes, there were days when there was no food at home and basic meals meant beans and potatoes. Free food furnished by the government usually consisted of canned ham nobody liked and honey that was as thick as motor oil. I spent many a night looking at the San Carlos skies wondering about a better tomorrow, one possibly filled with happiness and joy. In the first 13 years of my life in San Carlos, I had seen too much sorrow and pain in the faces of Apaches. It seemed like everything was done at a snail's pace and I began to see the idiosyncrasies of grown adults who were determined to see others fail. As an observer from a detached perspective, I began to see holes through my dreams and wishes. However, nothing stopped me or prevented me from succeeding to ensure my survival and happiness. As a youngster, I always avoided physical violence to settle differences with my buddies.

My dreams were confounded by value conflicts. Attending the holy roller churches usually instilled fear in me. It was as if HE was watching every move I was making, and the Christian upbringing I had was in serious conflict with my own Apache traditional beliefs, such as using eagle feathers and cattail pollen to pray with. Going to hell became an alien concept to me as I got older. Perhaps the dark winds of the Apache witchcraft could be considered hell. However, being around Apache medicine men created a feeling of well-being. It seemed as though Apache spiritual paths made you more at ease, more whole. There wasn't any shouting here about the world ending. To dish out Christianity was to live in constant anxiety.

Somewhere, I rode the fence to get a better bearing on my values. I was being pulled in all sorts of directions. My grandmother was a devout Christian while my grandfather had a traditional background. He never paid attention to the Christian doctrine. Oh he'd listen to the Mormon missionaries when they came on their Schwinn bicycles. Johnson Irving, or my 'she-choo' (grandfather), lived a hard life, having worked all his life, one filled with some pretty good experiences. He never tried to pass judgment on anyone nor did he involve himself with the bickering that seemed to divide many of the people on the reservation. He basically minded his own business. His legacy lives on today in Payson, where many of his blood relatives made something of themselves with a brand new casino, after having lived in deplorable conditions for many years. Johnson's brother, George Campbell, who is also long deceased, should receive credit for the successes of the Tonto Apaches in Payson. Descendants of his family, who are all members of the jil'she'ii'eh or the scrub oak/manzanita bush people, run that reservation.

* * *

Now grandma Ivy sure could put a spell on you with her Christian beliefs. Every now and then, she'd backslide and hit the hootch and get crocked. The fact that backsliders could return and repent wasn't such a bad deal after all. And of course, there were traditionalists who didn't touch a drop of booze or beat the hell out of their wives. The traditionalists maintained a strict order of living without fear of hell. I liked this and that was why I sat in the inner circles of Apache men who sang the ancient holy songs to the great spirits. Some of the old guys could deliver some fantastic eulogies at funerals. I can still hear their voices ringing in my ears. Very much like the famous John Kennedy speeches; these eloquent speakers pointed their hats and fingers to the skies, shifted their weight, wiped their spit off their chins and hoisted their hats up to the high skies for emphasis. This was all done in dignity. There are very few orators left in San Carlos today.

Dreaming can literally drain you and dreaming in broad daylight in San Carlos was also an exasperating experience. Summer vacations in San Carlos were a welcome break which allowed me to think about how I was going to survive in the future. My grandfather had some grand plans for me to be a carpenter. That was my early immersion in career education. He really instilled in me the work ethic that is missing in most work places today. Grandpa managed to whip up some nice wooden furniture at home. I honestly believed that he may have known that Jesus was a carpenter. I spent my time sawing boards and making furniture to my grandfather's amazement.

My dreams were further projected along after seeing Russ Graham drive a Greyhound bus that used to drop us off at the Peridot Junction in lower San Carlos. There was no encouragement to be a teacher or scientist or a lawyer. I was more interested in driving a Greyhound bus, perhaps on a one-way trip out of San Carlos forever. I spent a good portion of my life traveling these stainless steel buckets especially on the way to pick the annual harvest of cotton in Phoenix. At one time, my grandparents wanted me to be a cow puncher up in the mountains of San Carlos. At one time there were even plans for me to live with the late Leon Randall, a famous cattle man of San Carlos. Leon's parents had a big ranch in Cutter, west of San Carlos on the reservation. These grand plans never materialized as I continued to explore other options for my self. Had I taken advantage of this offer as a ranch hand, I would probably be one of the biggest cattle barons of Apache land today. However, horses always terrified me anyway. I would have washed out long ago. Couldn't have cut the mustard.

At the age of fourteen I really began to open my eyes and saw for the first time what possibilities there were for careers. Seeing Apache Orion Dillon behind his surveying equipment and sitting in the San Carlos hospital watching all the high strung nurses was an enlightening experiences. Mrs. Anderson, the white nurse, was known for jabbing cotton swabs dipped into iodine down your throat just to treat a sore throat. To date, I can still smell the iodine and all the other hospitals where I spent times getting my head sewn up from skull fractures and falls. At this time, I began to think in terms of 'success' and the 'future'. After all, I had sold the highest number of cans of Cloverine salve with small placards worded with biblical sayings which were highlighted by brilliant sparkly flakes with a picture of Jesus at the Lord's Last Supper. Even at Globe High School years later, I was the top seller of a fund-raiser that sold candy bars. The late Phillip Cassadore was one of the driving forces in my life. He never said a word to me when I was young. He was a big wig in the tribal government when he was young and my grandparents always consulted with Phillip about problems. I always emulated Phillip since he was the only person that I saw with a black tie and a white shirt. Just seeing people like Phillip made me think about how I wanted to look when I grew up. Part of this success was understanding poverty. When I reached fourteen years of age it seemed like there was never any money to do anything. Coming from a welfare-dependent family didn't help matters either. Waiting for my grandparent's government checks at the end of each month became a habit. Keeping charge accounts at Higgin's Trading Post was a common practice for my grandparents. Run the tab up for three weeks and then broke for another four weeks. It was an endless cycle. San Carlos was really poor at this time. Even to date, San Carlos continues to experience a high rate of unemployment. Each month when the checks arrived at the store's post office, it was quickly confiscated by the store to assure proper payment for the monthly purchases on credit. I am sure my grandparents were aware of budgeting during these times but it seemed like we never had any money to speak of. Money as a teenager meant status in San Carlos and only a few had money in their pockets. My dreams became somehow connected to the thought of having large sums of cash. I can safely assume that by that time, my values were slowly changing and this concept of money was becoming a critical factor in how I was going to live and grow up. However, the traditions were not forgotten as I continued to sit around the sacred drums at Holy Ground, where the songs were sung into the night for a spiritual renewal for everyone.

Apache forest firefighters seemed to have large sums of cash all the time. These men spent much of their summers battling fires throughout the United States. I never wanted to be a firefighter but I always enjoyed their presence in San Carlos. Summer fires in America usually brought prosperity to San Carlos even momentarily. These firefighters would usually arrive back to the reservation in slick brand new Levis and cowboy boots. Their sense of sharing was different because they seemed like they were the economic kingpins. It wasn't unusual to get a brand new 5 dollar bill from these guys. The best time to hit them up was when they were slightly tanked up from drinking raisi'in jack and malt liquor. Their prosperity worked well for San Carlos and nearby Globe—kinda like accidents happening for the police. There was a mini-Mardi Gras in San Carlos after payday for the firefighters.

Since bank accounts and checkbooks were unheard of in those days in San Carlos, these fire busters usually carried their big fat rolls of cash in their shirt pockets. If you asked them for money they'd always remark, "You been good at home?" and of course the reply was always in the affirmative. One way to work these guys over was when they were passed out from drinking too much. Cash was usually stowed away in their boots. Ever slip a pair of these cowboys boots off? Taking off a pair of boots off a drunken firefighter was like bartering with a mad and an enraged bear in the forest.

In 1957 or 1958 I was selected to attend a work camp on the reservation in Point of Pines. This place is located in the higher elevations where the mountain streams carry trout and pine trees stand tall for miles and miles. This was an opportunity to make some extra cash before going back to school that fall. About 30 boys were selected from the community of San Carlos and Bylas. We went to the mountains that summer some 60 miles east of San Carlos to cut juniper trees which were to be used for fence posts for the tribal ranch. The transition from the Sonoran Desert to the pone forest was a good experience. And the hot summers in San Carlos down below with temperatures of over 114 degrees made this work experience a good respite. Near Point of Pines is the Black River known to this very day for its excellent fishing. To the east of Point of Pines is Hanagan's Meadow, which sports a pine forest jungle which makes for an excellent summer vacation site. In 1957, Point of Pines was still a primitive part of Apache country. Not far from our work camp was the University of Arizona's field camp for archeological studies. Students and scholars from Tucson came to the camp for the summer to study the ancient people of the high country, who are known as Mollogons. The university dug for scientific purposes, excavating old prehistoric Indian ruins and possibility for looking for the missing saber tooth tiger. Each evening when we'd come back from the fence post cutting, we'd manage to hit the university's canteen store. There were lots of candy bars including ice cold 'soda water'. We even sneaked a peak at the young pretty university students clad in plaid Bermuda shorts. This was my first experience with croquet using wooden mallets to drive balls around a course. Volleyball was just as exciting too. The word in our camp was that many of the Apache laborers who had been hired by the university to do the digging for the project were being bothered by nightmares and ghosts. Apaches are very superstitious and we had a chance to hear some pretty good stories by these diggers across the road from our camp. Each night it wasn't unusual for some of the older boys to scare the hell out of us. One night everyone was woken up by a hooting owl which was perched on a tall pine tree next to our camp. You could hear it screeching away and the full moon added to the full effects of our fears. According to Apache superstitions, owls are messengers of bad news. Not long after an owl visits you, a relative or someone you know will die.

When we lived in Thatcher that one year during cotton harvest, an owl brought us some bad news. Not long after that, one of our aunts was run over by a Southern Pacific railroad engine. That night in Point of Pine, the owl talked to us all night. One of the boys said that owl was talking and saying "I'm your grandfather" over and over. The suspicion was that the Apache boys who came from neighboring Bylas 18 miles east of San Carlos were at the camp practicing witchcraft. Obviously everyone got scared and made a dash for the big Army tent which had been erected for us. We went inside and cowered all night. I could hardly wait to see daylight during that summer.

Each morning we boarded trucks which took us to the work sites five to ten miles east of Point of Pines. On one particular morning, as the truck was rolling down the dirt road, someone spotted a rattlesnake that was crawling across our path. There was a loud pounding on the cab of the truck from the boys who were closest to the cab. The snake killers wanted the truck stopped. The snake was a beautiful Western Diamondback, a species indigenous to the area. It was about 7 feet long and about 3 inches in diameter. He did look somewhat sinister as he lay there looking at us with his tongue feeling our body heat. As he continued to slither across the road about 20 sharpened axes slammed into his body. He didn't have a chance and within seconds the beautiful snake had turned into thousand pieces under the watchful eyes of laughing Apache boys. I hated killing things and this had happened long after my grandfather had me shoot a female dog when I was eleven years old. I asked one of my friends why the snake was killed and he said that the snake would have bitten someone in our work crew. I had a problem with this as we were some 4 miles from our work site. I also knew that if the snake had reacted quickly he could have inflicted some major damage to all of the assailants with the axes. Fortunately, this wasn't the case.

The wood cutting was hard and you had to seek out juniper and cedar trees which met the specifications for becoming a fence post. These type of trees never rot, therefore, they are good candidates for holding up the thousands of miles of barb wire which held back the tribes prime graded 'A' beef that probably made its way to the fancy restaurants of New York.

Each of us carried a giant black crayon, the kind they give you in kindergarten class. When one of the trees was chopped down, you'd trim it and write your initials on the bottom part of the post with the fat crayon. Putting my "DD" on the bottom of the tree was easy but dragging it was hard. It usually required the assistance of other boys to complete this job. This is where I began to see teamwork for the first time of my life. After a week of this slave labor, it got very tiresome. Each evening it was back to the camp where we would have a shower under the makeshift stalls erected for us. There was no room for privacy at the work camp. The outdoor john pretty much gagged you when you sat down. For the first time, I participated in a camp insurrection. One of the boys, who was to become a tribal leader, was instrumental in organizing this protest against the white camp director or field boss. We had been eating macaroni and stewed tomatoes for about 5 days in a row. The cooks brought us the stuff out to the work sites each noon. We got totally sick from this repetitious menu. It was pure slop. We organized and approached the Apache cooks who told us it was pretty much out of their hands. Finally, we met Pinocchio himself. Everyone at the camp gave this name to the camp director because he had a snout like the fiction's character. He refused to listen to our demands. We threatened further retaliation if he didn't budge. Most of us were between the ages of fourteen and sixteen. No sooner had we met with the camp boss, our menu was drastically changed the next day. This time it was Dutch oven biscuits, iced pop, cooked meat and hot vegetables. Our demands had been met. Having a flare for protests, I applied the same techniques after my obligation to the U.S. Army and the Illinois National Guard. After 5 weeks in Point of Pines, I grew tired of the routine. It was manual labor at an early age. If there was something to be learned from this it was that life wasn't a joke.

One day I received a visitor at the camp site. Orion Dillon, the Apache surveyor who worked for the Bureau of Indian Affairs in San Carlos. He handpicked me to assist him with surveying the wide opened spaces of Point of Pines for a juniper eradication program. Junipers are known for killing all the grasses underneath them. This eradication program allowed the range grass to grow without interruption. I was Orion's assistant and rode his jeep out to the range early in the morning. Orion operated his surveying transit while I ran out front hundreds of feet driving wood stakes into the ground with a hammer. We were preparing for another work crew that was coming to dig out the trees by shovels.

I knew Orion in the 6th grade from my 4-H days when he was one of the sponsors for the club along with Mr. Owens. I also went to school with Orion's sister Norma Jean all of our elementary and high school days. Orion was one of my earliest mentors and he took a real interest in me. I had a lot of respect for him because he emulated everything about education. Riding with him in his jeep in the brisk morning in Point of Pines was a real treat. In Point of Pines you can see for miles and miles. To the east toward Hannigan's Meadow mountain range and to the north toward Whiteriver.

As Orion's helper, I would walk way ahead of him while I kept my eyeball on him as he peered through his surveying instrument a quarter of a mile a way. I could see him waving left or right and down for 'ok'. He showed me the aerial maps of the area as well.

The following summer, I drove a hay bailer for Mr. Leminger. This was strictly illegal but I had a hell of a time seeing all those bales pop out the rear end. From the age of thirteen on, I kept myself busy each summer doing something useful in San Carlos.

In the summer of '59, I went to Prescott, where I lived with my mother. My stepfather, the late Charles Begay, was in the VA hospital in Prescott and I had the opportunity to see him often. My mother told me Charles was my real father. I have never been able to confirm that to this day. Prescott was a good break from the hot summers of San Carlos. My aunt Mamie had married into the Yavapai Tribe in Prescott, so I spent time with many first cousins there. That summer I met the late Sugar Rice, nephew of my aunt on her husband's side. I spent part of July having a crush on Shiley Bonnaha, a Yavapai who spent much of her time riding her bicycle around the reservation. Sugar and I spent a lot of time sneaking into the snooker pool halls of Prescott where I witnessed Sugar Rice beat all the old farts at pool. Sugar managed to make enough money off of these pool hustles to make the Matinees in Prescott. The late Mickey Rice, brother of Sugar, showed me more guitar licks the summer.

I left Prescott in late August to return to the hot dusty town of San Carlos, where I had Globe High School facing me for the 9th grade. I was apprehensive about high school that fall. I continued to live with my grandparents in San Carlos while I caught Fergus Sneezy's red eye special to Globe High each morning.

During registration my first year in high school, there was a major change in my schedule which affected the outcome of my life. Lyle Thompson's shop class was full at the high school. "You're late", they told me as they readjusted my schedule to take chorus. Although I enjoyed the guitar which I continued to perfect at that time, the thought of joining music class was such a sissy idea that I wanted out. The teacher was a young 21-year old Anglo. I ended up trying to pick my seat out in boy's chorus. The young man who was teaching chorus spent some time adjusting the seating arrangement. I knew then and there that I wasn't keen on the idea of staying in chorus. I was so disruptive that on several occasions I got dragged to principal Hugh Summer's office, where I got the Globe Tigers board of education on my ass, literally. Like a disobedient jail bird, I was taken back by the teacher, who by now had run out of steam in dealing with my behavior.

"I'm not taking this from you. You're not gonna mess this up for me", said he. Chorus was such a wimpy class I thought. Little did I know that the second year of chorus had many of the frontline football team of the Globe Tigers in it. People like Johnny Alvarez, wide receiver, was there by me. Soon, the young teacher befriended me that year by taking me to his home, where I met his young wife who was no more than 27 years old. They had 2 children, one being three years old and the other one about one year old. They lived two blocks up the hill from the high school in Globe. It had been a long journey for his family which had just completed a brief stint in Broadlands, Illinois, where the young choral teacher taught music to a basically rural farming community. Asthma had caused such havoc with the two young children that a change in geography was required.

The young family had arrived in Globe that summer of 1959, when Sugar Rice and I were hustling the snooker players in Prescott.

Soon, I was staying at my choral teacher's house on weekends. About this time I was trying to figure out why people had toilets in their homes. After all, I had an outhouse in Gilson Wash complete with a Sears catalog. So, I couldn't figure out the handle on the commode. My environment completely changed that year as I spent more time in Globe. I began to enjoy chorus more. I also met more people in Globe who were non-Apaches; mainly young people from the middle-class families. One of the first dates I had in Globe was with the daughter of a prominent physician. Not long after this, I also experienced prejudice from a white family. I had gotten to know another Anglo girl, named Patty, who was one of the most popular girls at Globe High. I had taken Patty to the movies and even a carnival the following summer. Not long after this encounter with Patty, the choral teacher who was taking care of me, got a phone call from Patty's mother. I was told that I was not to be dating Patty anymore. As it turned out, it was Patty's stepmother who had called. Patty's real mother had been killed in a head-on collision by a car load of drunk Apaches a few years prior my arrival in Globe. This was an overt expression of racism that made me feel bad and sorrow for Patty. This was the time when I began to question my own feelings toward white people in the town of Globe. I thought that all of us Indians weren't alike though. My world began to crash down upon me for the reasons that I couldn't understand. Not long after that, the choral teacher and his wife told me that they had resolved the situation with Patty's stepmother. I saw Patty at the school and talked with her about the situation and before long we were dating again. During my second year at Globe High School I was dating other Anglo girls as well. I was gradually accepted by Patty's mother. As I look back, I was glad that I became a part of the process which changed some of the negative attitudes toward Apaches in Globe. I dated Janice, daughter of another prominent business man in Globe. I was easily accepted by this family, and I frequented the girl's home in Six-Shooter Canyon. I could not believe the latitude I had with dating all the Anglo girls of Globe. I had many sincere relationships during the time I spent in Globe until the summer of 1962.

I kept going out to the reservation to stay with my grandparents in 1959 and the spring of 1960. The choral teacher and his wife bought me a large plastic zip up bag to carry clothes in. My grandfather's stove still filled up the one-roomed frame house in Gilson Wash and I didn't like my clothes smelling like mesquite smoke anymore. Sometimes, the young white family would go out to see my grandparents to visit them. After school, I would be taken out to San Carlos after chorus practice or some local event in Globe. With other Anglo families of Globe, I attended the First Christian Church on Broadway Street. Bob Sypult and June Norman whom I had gone to school with since junior high, were members of that church as well. June was striking and attractive daughter of a prominent Globe family photographer. I was good friends with her and her brother. I really began to get a sense of the word 'family' during the time in Globe. The choral teacher and his wife made a special room in the back of their home for me where I set up my room ... the first room in my life where I didn't have to sleep between my grandparents anymore.

I got my first high school job in the fall of 1960 at Cox' Lumber Yard on Broadway in Globe. Al and Mildred Cox were First Christian Church members who had gotten to know me well through the chorus teacher. The chorus teacher was also the choir director for the church. His wife sang with him at community functions as well. I started to earn about $2.50 per hour at the lumber yard and started to save my money in the Valley National Bank in Globe. My savings pass book allowed me to control my money for the first time. The following summer of 1961, I lived with Al for a few weeks during Al's wife absences for a visit back to the Midwest. I lived in a more prominent section of Globe in Skyline Drive east of Globe where I learned how to cook that summer and prune fruit trees under the watchful eye of Al. Enter Kathryn B., a gorgeous blond girl who took my soul that summer. Kathryn and I had been in chorus together for the past 2 years. She threw a birthday party for me at Al Cox' beautiful home on July 26, 1961. Sex was still such a taboo for me at the time even though I had to learn my patience with Kathryn. Nothing catastrophic happened that summer except some heavy kissing overlooking the night lights of Globe from 'G' hill.

Back in high school, our chorus department featured its first Broadway musical called *Lil' Abner* with Brian Bunney of San Carlos taking the lead role of Lil' Abner. It was a first class production by the young choral teacher who had gone west to seek a better life for his children. The musical was produced on the floor of the Globe High School Tigers. This was one of the two musicals ever produced at the high school for several decades thereafter. The other musical was *Bye Bye Birdie*, in which I had the leading singing role of Conrad Birdie. I even played the guitar for the role during the 1962 production. Globe finally made a mark by having refined music brought to its town by the young choral teacher from Illinois. I played guitar for the young couple on certain songs at local luncheons in Globe. Not long after this, they took me to Scottsdale to a classy place called Portofinos, where I met the world famous folksingers Bud and Travis, Liberty recording artists and Arizona's current official songsmith and balladeer Dolan Ellis. Dolan went on to join the New Christy Minstrels after his debut with Bud and Travis. Travis was a large influence on the style of music I began to play after that, especially during the folk scene in the Midwest during the mid-60s. I finally caught up with Travis Edmonson in 1975, I spoke with him on the phone to his home and brought him up to date about my music.

In spring of 1962, I stayed with the young Anglo family most of the time except to visit my grandparents every once in a while. The young couple who already had children of their own (Brad and Dawn Ann, who later became a wealthy model in New York City) confronted me one day and wanted to know if I would like to be adopted. I just couldn't believe that I was at that point where I was to make a commitment for adoption. I didn't want to be adopted by the white family and I was afraid they had plans to take me away from my grandparents. I talked with my grandparents about the young couple's proposal for adoption. My grandfather wasn't sure what he wanted for me. He did tell me that he was getting older and he could no longer take care of me due to his falling eyesight. My grandmother had gotten bedridden due to arthritis for the past few years, so she was relegated to staying in bed most of her life. Besides, I had gotten too accustomed to living with the young couple and their children in Globe. I didn't see any reason in turning back at this time. My grandparents weren't really sure and my grandfather said he would give me an answer very soon. All this was occurring during my sophomore year in high school. One day when I was in Mr. Joslin's biology class at Globe High, one of the student worker has brought a message to the teacher. It was an early afternoon. I was called out to the hallway, where the chorus teacher stood with a drawn face. It was not a pleasant situation from all appearances. The chorus teacher told me that my grandfather had suffered a stroke and he was still alive at the San Carlos government hospital. I was excused from class that afternoon and was taken to the bedside of my grandfather, the ace road builder of northern Arizona. He laid there very still under the oxygen tent with his mouth wide open and he appeared to be asleep. I was crying very hard at this time because I knew he was dying and this would be the last time I would see him. One of the things that really bothered me was that he never gave his permission for me to be adopted by the white family in Globe. He never did. I came that afternoon to the hospital to see him in hopes that he would somehow give me an answer. I talked to him and somehow I could tell he was listening to me. I told him that I loved him and that I hated to see him this way. I also asked him if it was alright to be adopted by the couple. He lay there very quietly without movement. I left him in the hospital that afternoon and went back to Globe with my choral teacher and his wife. The next day, while at school, my choral teacher came to my classroom bringing the ultimate news to me—the death of my grandfather who had raised me ever since I was two years old. I first cried and then bawled like hell down the hallways of the high school. I could not believe that life could betray me at this point in my life. The choral teacher and his wife were very supportive of me during this time, and so were the members of the First Christian Church in Globe. The funeral was held at the old wooden shack where I lived for many years in Gilson Wash.

They brought his body back in the afternoon for an all night wake. I looked in the casket and saw my grandfather Irving. It was the end of an era for this man who had brought so many people into the world. I looked at his face real close, the make-up was caked on his lips and somehow he didn't look natural to me with his Wall Street blue suit and neck tie. He should have worn his old blue work shirt and faded Levis for this final journey. He was really dead and I couldn't believe that he was gone. My grandmother Ivy was there with me as well. She was really heartbroken for seeing Johnson leave this earth. Many people from Globe came to the funeral. I saw my grandfather one last time before they closed the casket. I look very much like my grandfather today and I am also beginning to see the very first stages of my grandfather's baldness. Grandpa was one of the few Apache men who were bald. He was a rarity of his time.

After my grandfather's death, my life went into a drastic transition stage from my reservation days to an odyssey that was to lead me beyond the railroad tracks of the Southern Pacific and the cool running waters of the San Carlos River to the new horizons of a new life away from the reservation.

I was adopted by my high school chorus teacher and his wife in 1962 and my name was changed from Don Denny to Don Decker, after my new parents, Donald and Barbara Decker of central Illinois. I was now part of a new family which gave me a new start in life. This was the biggest break in my life as I went on to my new family, which included a new 4 year-old brother (Brad) and a 6 year-old sister (Dawn).

There were some major changes the summer of 1962 as my adopted parents informed me that we were moving to Illinois. We had a long talk about a new start for everyone. My adopted mother talked to me about the benefits of moving back to Illinois that summer. She said this move would actually give me a clean slate to start with after living in Globe and in San Carlos for the first part of my life. I said good bye to everyone on the reservation in Arizona. I would see my last mountain in Arizona until 1967 when I returned to deliver a car to Tucson, for a medical doctor from Chicago.

Like every wish of a high school student, I wanted to stay and graduate with my high school classmates but I accepted the fact that I was moving. It was difficult for me to leave my grandmother Ivy and many of my relatives in San Carlos. In addition, I couldn't forget all of my girlfriends in Globe.

I arrived from sunny dry Arizona to a humid Illinois summer of 1962. I had been to Illinois prior to this in the winter of 1961 when my adoptive parents had brought me there for the Christmas holidays to meet my new family in Charleston and Casey, Illinois. This family included grain farmers named Bill and Florence Decker of Casey and all of their children (who were also farmers in central Illinois). They had a son who was the only college graduate from this farming community and had received a degree in choral music. On the adoptive mother side was a family who were all college educated. This made a good mix for me, as I was able to adapt to the new families I had acquired through my adoption. It was a large family which contained hundreds of Illinois traditional farmers and other skilled workers. The forte of the Decker and Jackson families was farming and education, respectively.

We relocated to Charleston, Illinois, a small farming community with a large university called Easter Illinois University. I arrived on a hot August day with the humidity hitting about 95%. Since I arrived at night, I woke up to literally thousands of acres of corn that dotted every square inch of the Illinois countryside. You could actually get lost in these cornfields as I was to find out later in my life. I spent what was left of my summer vacation cruising the streets of Charleston, Madiun and other small farming communities in central Illinois with my new acquired cousins Donna and Sharon Decker and Vicky McCalravey of Jewitt. They were all members of the huge Decker family. I was introduced to many of the farm kids, who always made me feel welcome. We went to summer teen dances and skinny dipping with some of the urban kids in Charleston at the nearby open pit limestone quarries east of Charleston. That fall I enrolled at Charleston High School, where my adopted father began teaching choral music. There I met Mary Kay, the daughter of a prominent university professor at the nearby university. She was no doubt the most beautiful girl at the high school and in the community. I couldn't understand why she took an interest in me when she could have easily dated one of the jocks. Throughout that last year in high school I also met Janice and then Emily, who became my first heartbreaker. I went to the high school's annual fall bonfire and got to know some of the Rudy high school boys who had a flare for tipping a few cold cans of beer down at the Embarrass River, 5 miles south of Charleston. I also ran around with a doctor's son who kept me in contact with many of the farm belles at Charleston High. Dick introduced me to the first prophylactic I had seen. He also had a propensity for "lifting" some pills from his old man's doctor bag, which we experimented with. I also attended the First Christian Church where I got to know some of the "Sunday school types", who pretty much steered me away from the trouble spots. Bill Harpster, a drummer at the high school band attended the same church. In later years, in the mid 60s, we were to form a rock band that played to capacity crowds across the Midwest. Bill also took me on my first canoe trip down the Embarrass River, where one time we were threatened by some drunk thugs. The scumbags pointed their rifles at us saying "Let's kill these motherf…." We didn't talk to them, instead we listened to their verbal abuse. I wasn't afraid at anytime because I had already been exposed to this type of behavior in San Carlos. After this incident, Bill told me that he was prepared to pop the fellow with the rifle in the head with the boat oar. Bill was later drafted to serve in the Vietnam War where he lost a leg. He got over it and continued to play in bands after his ordeal in Vietnam.

It was an exciting change for me to be in this small rural town. I truly had a clean slate to start with, and no one knew about my past. I was accepted by everyone in the community. Suddenly, I had forgotten about undertones of racism which I had barely overcome in Globe, Arizona. I went to one on the university dorms in the summer of 1962 and accidentally ended up in a room full of folksingers. I met Mike Enright from Scahnecty, New York who taught me a few licks on the guitar. He was more amused at the proficiency of my guitar playing because by this time I had perfected it. We became good friends even though I was still in high school and he was a big time fraternity guy. I got to meet more of the university students and particularly Mike's fraternity brothers from the Sigma Pi Chapter. I also met Tom Windsor from another fraternity, who introduced me to some very nice attractive sorority ladies. I kept close in touch with the university folk scene while still attending the high school. In the spring, I participated in Eastern's folks festival. Back at the high school, I took part in the musical production of *Lil Abner* in spring of '63, which my father directed. I spent much of my high school days goofing off. Suddenly, I was having too good of a time. One day the high school counselor got a hold of me and knocked me around. I was walking down the hallway and the counselor said, "Hey, Decker I wanna see you soon, Okay?" I wasn't sure what he was up to until he backed me up against the door in his office and wanted to know "what the hell I was up to". I was scuffing off too much at the high school, so this little reminder from the counselor sounded serious. That's all it took. When you're at the same school as your dad, there isn't much chance for error. However, I seemed to have maximized my position as a student and a son of the choral teacher at the high school. I wanted to cut up often to let other students know I was one of them and that I wasn't gonna be no angel because my dad taught there at the high school. Much to my surprise, my dad was the driving force in having other teachers discipline me. In the last 9 months of my high school career I more than made up for all the lost time at Globe High back in Arizona.

I saw my first severe winter in Illinois, where I didn't see the sun for almost 3 weeks one time. That was my first test at understanding the elements. Never had I seen the temperature dip to 20 minus below. It was during this winter that I was introduced to the famous "lick the pipe" trick by Illinois farm kids. I went out to an ice cold frozen water pump handle and was encouraged to stick my tongue on the handle to experience "how cold it was". I licked the pipe, except my tongue refused to come back into my mouth. I was stuck there while several local boys stood around laughing at my predicament. I was in a helpless and critical situation. I panicked. I made a quick jerk on the handle and separated about 1 square inch of my tongue. This incident was a valuable lesson on the hazards of winter life in Illinois. I got frost bite on my ears as well.

Some time during that year of 1962, my uncle Johnny Decker of Casey, Illinois took me to my first pool hall, where he introduced me to snooker and some of the farm folks who came into town to shop and shoot the breeze. In one year I had learned how to speak Illinois "farmanese". The farm folks still have their own expressions that they use to communicate with. A favorite of mine is "Gol darnit" and "It ain't rightly so". And if you made a profound statement or some other type of emphatic statement, the usual reply was "Weell". You let the "e" in the "well" drag out which ends up sounding like "Wheel". Much of the farm talk reminded me of what I had heard on the "Hee-Haw" show. Getting to know my new relatives was quite an experience. Some of my adopted relatives continue to live in the farm communities of Casey, Greenup, Charleston and Jewitt, Illinois. My adopted father was the only member in the whole Decker family who went to college to receive a Bachelor's and Master's degree. On my adopted mother's side, most of her brothers and sisters received college degrees, including her mother and father. The farm people are truly genuine people though. They are generous and caring people who still believe that the nuclear family is an essential part of the social organization. Their Sunday get-togethers in their respective community parks still top social events in America today. If not at the park, the get-togethers take place on the farms. The late Phil Cooper who was married to my aunt used to host one for the largest Christmas parties each year. Phil was one of the biggest soy bean farmers in America before he died in the 90s from an accident. Most of my father's family members were big time farmers at one time or another in the Midwest. My grandfather, the late Bill Decker of Union Hills, near Casey, was also a well-known farmer in the Midwest. Farm people have close-knit families. This closeness is what sustains their survival. Their kinship values match those of American Indians. It is for this reason that I felt never any different when I was adopted into the white farm family. On my mother's side, the non-farming family also carried on a strong kinship bond. The Jacksons were from the Windsor area west of Charleston, Illinois. My adopted grandfather Jackson was a band teacher in the public schools in Charleston until he retired in 1960. In addition, my grandmother Jackson was an English teacher for many years. She also cooked the best chicken in the world! The couple devoted much of their time to the education of farm children in central Illinois. All of their children went to college and received degrees. It was through this union that created a by-chance encounter which changed the whole world for me. Had it not been for the allergy problems of my little adopted brother Brad, who is now 38 years old, my father and his family would not have moved out to Arizona in the early 60s. However, this marriage of my adopted parents was a grand design by God to make it possible for me to escape the harsh life of reservation. Coincidence or not, I accepted the adoption without question.

After high school graduation in 1963, I had several things waiting for me. The draft for one. The Vietnam War was still in its infancy in 1963 but soon the giant cancer which was to consume the nation for a decade was knocking at my door. I went to see Betty Brown at the local draft board and registered for Selective Service. I was hoping they wouldn't be too selective as I was making plans to attend college at Easter Illinois. The summer of 1963 I spent working and making payments on a '57 Chevy, which kept me occupied. I kept up with the folk singing scene at the university as I continued to jam with Mike Enright and some of the others at the university and around town in Charleston. I was determined to fulfill those dreams I contrived on the railroad tracks of San Carlos and I went to Chicago in 1966 where I stayed in Old Town. It was there that I met Judy Collins at the Poor Richard's Bar on north Sedgewick in Old Town. Dave van Runk, a blues singer, was doing a heavy stint in the area as well. Others included Steve Goodman and Jose Feliciano singing at Easy Street on the north side. I didn't know these performers by their names and it was only in later years that I recognized their faces on record albums. I missed seeing the Beatles by 10 minutes in Old Town. Had I stayed around at John's Leather Shop on north Sedgewick that afternoon, I would have had a nice chat with the boys from England. I got there right after they had left the leather shop. The group had been in Chicago to perform at Soldier's Field. I was told by the shop owner that the Beatles were alone that day. That night, the boys performed in front of several thousand people. I made my debut at an open-mike function downtown Chicago at the Gate of Horn. It was an off night and other famous folk singers had sung there, such as the Kinston Trio, The New Christy Minstrels and Bud and Travis. I sat for a good 2 hours before I was introduced among all the other amateurs who had brought their guitars. If you could get heard at the Gate of Horn, you could get possible jobs at other places in "Chi-town". I finally staggered to the stage with my guitar in hand. It was no use. I was crooked from too many beers. I was only twenty at the time. After a dynamic introduction by the M.C., who said I was Geronimo's great grandson (I think he made this up because I told him that I was from the San Carlos Apache Reservation in Arizona), I forgot the versus to the songs and about midway through one of the songs, I got a nice applause from the crowd. I got a quick escort to the dressing room after which I ended up hitting all the bars selling my "wares". The next morning I woke up at Judy's house in Old Town. She was a friend of my friend Marlene from Eastern Illinois University. I tried my luck at becoming famous as a folk singer just that one time in Chicago without much success. After two weeks in Old Town, I went back down south to Charleston, Illinois, where I joined a hot rock-n-roll band. Bill Harpster, Red Taylor, Jimmy Hite, Gary Tate and myself formed this tight band playing Rolling Stones and Paul Revere Songs. We became well-known in Illinois and played to capacity crowds in town like Champaign, Tuscola, Macomb and other towns across Illinois. We rehearsed and learned all sorts of songs. We booked ourselves in small farming communities all over Illinois. One night, we played at a battle of the bands with REO Speedwagon. At this time, our band was becoming well-known. A favorite hangout for this band was at the Red Lion Inn on Green Street in Champaign, next to the campus of the University of Illinois. Our group, The Rhythm's Children, was well received all over the Midwest. We were also the hometown band of Charleston, where we managed to play to a full house of teenagers almost every weekend. Prior to this, I remember Jimmy Hite's father coming to a pizza place in Charleston where his dad tried to coax him into coming home after playing at a job. Dr. Hite, a local physician of Charleston, was thoroughly pissed that night when he walked to my car and found Jimmy's guitar case tucked away in the back seat. Doc Hite took out some wire cutters and cut all of Jimmy's guitar strings in front of us. This was around 1965 and the band continued until 1968.

Our band became in heavy demand. Where we once played for $100 per night, now we turned $600 per night. We were now all old enough to play at a bar in Sidel, Illinois every Sunday night when most bars were closed across Illinois. Sunday nights were jumping at Elsie's in Sidel. Louise Taylor of Charleston, mother of bass player Red Taylor, was our greatest supporter in the mid-60s, when she opened up a teen club dance hall which featured non-other than The Rhythm's Children. Louise even rented several halls in Charleston which became our "home".

I quit the band in late 1966 only to have Tom Kelly replace me. Tom later went on to be lead guitar player for the Dan Fogelberg band. Fogelberg was also a product of the central Illinois music scene, including Irv Azoff who is still a big-time band manager for groups like the Eagles and others on the west coast. Azoff was originally from Danville, Illinois. The Rhythm's Children (without me) went on to win a state amateur talent contest at the Illinois State Fair in 1968 where Jim Hite got so good that he played the lead part to Eric Burton's song "Monterey". The group played in front of over 27,000 people during that contest. Ironically, I had joined a temporary folk singing group about the same time, called the Marcus Kenyon Singers of Charleston. We rehearsed for the same talent contest as The Rhythm's Children but in a different category. Earl White, Tom White, Glen Gabbard and I hastily assembled this group which went on to win first place in the amateur contest at the Illinois State Fair. That evening we performed in front of 29,000 along with Paul Revere and The Raiders and Sam the Sham and the Pharaohs. I remember Mark Lindsay from the Raiders jumping off the bus next to me at the back of the stage. I met Sam the Sham because he was in the same dressing room as our group. We sang two folk songs that evening with two guitars, an upright bass and a tambourine. During the fair, Earl White, tambourine player for the folk group bummed a cigarette from the Governor Otto Kerner. Thirty-two years later in 1994, on an evening broadcast of *Unsolved Mysteries* on NBC I see my good friend Glen Gabbard, who was the guitarist of the folk group I joined in 1967 which took first place at the Illinois State Fair in 1967 and who is now the chief psychiatrist at the Menninger Clinic in Topeka, Kansas, talking about serial killers. Glen's father was the drama professor at Eastern Illinois University, and he was the one who helped us with the choreography of the routine we did with the songs we performed at the Illinois State Fair. Glen's parents went on to Broadway, where mother Gabbard won a Tony in the mid 1990s. Sometime in 1994, Glen caught up with me in Flagstaff, Arizona, where he filled me in after I had written him a letter telling him I had seen him on *Unsolved Mysteries.*

In 1966, while still in Eastern Illinois, I had the opportunity to deliver a brand new Cadillac to Tuscon for a prominent dentist of suburban Chicago. I drove the car non-stop except for a wink at a Holiday Inn in western Oklahoma, to the San Carlos Apache Reservation. I drove up to the front of the San Carlos Trading Post, where I was greeted by Travis Noline. I felt great just to be able to step out of that car in front of a bunch of Apaches who were sitting in front of the store. Travis was the first to greet me. He asked me a lot of questions. I told him how I went out to seek my fortunes in the tall buildings of Chicago. Driving a new Cadillac that didn't belong to me gave me a lot of latitude in bullshitting my way through. I still hadn't gotten my college degree either. As a matter of fact I had just flunked out of Eastern. It was impressive though as I drove the giant Coup Deauville up and down the dirt roads of San Carlos even for a few moments, before I delivered it into the hands of the dentist at the Tuscon International Airport. I got paid $200 for delivering the car plus a free one-way airline ticket back to Illinois from the dentist and his wife. It was fun driving that Cadillac across the country and into San Carlos.

Earl White, another member of our temporary folk group, went to Vietnam, where he served with distinction. In The Rhythm's Children group, the drummer, Bill Harpster, was in Vietnam from 1966 to '68, where he had part of his leg blown off by a misfiring mortar round. Bill came back in 1968 to pick up where he left off and played for The Rhythm's Children. The band finally disbanded that year.

In the fall of 1967, I moved to Indianapolis where I enrolled in the Herron School Of Art of Indiana University. There, I continued to hone my art and guitar playing abilities at night while I attended school and worked at J.C. Penney downtown Indianapolis in the display department. At J.C. Penney, I worked under a well-known window dresser from New York, Ivan Taylor. Taylor spent time in the Big Apple working stores like Boniwitz Teller and

Macy's, dressing mannequins. I quickly learned the fine techniques of window dressing. On weekends, I played the coffeehouse scene at a place called the Glory Hole on North Meridian Street. At the "Hole" I met all sorts of musicians. At the Black Curtain Theater, I sang to dinner club guests who paid to see a theater production. It was during the seat changes that I was introduced for a few songs. The owner of the theater really wanted me to succeed and so he coached me with a script he had written for me in between two songs. I was a featured entertainer at the Beef Eaters on eastside of Indianapolis, singing in between sets of a piano player named Watkins, a regular on the Smothers Brothers CBS Comedy Show. The only difference between the Beef Eaters and the Glory Hole crowd was that the Beef Eaters crowd had diamond rings on.

Back at the Herron School of Art, I met Bix Smith and his brother, Stan. Stan's girl friend was a student there as well. These brothers also played exceptional guitar. We spent many nights playing jazz. This technique was a new concept to me. I had never tried jazz before. Bix was much older than I was and he had also studied art in France. Bix also had a roach bamboo cage which he used to cage all of the Talbot Street roaches which invaded his apartment. Talbot Street was where all the art students lived that attended Herron. Bix's roach cage was a good conversation piece and provided the backdrop for Bix's jazz and blues songs. It was during this time that I had my first experience with "pot". No need to describe the whole incident since most people today have experimented with this drug. I was a virgin of pot though. All it made me do was get hungry and drink lots of liquid. The effects were definitely different than Neesto's tobacco on the San Carlos Apache Reservation. Bix Smith was truly a remarkable artist and I often wonder what became of him after all these years. He was about forty years old at the time and I was just a mere twenty-four. When Brix arrived at the Herron School of Art, the professors were no match for Brix's techniques. One day, Brix and I got pretty thirsty and he told me how his teacher made him go outside to do sidewalk etchings with chalk. Here was Brix, who could draw circles around his professors, and now he had the task of lowering his standards. We got pretty looped that day and he brought out his portfolio of his art work which was a collection of years of art. His lithographs were fantastic. Some of the images I recall were of black people in the south and a revival meeting where people are reaching up to the sky. All of the prints were done in Europe.

Bix had the bright idea of having me carry these prints to north Indianapolis where the rich people lived. I went to the richest part of "Naptown" (colloquial for Indianapolis) and knocked on doors for a whole day. Surprisingly, I made it into the majority of these homes. In one home, a lady bought many of Bix's prints. She bought the one with the clown at the circus. She continued on with her selections and wanted to know who had done the art work I was peddling. I explained who Bix was and she bought several hundreds of dollars worth of prints and paintings on illustration boards. The lady paid me in cash. I finally asked her what her name was and she said her last name was STOKELY. I stopped selling Bix's artwork at that house because I knew I had sold enough for our re-supplies. That evening, I got back to Bix's who was now anxiously waiting for me and wanting to know if we even got a few pennies for his work. I told him I had a couple hundred dollars in my pocket. He said, "Injun, you got to be kiddin'". I told him that I made my biggest sale at a lady's house whose last name was STOKELY. Bix said, "You know who the STOKELYs are?" He explained that "They own the whole cannery here in Indianapolis that cans your vegetable soup you had here and probably out in Timbuktu, Arizona, where you used to live. They're one of the richest families in the world." Well, that really impressed me knowing that I stood right in the hallway of the STOKELY home. As I remember, Mrs. Stokely was very kind to me. She didn't act any different than any of the other people I knew . By this time, in 1967, I was still putting "two and two" together and started confirming everything I thought of when I used to sit on the railroad tracks in San Carlos years back. These rich folks weren't any different from me. Sure they had a lot of money but they recognized good art work too. The art work was done by an unknown poor person who probably never had much money either. Bix Smith's artwork is probably worth a lot of money today.

The Herron Art School scene was an educational one as well. At a local café near the school was where some of the art students hung around. On one occasion, I ended up sitting with several of my friends from the school, and one of the students sitting in our circle wanted to know if we would like something to eat because he had a friend there who would pay for it all. Of course everyone jumped at the opportunity, and we all ordered our meals and an older gentleman came over to visit with all of us. Our one friend from the school was very chummy with this man who paid for the burgers. We gorged ourselves to our hearts' content and even ordered up a dozen more beers to quench our thirsts. Finally toward the end of the evening, our art student friend bid us a good evening and left with his older male friend. After the situation quieted down, one of our other friends said, "You know the old man's faggot, don't you?" It was a real shock to everyone that one of our friends was taking advantage of a gay person. About a week after this incident, I heard loud sirens on a nearby street not far from my apartment. I went out to the street and saw a man dangling out of a window 4 stories high. There were many spotlights on him from below. There were also fire trucks which were in the process of extending their long ladders to the dangling man above. He was naked with the exception of the bed sheets that were tied around his chest preventing him from falling to the sidewalk below. Slowly, the ladder extended itself out to where the man was dangling. He was very still but alive. I walked up closer to the trucks and got a good view of the man. It was the man who had bought all of our sandwiches and beer at the local pub a week before. I could have been none other that what's his name, who hung around with this man the week before, I thought. It was a crude joke pulled on a perfectly innocent man. The dangling man was the point of conversation for many weeks thereafter around the campus.

All of 1968 I flowed with the situation in Indianapolis and contemplated my future almost each day. Now I had seen the true city with all of its blight and chaos. The midnight sirens were too threatening. On the eve of Martin Luther King's death, all of the cars parked on North Alabama street had their windows broken out. I was never able to pinpoint who might have broken all those windows. Perhaps some angry blacks who were frustrated over the sad news of King's death or some crazy white folks from the suburbs. Robert Kennedy also came to Indianapolis just prior to his death for a rally at the Marriott Hotel on North Meridian. I missed that opportunity to see him only to hear that he was killed in California shortly after his Indiana visit. After having spent my formative years on the reservation, I was beginning to really understand the complexity of this new world. Now, it seemed more complicated than ever. There were too many variables to contend with. The fast pace of the city. I had ridden the same bus from the north side of Indianapolis to downtown everyday for almost two years. I saw the same faces getting on the bus each day. A woman that really attracted me on these bus rides usually sat in the same seat every morning. I wanted so much to go out of my way to meet her. Somehow, this seemed like a remote idea for me. It would have required a lot of nerve to meet this seemingly single lady who shared the same ride with me each morning. I passed up the opportunity and instead read the morning paper which I picked up from the corner newsstand where the newspaper man always had a warm fire burning inside of a 50 gallon can. You won't see that in Indianapolis anymore. It's history as they say. I went down to J.C. Penney and worked my 8 hours each day. It was here that I met Christine, a young 16 year-old female. I was twenty-four years old at the time. Her father was a tile setter in Indianapolis and she attended a private Catholic school locally. We worked together at J.C. Penney, and we spent a lot of time together at her home with her family. I took her to her senior prom at the school, where she proudly introduced me to her classmates and teachers. It was understood that I was much older than she was. I respected this. However, I did not negate the fact that we had warm feelings for each other. Christine and I spent several months together in non-intimate situations. It was an opportunity that I never took advantage of knowing that it could have cost me several years in the Indiana State penitentiary. More important was that I got to know her family really well and her mother listened to all of my personal problems. It was too late. I became big brother to Christine, whom I had grown attached to earlier. Christine almost came close to losing her will power once though. Now, after all these years, I can't remember her last name or where her family lives. If I could only see them once again.

In 1968, I continued to pursue my dreams in Indianapolis. I stayed at Herron that spring but I had switched jobs to a silk screen company at the Gardner and Sons factory downtown. We printed radio panels for the South Vietnamese Army and banners for Burger Chef. The work was tedious and demanding. One of my foremen ran a hotel in Rome during the World War II. He told me some stories of how he saw a young Frank Sinatra there during the war singing in the clubs for the troops and their girl friends. In the morning, I had lots of enthusiasm for the job at the printing company. I got up early and made it on time to work every morning. I can truly say that this is one of the few jobs I have ever had for which I showed excitement. It was during this time that I began to really doubt my future goals. I wanted to be a teacher and go back and teach on the reservation in San Carlos. I spoke with the foreman, Harry, who said I couldn't go back to college because I wasn't "cut out for it". He even took me out for lunch one day down at Joe's Mexican Café and attempted to talk me out of leaving to go back to Illinois to complete my college degree. He even introduced me to a very important person from the Eli Lilly pharmacist company, which was headquartered in Indianapolis. This gentleman assured me that I didn't need a college degree. Actually, what was occurring was that Harry was losing a good worker at the silk screen company. By coincidence, Eli Lilly was one of my supporters as a young child on the San Carlos Apache Reservation through the Save the Children program. In 6th grade, I remember writing them thanking them for buying clothes for me. I finally resigned from the printing company and went back to Illinois to work on a construction crew to save up enough money to continue to pay for my '67 Chevy which I had bought two years before.

My first big job was to work on a church which was being built in a subdivision south of downtown Charleston. This was a special request by the subdivision owner. We had to build a church identical to the one in the movie *Hello Dolly*. As a matter of fact, the plans were sent directly from the California movie company. I worked with an all-Amish work crew from Arcola, Illinois. I got to know them real quick. They asked all sorts of questions about Indians in the West. The church had some big pillars out front with a steeple on top. It was a beautiful church that was sure to generate a lot of interest in the city of Charleston. We completed the church and moved on to other projects such as building a home for a prominent man who owns one of the largest candy bar factories in the world. After completing the floor for the house, a refrigerator was moved in and stocked with ice cold beer. It was a nice gesture on the part of the owner who wanted to quench our thirst after a hard day's work under the hot Illinois sun. Many of the Amish men loved their beer. Anyone who says Amish people don't drink beer is tipping a few too many beers himself. The following winter of 1969, I was working in sub-freezing weather in Champaign on the roof of a house when I smashed my thumb with a hammer.

My thumb split open and I tore the nail off of it as well. I knew I had to stay on top of the roof because I had car payments due for the '67 Chevy. It didn't take long for me to decide that I didn't belong on the roof anymore. I cried while holding my thumb. As I started to walk on the slanted roof, I accidentally slipped and fell off of the roof, landing in a pile of snow near the edge of the house. It was too much in such a short amount of time. I threw the hammer as far as I could and got into my car, which provided a respite from the howling wind. I quit my job as a carpenter. It had been a long 7 months of hard work outside where I had also experienced heat exhaustion.

I was determined to give up the car payments which has kept me a prisoner for several years. In January of 1970, I entered Lakeland Community College in Madiun, Illinois, 10 miles west of Charleston to finish up my college degree.

This was a good route for me since I needed to raise my grade point average before asking Eastern Illinois to admit me back. This was a new era for me. After flunking out two times, I was determined to tough it out. I registered and took two classes that spring season. It was still blowing snow outside in January but I felt comfortable sitting in the college building where the steam pipes were banging around to keep us warm from the snow storm outside. I kept thinking of my construction buddies outside. I was now attending a junior college to raise my grade point average to eventually reenter Eastern that coming summer. In philosophy class, a plumber in the back seat had it out with Joe College up front. It was truly an interesting class. The course was one of the required courses for my major. We got into some lengthy discussions of how it should be and what is right and wrong. It was this educational setting which got the wheels turning inside of my head. I ended up in the same philosophy class with a super guitar player named Donny K. He was a Polish so everyone called him "Donny K". I was really glad to know that another person who could have easily made hundreds of dollars playing guitar in night clubs would actually be sitting in a philosophy class for a whole semester. It got an "A" out of English and barely passed philosophy. I raised my grade point average high enough to get readmitted back into Easters Illinois University. I took some easy courses concentrating on art. I loved every minute of it. I was truly becoming someone. Here, I had taken an extra three to four years to figure out what I wanted to do with my life. After all, I didn't want to be a perpetual student at Eastern. I honestly believe that others were batting for me as well, such as administration people from Eastern who personally knew my parents.

Considering the fact that by 1969 most of my fellow high school classmates were on their way to making their first down payment on a house, I didn't have a penny to my name. Now, I was the older student in my department. My last two years in college were serious but attached with lots of fun. I made a fantastic, surrealistic movie in John Linn's art history class. I got Shiela to model in the nude for me in a junk yard south of Charleston. It was a 3 minute 8 millimeter movie about the contrast between the beauty of the human body and discarded objects. Dr. Linn loved it. I got an "A" for the class plus loads of credibility from a professor who didn't spend lots of time talking with students. It was my last year in college when my painting professor told me that I "wasn't anymore Indian than the man in the moon". I quit painting Indian symbols on my canvasses and branched out to free-form painting that had lots of slashes and wide use of colors. I participated in numerous art exhibits in the region with much success. On campus I was involved with the organization of a special workshop addressing the problems of Indian education. Several professors on campus and other individuals assisted with this event, which attracted a large segment of the student population at Eastern. For the first time, the issues concerning the welfare of American Indians came to the forefront on our campus. Obviously, the Vietnam War was also a main concern to many of the students. By now, my former roommate, Terry Shoot had been killed in the jungles of Vietnam. He was only nineteen years old when he went there. I buried him in Charleston. In 1968, the Illinois National Guard was placed on an extended standby status due to the disturbances at the Democratic National Convention downtown Chicago.

I was attached to one of the units in Illinois and I became more aware of the problems in our country. After Terry was killed, I changed my thinking about our purpose in Vietnam. Our presence had been wrong from the beginning. In 1970, several students were wounded and killed at Kent State University in Ohio. At Eastern Illinois, there was a large demonstration out in front of Old Main. It was a stand-off between the conservative students and the hippie elements on campus. Rather, they were conscientious students who were bringing about an awareness of the stupidity of that war in Vietnam. The demonstration was also to honor the students who were injured at Kent State. In front of Eastern's Old Main, both elements of the student body were arguing about the merits of lowering the flag down to half staff while others shouted, "Hell no, it stays on top". Someone from the administration read the official riot act from the governor of Illinois and demanded that the students disperse. It was an attempt to diffuse the intense encounter of the students. After no one would move, I grabbed the bullhorn from one of the administrators and told the crowd that if there was anyone who should decided how the flag should be displayed, it was me. I told them I was an American Indian and I wanted the flag to be taken off of the staff completely because everyone else at the site was trespassing on Indian lands! Of course, all of the factions started laughing, knowing that the whole scenario was not necessary. The Vietnam War dragged on for years after that until 1973. Even Bill, the drummer from the band I belonged to, had been drafted years before only to return home with part of his leg missing.

I finally graduated from Eastern on a hot August day in 1971 exactly nine years after I arrived from the San Carlos Apache Reservation. It took me a little longer than normal but I figured everyone else had a head start of at least ten years on me—emotionally. I had already been married one year when I graduated from college. I had to jump through a minor hoop prior to graduating from college. It seemed that I was missing 3 credits that spring of 1971. So I ended up taking a Botany class the summer of 1971. My professor was good about the whole situation because I had told him that the university should have notified me earlier about the deficiency. The Botany professor said I could do watercolor renderings of cross-section of microscopic slides that summer. I got an "A" from the class.

 I got my first teaching job as an art teacher at the Fairview Heights William Holliday School in Illinois across from St. Louis the fall of 1971. We stayed there until spring 1974, when I accepted a position as Indian Counselor at Eastern Arizona Junior College in Thatcher, Arizona. I brought a new born son and my wife out West in the fall of 1974 and ended up near my native lands of San Carlos after spending 12 years in the Midwest chasing rainbows. I took all of that experience and attempted to mold it into something I could utilize out in Indian country. This meant counseling Indian students at various colleges and universities in Arizona. Arizona, in 1974, still appeared primitive to me. A huge August rainstorm greeted my family as we arrived in the Gila River valley near Safford, Arizona that fall. It was a full circle that I had made from the dusty community of San Carlos Apache Reservation in Arizona to the outside world. My ambitions were validated finally.

* * *

Guillermo Bartelt

Negotiating the Traditional and Modern Self

> *We are what we imagine ourselves to be.*
> *The Native American is someone who thinks of himself,*
> *imagines himself in a particular way.*
> Scott Momaday (Kiowa), Author of "House made of Dawn".

The value of autobiographies in offering "an unparalleled insight into the consciousness of others" has long been recognized by such literary critics as Roy Pascal (1960), who stated quite candidly that "even if what they tell us is not true, or only partly true, it is always evidence of their personality" (p. 1). Thus autobiographical accounts are unique opportunities to examine cultural systems from an insider's perspective, and the statements of members of traumatized cultures, such as American Indian communities, provide windows into the tensions of culture change. Such tensions appear to emerge in the attempted accommodation of competing scripts for the presentation of the self in the written autobiographical narrative of an Apache/English bilingual male in his sixties. The narrative reveals movements between a tribal orientation and a modern individualistic conception of the world, resulting in syncretistic constructions of the self that appear to be at odds with each other. Very much evident in the text, a 20 000-word first draft written in informal, at times even non-standard, English, entitled "Apache Odyssey," is a series of collisions of the impromptu iterative Apache story telling tradition with the English rhetorical demands of concrete detail and a strict linear progression. The resulting disturbed sense of identity could be seen as emblematic of the struggle of a Native community in transition and of its collective suffering.

This study attempts to analyze the constructive processes in this autobiographical narrative, which are constrained by the convergence of what Scollon and Scollon (1979) have termed reality sets—particular worldviews or schemata, invariably at odds with each other, and thus giving rise to conflicting ordering structures. The approach chosen for this task is derived from an expanded ethnography of communication which allows for the interpretation of not only sociocultural but also psychological meanings of a text, accessed by the methods of interpretive sociolinguistics. Since narrative, as a cultural practice, reconstructs experience to make it acceptable not only to the decoder but also to the encoder, the negotiation of shared meanings becomes all the more problematic in a bilingual context. In other words, an acceptable sense of the self for presentation to others and, perhaps more importantly, to oneself depends in this case to a large degree on how well biographical events fit the canons of not just one but two very diverse cultures.

The canon of a culture provides, as Bruner (1990) has pointed out, the appropriate concepts and categories into which individuals are socialized and which then continue to be reestablished through interactions based on particular discourse preferences. One such structure is narrative, a cultural practice which serves, among other things, as the function of reconstructing experience and making it acceptable to the interlocutor and the narrator himself. Especially in autobiographical narrative we see culturally shared meanings negotiated. This process of re-contextualization becomes especially challenging for individuals with problematic or disturbing life experiences which demand at least a partial canonization through a relation to the established categories of the culture. Further complications are introduced when this process involves bicultural individuals, such as American Indians, who must come to terms with the integrative pressures of competing sets of cultural prescriptions.

The (re)-construction of past events, or looking at social reality for a second time, invariably involves the attempted resolution of certain problematic actions or events. This kind of discourse production, in which the ordered configurations of mental processes require complex planning at the rhetorical level, can serve as a window on the nature of thinking itself. Chafe (1979; 1980a, b; 1990) has suggested that thinking involves foremost information, the self, and consciousness. In this conceptualization, the self is involved with the fulfillment of needs directed toward the maintenance of the organism, and consciousness activates available information in the service of the self. Activated information of this kind can be discovered, Chafe points out, in certain focuses during language production which he has called idea units. At the spoken level, such units consist of clauses marked by final rising or falling pitch and various hesitation phenomena such as filled and unfilled pauses. These prosodic and temporal criteria serve also as boundaries for larger chunks of discourse called centers of interest. Whereas idea units are focuses of consciousness defined by information processing limitations, centers of interest are sentential links representing mental images in the discourse chain that are too complex for a single focus to handle. In a similar vein, Gee (1986) identifies narrative utterances with one pitch glide as lines and larger chunks of meaningful information as stanzas. At the informal written level, nonstandard punctuation and paragraph breaks can be considered as markers of structures similar to idea units and centers of interest.

Experimental work in speech production by Dechert (1980) and Goldman-Eisler (1968) clearly indicated that larger episodes marked by a significant amount of intonation contours and temporal variables were greatly indicative of the narrator's attitude toward the underlying experience giving rise to his narrative. Although such prosodic markers are not available in extemporaneous writing, the attempts to express distancing from or solidarity with the topic can certainly be isolated. Furthermore, if the experience represents a disordered event with which the writer has not fully come to terms, his attempt to narrate the sequence will produce considerable processing loads resulting in digressive discourse strategies reflecting processing difficulties at the time of writing. The recollection of disturbing events may create so much experiential disorder for a narrator that he may be incapable of presenting them in single centers of interest. As a result, he may feel the need to insert into a particular episode what appears to him to be crucial context information, producing digressive presentational activities.

To determine the connections the narrator is trying to make in the linearization of events, it is necessary to examine the points in the account where the main story line seems to be elaborated with seemingly unnecessary information which may even distract from the flow of information. In the following excerpt, the narrator recollects the imminent threat of being removed as a child from his home environment to be sent off to a distant boarding school:

Since the advent of time many children from the 'rez' (short for 'reservation') have attended Phoenix Indian School. As of this writing, the Phoenix Indian School buildings have been razed to make room for a show-case community center for the greater metropolitan area. Many of the children attending this school were referrals from the Bureau of Indian Affairs' social adjustment programs. Those who were displaced in home environments such as parental abandonment were first to go. Second, the juvenile offenders who had brushes with reservation laws, and third, children of traditionalists who thought it was the thing to do. This group usually followed the mandates of their parents. In July, the Bureau of Indian Affairs (BIA) always placed a list of eligible students who were to get on school buses at the two stores in San Carlos bound for distant government boarding schools in Nevada, California and Arizona. In mid-August, Apache children as young as ten years old would line up for roll call in front of the school offices in the government school compound in San Carlos.

When I was bound for 7*th* grade, the BIA had me earmarked for enrollment at Phoenix Indian School. The only chance I would have to see my grandparents would be once in a nine month period—Christmas. Big Christmas present! So, many of the children sent to these types of schools were outcasts in San Carlos. I remember sometime in July of that dreadful year, my grandfather took me down to the local trading post and bought me one of those ugly blue metal suitcases with a fake brass border around the edges that you still see in the bunk rooms of cowboys today. These suitcases had a paper tray in them. At each end were snap latches with a locking devise about mid-way across the case. We went through the whole store and bought Levis, shirts, socks and underwear. They were all too big to fit me ... but what the hell, right? I wasn't gonna be around anyway. Along with my personal belongings, I packed the suitcase in the second week of August in preparation for the much-talked about Phoenix Indian School. I was ready for it.

My grandfather took me down to the school ground that hot August day to catch the bus. There were about ten buses there all heading west to Nevada, California and Arizona. Each bus had a number on it to signify its destination. The school officials took my blue metal suitcase and shoved it underneath the back seats of the school bus. I climbed up the front of the steps finding a seat in the middle of the bus. It was loaded with other Apache kids as well. Everyone was clean and dressed up for the long hot trip. I remember I had on a cowboy shirt with fake pearl buttons and a set of PF Flyers tennis shoes that were by now baking my stinking feet. My Levis were too long and the cuffs were rolled up 3 times, if not more. I sat next to a kid who I may have seen a few years back picking his nose in his dad's car on the way to Globe when I was hitchhiking with my grandfather. He was still licking his runny nose.

It was hot and miserable inside the bus. I looked out the window and I could see my grandfather standing there staring at the bus. He couldn't see me. He was probably wondering how I was going to make it in the boarding school. The noise in the bus suddenly came to a halt after an adult came on board with a clipboard in his hand. He got everyone's attention in Apache and said he was going to read off names and that we had better pay attention. He began reading the long list on his official-looking clipboard. There was a string tied to the metal clip and the other end had a long pencil tied to it. The names were in alphabetical order and when he came to the D's (Denny was my last name at the time), he didn't call my name at all. I was waiting for him to do so because I kept track of everyone's name on the list. I sat there the whole time wondering what the hell was going on. It must have been an hour before someone came on the bus and said, "Don Denny, off the bus".

I slowly walked off the bus and soon felt the cool breeze hitting me underneath the tamarack tress which shaded the bus I had been sitting on. I must have felt relieved because my heart wasn't really set on leaving San Carlos. I had already heard some horrible stories about these distant schools. My grandfather walked up and spoke to the man with the clipboard. I couldn't hear what they were saying except I heard the man say he didn't know what was going on.

The next thing I know, we were all walking to the back of the bus where one of the older boys tossed my metal suitcase to the ground. It made a large thump and I could visualize my white oversized socks doing somersaults. My grandfather quickly lifted the blue suitcase to his shoulder, and we started walking toward home in Gilson Wash. Grandfather didn't say much, but he got stronger as he carried the huge suitcase without stopping for a rest.

The macro illocutionary act of this part of the autobiographical narrative attempts an expression of Apache identity by appealing to a collective discourse of suffering which is derived from the ethnohistorical significance of the government boarding school system for American Indians. In his introductory idea unit, the narrator's formulation "[s]ince the advent of time many children from the 'rez' … have attended Phoenix Indian School," acknowledges the boarding school phenomenon in the lives of Apaches as a cultural topos, in a similar sense that Treichel (2004, pp. 23, 255) has applied the term to the role of a shared inventory of stories about imagined communities which contribute to identity formation and maintenance. Since the late nineteenth century, the Bureau of Indian Affairs has resorted to physically removing Indian children from the influence of their linguistic communities by placing them in boarding schools far from the home reservations in the West. The first two such institutions were Carlisle Institute in Pennsylvania, founded in 1879, and Hampton Institute in Virginia, founded in 1881. Both schools emphasized vocational skills combined with a basic elementary education and enrolled students from all tribes. Since it was often impractical and expensive to send many Indian children from the Southwest to such distant locations, regional boarding schools were established at Albuquerque and Santa Fe, New Mexico; Tucson and Phoenix, Arizona; Riverside, California; and Lawrence, Kansas. The boarding school became an effective device for the teaching of English by punishing students for the use of their native languages and by prohibiting all signs of an Indian identity such as tribal dress, religious practices and long hair on males. In addition, the intertribal and multilingual context of the boarding school student population made it necessary to resort to English as a lingua franca outside of the classroom in such places as the dormitory and cafeteria and in extra-curricular activities. Many Indian students remained in the boarding schools for a period of eight years under military discipline without being allowed to see their parents. The ethnohistorian Edward Spicer (1962) describes the boarding school situation in this way:

Out of touch with parents and other Indian adults, and under the instruction of men and women who were officially and usually personally antagonistic to native Indian ways including language, as well as unequipped for learning the Indian languages, the students in periods of three or four years learned how to speak English and, somewhat less effectively, to read and write it. (p. 44)

Although today's boarding school curricula attempt to match the offerings of public schools and the practice of native traditions is no longer discouraged, such was not yet the case in the 1950s, the era to which the narrator refers. Horror stories about the boarding school experience still make up a substantial part of the oral tradition of many older individuals in American Indian communities. Memories of the alleged physical and psychological abuse have given rise on the one hand to life-long resentment and on the other hand to proud claims of overcoming adversity. In their oral autobiographies many American Indians even credit the harsh discipline as a valuable character-building experience, much as military service in retrospect often adds to self-esteem. The narrator gives a hint of this view when claiming that "traditionalists" were in support of this kind of educational experience for their children. In any case, the boarding school as a cultural topos remains a source for the discourse of suffering in the collective American Indian identity formation processes.

Even though the narrator narrowly escapes this potentially harrowing experience, he feels compelled to add his story to the large storehouse of boarding school tales in order to access this crucial identity marker. In other words, in spite of the intervention of fate, even the partial amount of suffering, qualifies him not only as a full-fledged member of the indigenous community but also as a quasi member of an acknowledged and venerated group of survivors. Indirectly, his explanation regarding the students' criteria for boarding school attendance as "[t]hose who were displaced in home environments such as parental abandonment were first to go" also reveals his own troublesome parental circumstances. Thus his status as an "outcast" in his own community intensifies his suffering and at the same time amounts to a subtle accusation of child neglect, perhaps even abuse. Since only the grandparents are mentioned, the natural parents were apparently unavailable or maybe even avoided as nurturers. Nevertheless, the prospect of being separated from his familiar surroundings for nine months and only being able to come home for Christmas is remembered as "dreadful" and taps into a shared narrative schema of suffering, whose detailed explanation to Native decoders would be certainly superfluous. However, in his aim to address non-Native readers, he feels compelled not only to explain the pain of separation but also to confront white society by inserting such sarcastic comments as "[b]ig Christmas present."

In his further attempt to explain this Native schema within English rhetorical constraints of the flow of information, the narrator seems to encounter a problematic task for this episode. The desire of creating a believable account for non-Native readers causes the narrator to appeal to English rhetorical expectations of concrete specifics by inserting seemingly trivial and distracting details about objects which are not crucial to the center of interest. This discourse strategy seems at first to be at odds with preferred Apachean narrative techniques which rely on redundancy for emphasis and foregrounding. This rhetorical feature emerges especially in contexts such as persuasive arguments, the underscoring of emotions, and the repetition of main ideas in stories and of punch lines in jokes (Bartelt 1983). A similar strategy in the mode of argumentation was noticed by Scollon and Scollon (1979) in Canadian Athapaskan, which also belongs to the Na-Dene family, when they observed the emphasis of the discourse lying in the process rather than the outcome. From an outsider's point of view, discussions seem to lack logic and proceed in circular and holistic ways. Particularly in public meetings, portions of texts are repeated with only subtle changes in detail. Apparently, these changes become only important when the discussions require the presupposition of new underlying assumptions for the foregrounding of the arguments. Scollon and Scollon (1979) note:

The method of argument was for one to say first something like, "We have a good chief." The second would then agree saying, "I agree that we have a good chief but there are other good people." Thus it was only implied that this chief might be replaceable. The first would then say, "I agree that there are other good people but they don't know how to speak for the people." This would be answered by "People should tell their chief what they think, then he can speak for them." (p. 186)

The Scollons claim that the main concern of the speakers is the avoidance of a rapid integration of new details and the sudden shift of presuppositions in order to ensure a fully assimilated discourse in progress. To an outsider, on the other hand, the discourse appears simply disorganized because the speakers do not seem to stick to the point.

The transfer of this foregrounding strategy, resulting in a peculiarly redundant nature of English writing produced by Apachean speakers in Arizona has been documented in Bartelt (1983, 1986). However, this feature, which usually emerges in written English as the repetition of key lexical items and phrases for the expression of emphasis, even to the point of violating Grice's maxims, appears only indirectly in the boarding school text. Instead of repetitions intended to avoid the rapid integration of new details, the narrator offers digressions in the form of seemingly trivial detailed, and at times even redundant, descriptions which, nevertheless, attempt to contextualize an event which still does not make much sense to him.

Thus in the same center of interest which begins with an explanation of the suffering caused by the extended boarding school attendance periods without being allowed to visit relatives, the narrator somewhat abruptly switches to a focus on his suitcase and its contents. The idea units containing such textual structures as "ugly blue metal suitcases", "fake brass border around the edges", "paper tray" and "bunk rooms of cowboys" divulge a need by the narrator to underscore a state of poverty. In the same vein, the pseudo interior monologue "[t]hey were all too big to fit me … but what the hell, right? I wasn't gonna be around anyway" discloses a not so subtle implication of indifference on the part of his own kin. This shift to the use of greater detail of seemingly unimportant objects can be regarded as a type of foregrounding which causes some part of a text to be perceived as standing out against a less determinate background. As originally proposed by Prague School poetic theorists such as Jan Mukarovski and Roman Jakobson, foregrounding was primarily recognized as a demonstration of how literary language is structured to impede and prolong perception. Since then, stylisticians such as Roger Fowler (1996) have extended these insights to all forms of discourse in which signs become palpable while the objects they designate are backgrounded into subordinate importance. In the case of the boarding school episode, selected adjectival and compound noun sequences produce a perceptual salience that invites independent notice and interpretation of a significance which appears to be additional to the initial focus of the center of interest.

These foregrounding constructions appear to be presentational activities which are inserted into the main story line in response to a perceived explanatory need by the narrator for the creation of coherence more for himself than for the decoder. Even before he has really fully finished elaborating the main topic, he feels the need to enter into digressions. By doing so, he not only realizes the enormity of his experience but also communicates his desire to make some sense of it by seeking to blame two external forces beyond his control. First, the Bureau of Indian Affairs school personnel, who dehumanize him by "earmarking" him like cattle, fail to acknowledge his personhood when his name appears not to be listed on the "official-looking clipboard" which had "a string tied to the metal clip and the other end had a long pencil tied to it." The seemingly redundant details of the clipboard provide a heightening of the suspense and ultimate relief from a situation on which his "heart was wasn't really set." The clipboard seems also symbolic of the power of the state as well as the disconcerting randomness of human events. Second, in this scenario the guardian, his grandfather, becomes a quasi-accomplice rather than a protector. Seated behind the tinted window of the bus, the narrator is no longer visible to his grandfather, whose stare appears not only helpless but also alienating. Not having been able, or probably willing, to prevent the imminent removal of his grandson from his home, the grandfather is nevertheless presumed to have been concerned for the narrator's well being. However, the adverbial hedge "probably" infuses a certain amount of caution, perhaps even alienation, in that assumption as well.

The continued foregrounding of his "blue metal suitcase," which is forcefully "shoved" by the "school officials" supports the plausibility of his implicit point about his powerlessness and exposure to potential violence as one of the causes of suffering. Particularly telling is the mention of the precise place on the bus, "underneath the back seats," to which his belongings had been relegated. The foregrounding process is still preoccupied with his personal belongings when in the next idea unit the clothing worn for the bus trip becomes a vehicle to express the suffering of poverty and neglect. Thus, to be "dressed up" for the trip implied such discount clothing items as "a cowboy shirt with fake pearl buttons" and "PF Flyers tennis shoes" that were making his feet smell. To round off the humiliation, the narrator returns to the oversized Levis which his grandfather had purchased for him at the trading post and whose "cuffs were rolled up 3 times, if not more." The personification of his clothing when he visualizes his "white oversized socks doing somersaults" as his metal suitcase is thrown off the bus creates a parallel which heightens the expression of his suffering. The "large thump" his suitcase makes as it gets tossed to the ground is emblematic of the harsh treatment and ultimate rejection he experienced during the loading of the bus. In the final idea unit of this center of interest, which concludes the boarding school episode, the metal suitcase becomes almost symbolic of the grandfather's burden of having to continue raising his grandchild without assistance from the state. Notwithstanding the optimistic tone which is infused when the grandfather seems to become stronger in spite of the weight of the suitcase on his shoulder, the perception by the narrator of himself as a burden on his grandparents is further underscored later in the text by their encouragement of his getting adopted at age fifteen by white people.

This episode presents the narrator with a dilemma. In addition to his own tribal membership, which he communicates with the idea unit "[i]t was loaded with other Apache kids as well," his reconstruction of the boarding school experience, albeit aborted, becomes an extremely important additional ethnic identity marker in the presentation of the self. However, the detailed digressions pursue intended specific underlying indictments of some harsh realities of reservation life, the disclosure of which to outsiders might be perceived by fellow San Carlos Apaches as bordering on ethnic disloyalty. Thus the foregrounding processes as strategies intended to strengthen the claim of suffering end up taking a direction somewhat at odds with the Apache canon and could be interpreted as endorsing the common Anglo prejudices about life on Indian reservations, especially at San Carlos, as being poverty-ridden and likened to "concentration camps". Ironically, Apaches, like other tribesmen in the Southwest, who are keenly aware of such condescending attitudes, usually regard their reservations as safe havens in a hostile white world. Therefore, since it is highly unlikely that residents in such communities would view themselves as living under harsh conditions, it appears to be the case that the narrator has had to distance himself from his childhood environment and ethnicity sufficiently enough to make the connections he requires for his presentation. His later biographical particulars, especially his being adopted by a white family and spending a significant portion of his youth in the Midwest, may have prompted him to reconstruct the boarding school episode with a conflicted perspective regarding his place in the reservation community. Thus his foregrounding constructions, though they may appear to be trivial, perhaps even confused, digressions, offer him an overriding order-creating potential in that they provide a contextualizing explanation for the particular claims of his personal suffering.

Engaging in foregrounding processes affords the narrator the confidence in his claims of suffering due to powerlessness and loss of humanity as clearly substantiated and now absolutely coherent. Thus the interruption of his main presentational activity to insert these seemingly trivial details contributes in the end through effective re-contextualization to the recreation of a conceptual order acceptable primarily to himself. Linde (1993) has pointed out that the principal task in creating adequate causality is for the narrator to establish a sequence of events with acceptable reasons which in turn make unacceptable the possibility of the randomness of life. For our narrator, the acceptable form of adequate causality for his personal suffering seems to be the notion of powerlessness in confronting a seemingly uncaring and arbitrary Bureau of Indian Affairs as well as the poverty and social instability of reservation life.

Among the first to point out a biographical process scheme which models extended structures of suffering was Goffman (1972, p. 43), who suggested the term "sad tale" for retrospective accounts of such dismal events in a person's past that the best the narrator can do is to show that he is not responsible for what has befallen him. About the same time, Strauss and Glaser (1970) developed the concept of trajectory for the work activities of medical professionals dealing with the care of terminally and chronically ill patients (cf., Strauss, Fagerhaugh & Suczek, 1985). Expanding that concept, Riemann and Schütze (1991) have suggested the application of the concept of trajectory to autobiographies exhibiting the management of disorderly social processes and processes of suffering. These phenomena typically involve chains of events which give the narrator a sense of loss of control over his own life circumstances. In such cases, he feels that he is able only to react to outer forces which he now fails to understand. This sense of loss of control and of constant fear may produce a paralysis of the speaker's former action capacities. Such an outcome would render him estranged from himself and with low self-esteem. A trajectory, then, may contain forms of management of deviant experiences, and in his attempt to come to terms with such experiences, our narrator also applies such a process in his biographical work in order to reintegrate himself into the cultural canon, which he apparently supports.

One of the strategies to achieve this reintegration is for the narrator to dissociate himself from the other players in the drama through the use of deictic expressions and modals. Thus the use of a distancing demonstrative in the classification of some boarding-school-bound children as "[t]hose who were displaced in home environments such as parental abandonment were first to go" is indicative of his own disturbing personal familial circumstances with which the narrator has difficulty coming to terms. On the other hand, the associating demonstrative in "[t]his group usually followed the mandates of their parents" is an attempt to embrace the more prestigious criterion of belonging to a traditionalist family, even though it appears that the absence of parents makes the first criterion more of a probability. Furthermore, as it becomes clear to the narrator in the alienating observation "I could see my grandfather standing there staring at the bus" that even his caretaker was willing to abandon him. The dissociation from him is evident in the selection of the distancing adverbial "there". To intensify the feelings of alienation, the narrator describes a child sitting next to him on the bus as "licking his runny nose" and as someone whom he "may have seen a few years back picking his nose" as well. Particularly, the choice of the modal "may" provides the narrator with a vehicle for dissociation from the other children with the same fate and with the self-appointed authority of a detached observer of reservation life. Also worth pointing out is the dwelling on the child's preoccupation with his seemingly uncontrollable mucus in the context of hitchhiking as the narrator's family's primary mode of transportation. This juxtaposition appears to function as a retreat into greater rhetorical subtlety. In other words, the shame of having to beg for a ride to town from tribal kinsmen and the humiliation of being exposed to a child engaged in objectionable personal habits underscores not only dissociation of the self but also the recycling of the theme of personal suffering.

The attempt at dissociation from the other participants in the event is reiterated as the narrator continues to take on the role of the detached observer. The fact that the school official with the clipboard in hand "got everyone's attention in Apache" is only remarkable if the narrator considers himself to be primarily an English speaker and as such he intends to draw a linguistic boundary which strengthens his dissociation from the other actors. Furthermore, as the failure of the school official to call his name intensifies his feelings of severe reduction of personhood and of powerlessness, the narrator attempts a separation of himself not only from the others but also from himself as a protagonist. This process of dissociation is possible through what has been termed reflexivity. It makes possible the process of relating to oneself externally, the most important function of which, according to Linde (1993, ch. 4), consists of the establishment of the moral value of the self. Actually, the simple act of narration itself already creates a split between the narrator and the world of the text by allowing comments on the actions of not only the other players but also of the protagonist himself. In this case, being trapped without the possibility of physical escape in a trajectory situation such as a degrading hot bus bound for an oppressive institution for a lengthy period of time has caused the narrator to doubt his own integrity. Yet, the process of narrative not only allows the speaker to present himself as being one actor among others but it also provides him with the rhetorical resources to present himself as a person in control, even if the protagonist is not.

However, this self-appointed role of the detached but moral observer brings with it the uncomfortable paradoxes of the unfolding narrative which force the narrator to identify with the protagonist, in this case, as a sufferer who was going to be exposed to antagonistic and, perhaps even, dangerous situations at boarding school. As a result, there is an attempt in the first center of interest to canonize the boarding school experience as a sort of rite of passage. The matter-of-fact assertion that traditionalists expected their children to attend boarding schools because the parents simply "thought it was the thing to do" attempts to place the institutionalization of these children off the reservation within an expected Apache cultural category. However, even though these children "usually followed the mandates of their parents," it soon becomes clear to the narrator that these events are too horrendous to fit into a "traditional" Apache cultural category. The implication that emerges seems to involve an accusation of traditionalists as having been downright uncaring as they turned over their powerless charges "as young as ten years old" to the cold school officials. Lexical choices such as a "line up for roll call in front of the school offices in the government school compound" resort to the defamiliarizing discourse of military conscription and describe a shock caused by this disconcerting event. This type of discourse containing higher predicates has been interpreted by Treichel (2004, p. 51) as expressive of a trajectory. Thus, for the children, the basic bonds of traditional Apache solidarity have been severely disrupted and no one can really be trusted any longer. Suddenly, moral rules of traditional kinship behavior are put on hold as the narrator begins to act toward his new environment with great fear and suspicion. Furthermore, his sense of physical insecurity then broadens, almost metaphorically, to include the hot and miserable conditions on the parked bus, an enclosure which in turn seems to serve as a symbolic foreshadowing of the imminent entrapment awaiting the victims bound for boarding school.

Yet, the perceived agent causing the most acute breakdown of social solidarity and threat to physical safety turns out to be the fellow tribesmen hired by the authority structure of the Bureau of Indian Affairs. The ethnic dimension in this recollection of treatment by school authorities becomes subtly apparent, as the narrator seems to exhibit considerable trouble in his lexical search for an appropriate way to refer to the Apache personnel whose mercenary actions directly effect the separation of children from their homes. Although clearly identified as Apache speakers, the narrator refuses to regard them as tribal kinsmen by referring to them with alienating lexical choices such as a "school official," an "adult" or simply as "someone." In Apache culture, in which everyone is considered to be a blood relative, the betrayal of even distant kinship bonds is considered by some a flaunting of ethnic solidarity and in the past was regarded downright irrational behavior.

Once again, this type of narrative re-experiencing involving events which might be felt to be traumatic or shameful seems to be inspired by the notion of suffering and at the same time by a need for a presentational order at the very moment it is processed. The narrator realizes at certain points in the ensuing narrative that the account would not be credible if he did not insert such seemingly trivial, but to him relevant, details. In a very crucial sense, these constructions make possible a kind of biographical metamorphosis in which encountering recollections, perhaps even repressed ones, becomes an enrichment of identity and a claim for reaching new levels of maturity. Such a claim is evident as our narrator implies a newfound introspection and inner strength as a result of the suffering on the bus. As he describes himself walking slowly off the bus, he "soon felt the cool breeze hitting me underneath the tamarack trees," coincidentally, a deciduous conifer whose bark is used for burns in indigenous medicine. This specific detail is strategic in that it is a further attempt to strengthen the credibility of his claim for becoming a "better" person and undergoing a symbolic healing in a culturally recognized way.

Although confident in his claim, our narrator seems to have some trouble with modal searches for the appropriate framing of his new awareness, which is made somewhat tentative with the hedge "I must have been relieved". These hedges are examples of what Lakoff (1972) has called problems in categorization, which can also indicate a continued state of experiential disorder, in this case connected perhaps to an unease with this not-yet-fully-worked-through aspect of the narrator's perceived personal development. Nevertheless, it is his transformation which seems to make him a moral and mature person, enabling him to face life's future turmoil.

In moving toward the completion of the boarding school episode, the narrator senses the unsolved status of certain biographical problems and thus feels compelled to reiterate his status as the detached observer by inserting the pseudo quote, "Don Denny, off the bus". Not only the harsh imperative tone of this utterance but more significantly the fact that the narrator must let someone else speak for him shows his having difficulty integrating the events into his imagined world. Relying on Goffman's (1974) dramaturgical perspective, Treichel (2004, p. 52, 138, 262) interprets the use of pseudo-quotes as further evidence of feelings of alienation whose experiential authenticity is thus heightened and in this way made more believable. Since this center of interest occurs between the last episode of the main story line and the coda, it serves as a kind of pre-coda in the narrative sequence. Particularly revealing in this segment is the implied harsh tone in the treatment of the children, the representation of which in the form of a pseudo-quote affords the narrator additional credibility in his claim to kinship with boarding school veterans. With this strategy, he attempts to secure for his suffering a measure of respectability in the context of the Apache cultural canon, at least from the perspective of a traditionalist. Thus, before he can end his story line with the production of the narrative coda, he again has to struggle vigorously with the basic difficulties of relating to his biographical identity.

In fact, the narrator seems to be so deeply involved with these difficulties of biographical identity that the attempt to summarize in the pre-coda is considerably protracted and the evaluation of his overwhelming feelings spills over into the coda. According to Labov (1972), the end of an extemporaneous narration of personal experiences typically serves to connect the world of the story to the moment of language production by emphasizing the outcomes of the narrated events and their relevance to the narrator's present situation. The elaborations in the coda represent the last opportunity for an evaluation by the narrator of the biographical processes in their impact not only on his life but also on the canonical social values which were at stake during the course of the disturbing events depicted. As revealed in the summarizing activities of the pre-coda, the impact involves a change in the speaker's identity as a more moral and mature individual. This biographical perception of himself could be considered at least partly self-delusional, since his formulation of the outcome seems to fall short of dealing fully with the supposed trajectory of suffering.

Yet, the impact of suffering is not so much defocused in the coda as it is shifted to the actions of the grandfather, whose description reveals an underlying skepticism regarding the canonical belief in suffering as a necessary prerequisite to maturity. This skepticism is intensified with the recollection that "Grandfather didn't say much" on the long walk home, in which a subtle dissociation from the cultural canon seems to surface. Then, what has begun as subtle skepticism culminates in an outright rejection of the cultural canon when the grandfather "got stronger as he carried the huge suitcase without stopping for a rest." The juxtaposition of the feelings of bitterness regarding the trajectory of suffering with the claims for having become a more moral and mature individual represents a paradox which remains unresolved at the completion of the coda. In fact, the unresolved nature of the outcome of the narrated events can be seen in the somewhat awkwardly abrupt abandonment of the boarding school episode without a summary or even an attempt at a transition, other than a paragraph break, as a signal for the end of the coda. Thus the issues of the boarding school episode appear to remain unresolved and the lack of explicit closure may indicate a need to re-narrate the same events. Such a need for re-narrativization would certainly conform to Linde's (1993, p. 21) concept of a life story as being retold over a long period of time and as having primarily a specific point about the speaker instead of a general point about the world of the text.

Particularly relevant to this analysis is the perspective on human information processing capabilities which suggests a schematic organization of the kind of cultural syncretism found in the boarding school text. With regard to the overall boarding school experience as a cultural topos, our narrator seems to be navigating conflicting conceptual abstractions which serve, as Rumelhart (1980) has suggested, as the basis for information processing, including perception and comprehension, categorization and planning, recognition and recall, as well as problem solving and decision-making. In the narrative, problems seem to have arisen with schematic hierarchies in which prototypes, representing invariant aspects are filled by instances of contradictory data. Proactive transfer may be influencing the uptake of information as existing protoypes give rise to biased expectations of how to remember the event. In their work on the role of syncretism in frame analysis, Scollon and Scollon (1979) have referred to converging worldviews as contrasting reality sets whose accommodation poses a challenge. The boarding school experience seems to provide a frame for reconstructing schemata from prototypes derived from Apache oral traditions in the context of Anglo-American majority cultural and rhetorical input. In other words, each schema is elaborated by filling in details and gaps in accordance to what the narrator believes they ought to be. In addition, the text makes possible the instantiation of elements from Anglo-American culture by analogizing them to variable constraints of general indigenous schemata (Minsky, 1975, p. 212; Rumelhart, 1980, p.35).

Central to these general schemata is the powerful stereotype of the boarding school experience, which has been evolving since the nineteenth century. In many ways, American as well as Canadian Indians have bought into this prototype as it guides the construction and maintenance of a pan-Indian subculture. In an important sense, any individual narrative about government boarding schools is in great part based on a script which conventionalizes aspects of this stereotype. For example, the historic authoritative government control over Native families is unlike any experience in the Euro-American educational tradition. This gulf underscores the uniqueness of the Indian boarding school system as well as its implied power as a symbol of experiences distinctively "Indian". Except to outsiders, the associated suffering does not need to be explained, and the prestige accorded survivors provides one of the perquisites in the presentation of the self to other Natives. In the past few decades, many boarding schools have been phased out, and the remaining ones now have pedagogical and cultural agendas more sensitive to the needs of Indian students. Thus primarily the narratives of older generations continue to provide an input which acts as a powerful stimulus for the activation of prototype schemata of suffering.

Into the general boarding school prototype schema, the narrator has embedded constituent parts or subschemata guided by the expectations of both English and Apachean rhetorical processes. In attempting to make his discourse believable to English-speaking decoders, the narrator becomes well aware of the crucial role of concrete detail. However, vestiges of Apachean rhetorical redundancy also emerge in his presentation of seemingly trivial particulars. In his response to these rhetorical demands, the narrator is forced to select some details which are not necessarily compatible with the nodes of the prototype schema but which nevertheless seem to make possible an explanation of the events to himself. It is especially in the foregrounding processes that the details reveal a sense of suffering at odds with the general script about the boarding school experience. Clearly, a finger is being pointed not only at the Apache community in general but also at his close kinsmen in particular. The same narrative in Western Apache, with its emphasis on redundancy rather than concrete detail, may have selected more compatible constituent parts, especially with regard to ethnic loyalty. Nevertheless, since participation in the boarding school experience is ethnically restricted, it is an ideal means in a culture contact situation by which the narrator can create a boundary of exclusion by stressing his Indianness. Therefore, notwithstanding the contradictions to the Apachean canons of boarding school experiences as tales of oppression, the narrator wishes to present himself as a traditionalist and perhaps even as a cultural entrepreneur, as Treichel has applied the term to certain elite individuals who take on a somewhat self-appointed role of perpetuating the culture (2004 p. 108; p. 275). Although it could be argued that the narrator fits into the concept of the marginal man, as suggested by Robert Park (1928) in early twentieth century American sociology, he does not seem to regard himself liberated by viewing both cultures with the distance of a foreigner and the closeness of intimate familiarity.

In a bicultural and bilingual context, discursive transfer can be regarded as one of the manifestations of the more general phenomenon of cultural syncretism. Thus, when in the process of cultural contact an unfamiliar social institution is introduced to a group, individuals may tend to identify it with an instance of a class of institutions known to them. A case in point among many American Indian tribes today is the spread of the Native American (Peyote) Church, which in its symbolism and ideology combines fundamentalist Christian elements with those from several indigenous cultures. It could be argued that such examples show how existing schemata act as constraints, selecting primarily compatible features of the newly introduced institution. The resulting gaps in the new knowledge structure may then be filled with typical features of an analogous indigenous institution. The operation of generic schemata in the reconstruction of information has been demonstrated in studies on social cognition (Graesser, et al., 1980; Higgins, et al., 1977; Rice, 1980). Also, the filling of gaps in knowledge with qualities typical of a domain in question has been reported in studies on the recall of narrative texts with details of people or events imperfectly known (Graesser, et al., 1979). The transfer of such highly valued cultural features as discursive norms could be viewed as part of this analogical process in the creation of syncretism.

This study has attempted an interpretive analysis of the constructive processes giving rise to the ordering structures in a narrative by applying an expanded ethnography of speaking method which accesses particular meanings as clues to states of experiential disorder. Convenient points of entry for the analysis of the presentational procedure of the narrative are provided by foregrounding processes in the form of concrete detail which are driven by English rhetorical expectations but which also turn out to be attempted repair mechanisms in response to implausibility and disorder within the recollections of the narrator. The seeming triviality of these details suggests the partial transfer of the preferences of an Apachean rhetorical device which relies on redundancy for foregrounding. Intended as a contribution to the growing body of research on life stories, this paper suggests that the examination of the self-deceptive as well as self-enlightening biographical schemes of a bicultural narrator can provide insights into the convergence of conflicting reality sets or worldviews resulting in cultural syncretism. Notwithstanding possible common features of boarding school accounts shared with other biography incumbents, such as the connection to external forces beyond his control, this particular narrator exhibits in his presentation of the self a curious skepticism regarding the canonized notion in

Apache culture of suffering from family separation as a prerequisite to greater maturation. Other than the explicit revelation of tribal affiliation as an identity marker and the implicit hint at solidarity of boarding-school-attendees as a re-defined community, it is suggested that the more significant window on converging reality sets is represented by the narrator's paradox in partially accepting as well as challenging the conventional Apache notion of "becoming a better person" as a result of suffering through a boarding school experience. The majority educational system, with its on-reservations day schools and off-reservation boarding schools as established ways to acculturate children, has been superimposed on American Indian communities. It is safe to assume that tribal cultures, in which traditional instruction continues to operate informally within extended families, have not fully adjusted to the strong-armed intervention of the state. Thus the unresolved nature of our narrator's feelings of bitterness regarding his trajectory of suffering as a dominant mode of experience and his desire to re-narrate the events in order to come to terms with them are fully understandable. In such re-narrations symbolic interaction concepts are not only actualized and internalized but also altered and developed further. Finally, interpretive studies about the impact of deviant experiences on the biography constructions of members of various bicultural ethnicities should be encouraged in order to gain insights into the nature of syncretism with regard to symbolic universes, which provide, according to Berger and Luckmann (1966), the ultimate and integrated meaning for individuals and their communities.

References

BARTELT, G. (1983). "Transfer and variability of rhetorical redundancy in Apachean English interlanguage". In: S. GASS & L. SELINKER (Eds.). *Language transfer in language learning*. Rowley: Newbury House. pp. 297–305.

BARTELT, G. (1986). "Language contact in Arizona: The case of Apachean English". In: *Anthropos* 81. pp. 692–695.

BERGER, P., & LUCKMANN, T. (1966). *The social construction of reality*. New York: Doubleday.

BRUNER, J. S. (1990). *Acts of meaning*. Cambridge. MA: Harvard University Press.

CHAFE, W. (1979). "The flow of thought and the flow of language". In: T. GIVÓN (Ed.). *Discourse and syntax*. New York: Academic Press. pp. 159–181.

CHAFE, W. (1980a). "The deployment of consciousness in the production of a narrative". In: W. CHAFE (Ed.), *The pear stories: Cognitive, cultural, and linguistic aspects of narrative production*. Norwood, NJ: Ablex. pp. 9–50.

CHAFE, W. (1980b). "Some reasons for hesitating". In: H. DECHERT & M. RAUPACH (Eds.). *Temporal variables in speech: Studies in honour of Frieda Goldman-Eisler.* The Hague: Mouton. pp. 169–180.

CHAFE, W. (1990). "Some things that narratives tell us about the mind". In: B. K. BRITTON & A. D. PELLEGRINI (Eds.). *Narrative thought and narrative language.* Hillsdale, NJ: Erlbaum. pp. 79–98.

DECHERT, H. (1980). "Pauses and intonation as indicators of verbal planning in second-language speech productions: Two examples from a case study". In: H. DECHERT & M. RAUPACH (Eds.), *Temporal variables in speech: Studies in honour of Frieda Goldman-Eisler.* The Hague: Mouton. pp. 169–180.

GEE, J. P. (1986). "Units in the production of narrative discourse". In: *Discourse Processes* 9. pp. 391–422.

GOFFMAN, E. (1972). "The moral career of the mental patient". In: J. MANIS & B. MELTZER (Eds.), *Symbolic interaction: A reader in social psychology.* New York: Allyn & Bacon. pp. 234–44.

GOFFMAN, E. (1974). *Frame Analysis: An Essay on the Organization of Experience.* New York: Harper and Row.

GOLDMAN-EISLER, F. (1968). *Psycholinguistics: Experiments in spontaneous speech.* London: Academic Press.

GRAESSER, A., S. GORDON, & SAWYER, S. (1979). "Recognition memory for typical and atypical actions in scripted activities: Tests for a script pointer and tag hypothesis". In: *Journal of Verbal Learning and Verbal Behavior* 18. pp. 319–332.

GRAESSER, A., WOLL S., KOWALSKI, D., & SMITH, D. (1980). "Memory for typical and atypical actions in scripted activities". In: *Journal of Experimental Psychology.* pp. 503–515.

HIGGINS, E., RHOLES, W., & JONES, C. (1977). "Category accessibility and impression formation". In: *Journal of Experimental Social Psychology* 13. pp. 141–154.

LABOV, W. (1972). "The transformation of experience in narrative syntax". In: W. LABOV (Ed.), *Language in the inner city* Philadelphia: University of Pennsylvania Press. pp. 354–396.

LAKOFF, G. (1973). "Hedges: A study in meaning criteria and the logic of fuzzy Concepts". In: *Journal of Philosophical Logic* 2. pp. 458–508.

LINDE, C. (1993). *Life stories: The creation of coherence.* New York: Oxford University Press.

MINSKY, M. (1975). "A framework for representing knowledge". In: P. WILSON (Ed.). *The psychology of computer vision* New York: McGraw-Hill. pp. 211–277.

MOMADAY, N. S. (1997). *The man made of words: Essays, stories, passages.* New York: St. Martin's Griffin.

PARK, R. (1967). "Human migration and the marginal man". In: R. TURNER (Ed.), *Robert E. Park. On social control and collective behavior. Selected papers.* Chicago: University of Chicago Press. pp. 194–206.

PASCAL, R. *Design and truth in autobiography.* Cambridge, MA: Harvard University Press.

RICE, G. (1980). "On cultural schemata". In: *American Ethnologist* 7. pp. 152–171.

RIEMANN, G., & SCHÜTZE, F. (1991). "'Trajectory' as a basic theoretical concept for analyzing suffering and disorderly social processes". In: D. MAINES (Ed.), *Social organization and social process: Essays in honor of Anselm Strauss*. New York: Aldine de Gruyter. pp. 333–357.

RUMELHART, D. (1980). "Schemata: The building blocks of cognition". In: R. SPIRO, J. BRUCE & W. BREWER (Eds.). *Theoretical issues in reading comprehension: Perspectives from cognitive psychology, linguistics artificial intelligence, and education.* Hillsdale: Erlbaum. pp. 33–58.

SCOLLON, R., & SCOLLON, S. (1979). *Linguistic convergence: An ethnography of speaking at Fort Chipewyan, Alberta.* New York: Academic Press.

SPICER, E. (1962). *Cycles of conquest: The impact of Spain, Mexico, and the United States on the Indians of the Southwest, 1533–1960.* Tucson: University of Arizona Press.

STRAUSS, A., & GLASER, B. (1970). *Anguish: The case study of a dying trajectory.* Mill Valley, CA: The Sociology Press.

STRAUSS, A., FAGERHAUGH, S., & SUCZEK, B. (1985). *Social organization of medical work.* Chicago: University of Chicago Press.

TREICHEL, B. (1994). "On the narrative management of experiential disorder in oral life story". In: G. BARTELT (Ed.), *The dynamics of language processes: Essays in honor of Hans W. Dechert.* Tübingen: Gunter Narr. pp. 143–160.

TREICHEL, B. (1996). *Die linguistische Analyse autobiographischen Erzählens in Interviews.* Tübingen: Gunter Narr.

TREICHEL, B. (2004). Identitätsarbeit, Sprachbiographien und Mehrsprachigkeit: autobiographisch-narrative Interviews mit Walisern zur sprachlichen Figuration von Identität und Gesellschaft. Frankfurt: Peter Lang.

Erika Gericke

Discourses as Identities: Applying Critical Discourse Analysis

Introduction

Language is socially determined, thus we speak of 'discourse'. Language is also a social process and, therefore, discourse can be understood as the whole process of social interaction, which includes the process of production and the process of interpretation. Hence, text—here Apache Odyssey—is the product of the process of text production. There are also social conditions which play a role when texts are produced and interpreted (cf. Fairclough 1989).

In this respect the central challenge for discourse analysis is the multiple layers of meaning between the literal propositional meaning of a statement and the act which it performs in the context (cf. Fairclough 1995). So, what are the multiple layers of meaning in Apache Odyssey which might give a glimpse of an Apache identity? How are text and context interwoven and reveal a picture of the identity of an Apache?

Apache Odyssey as Discourse

The autobiography by Don Decker can be viewed as a discourse, if one considers basic discourse features which can be found in the text, namely intertextuality, interdiscursivity, recontextualisation and orders of discourse. In this paper I attempt to show how these four discourse features work in Apache Odyssey.

According to Fairclough (1989) intertextuality is the relationship between texts, i.e. the relationship between a text and an embedded quotation. We find that Don Decker quotes history books indirectly when he writes, "To this day, the Apaches have never surrendered to the U.S. government even though some *books* claim of a surrender. (…) The government's relationship with the Apaches has been a sad history and great many *books* have documented this relationship" (p.12, emphasis by the author). Why are history books called upon as a source of reference considering that some history books are questionable—they claim things, which are not true? By indirectly quoting from these books Decker not only establishes himself as a knowledgeable narrator but also outlines the cultural-historical frame for the story he has to tell. The ambivalent attitude towards the White world becomes visible right on the first page of Apache Odyssey, when Decker quotes indirectly from two (kinds of) history books—he draws upon an American history book with false information and (non-specified) books which informs about the special relationship between the U.S. government and Apaches.

Regarding intertextuality we find three types of quotes in Apache Odyssey. Firstly, Apache words are given in English and/or Apache—for instance, "'Kay-Yay', which would be comparable to 'wow' or 'cool' or 'come on, tell the truth'" (p. 66). The reader might thus get a vivid picture of Apache culture. Quotes are also delivered when the narrator talks about near-death experiences—"'Do you know how to swim?' (…) This was just another chapter in my daily near misses with death in San Carlos" (p. 58). Significant others and important personal experiences are the third type of quotes which are found in Apache Odyssey—the following quote is about Decker's chorus leader who becomes his adoptive father later on: "'I'm not taking this from you. You're not gonna mess this up for me', he said. Chorus was such a wimpy class I thought" (p. 81). Near-death experiences and significant others play such a pivotal role in Decker's life that they are 'credited' with quotes.

Interdiscursivity is the second discourse feature, which can be detected throughout the autobiography. Bakhtin (in Fairclough 1989) understands interdiscursivity as a mixing of genres. A genre is language used in a particular form of activity, characterised by a particular thematic content, style and compositional structure. For example, Decker writes, "Somehow, our family managed to get by even with the meagre offerings of Social Security and government commodity food (*Please pass the canned ham*)" (italics by the author) (p.17). The change of tone can be perceived as a coping strategy for emotionally difficult experiences. This discourse feature is used as a means of dealing with emotionally difficult identity components[1]—such as experiencing poverty.

---

1   Although I use the word 'identity component' please keep in mind that identity is more than just the sum of parts

In representing a social event, a speaker (or writer) tends to incorporate it within the context of another social event (Fairclough 2003). This is called recontextualisation and is the third discourse feature perceived in Apache Odyssey. Decker draws upon various discourses—direct and indirect—in his discourses throughout his autobiography. Thus he links diverse parts of his identity with each other into a meaningful whole[2]. The assumption here is that the topic addressed is a relevant topic for his identity, hence discourse as identity. The following example shows how the author integrates the discourse alcoholism in his discourse about church:

'Holy Rollers' as we would call them, had a large following in San Carlos. Samuel Harris, an Apache minister of the Miracle Church in nearby Peridot was the main kingpin of this movement and is still today. Samuel had the flare of a politician when he preached. He had a dynamic voice which would command anyone's attention. There was no snoozing in Harris' church. To see this Apache native preaching energized the local community and it kept everything interesting. Holy rollers were ridiculed because they were so outspoken on issues affecting San Carlos, alcoholism being the top priority (p. 59; emphasis by the author).

The fourth feature found in Apache Odyssey is orders of discourse. Basically, orders of discourse denotes the interrelated institutional types of discourse (Chilton and Schäffner 2002). This understanding can be linked to Elias' (1996) concept of figuration[3] which claims that the interrelated discourses (parts of identity) give us a picture of identity as a whole. On the one hand, this is already detectable in Decker's recontextualisation—integration of discourses within a discourse. On the other hand, orders of discourse can be perceived when looking at the interrelation of the four discourse levels in Apache Odyssey.

---

2   Please turn to the schema of Decker's recontextualisation in the appendix.
3   A figuration is an interdependence of functional and social dependencies among individuals, which are due to living in a community inevitably and necessarily develop, continue, change and partly die.

Discourse Levels in Apache Odyssey

There seem to be four discourse levels in Apache Odyssey, which are a) the (pure) collective discourse level, b) the collective-personal, c) the personal and d) the intra-personal discourse level.

The (pure) collective discourse level

Decker draws upon the (pure) collective discourse level when he describes the geography (pp. 12–13), religion and rites (pp. 21–24) and Apache culture (pp. 66–68). His tone is descriptive—he describes the collective Apache identity. Decker uses dichotomous language, namely Apache/us and the White/them. Hence, he uses words such as 'white world' (p. 14), 'white people' (p. 34) and 'western expansion' (p. 12). Characteristic of his language on this discourse level is also the application of scientific, in fact sociological terms such as 'social organisation' (p. 16), 'social class awareness' (p. 17), 'status' (p. 17) and 'antithesis' (p. 43). So, regarding the terms Decker uses he establishes the two spheres, namely the Apache and White worlds on the collective level and he legitimises himself by presenting himself as a knowledgeable and analytical person who is competent in applying scientific language correctly. Throughout the collective discourse level he integrates segments where he shows the relevance of the described events for his own identity and the identity of other Apaches (pp. 23, 41). He legitimises himself by explaining why he is an expert on Apache collective matters, namely due to personal involvement (pp. 23, 65, 74) and he evaluates the matters on personal and societal level(s) (pp. 66–68). As one would expect, Decker draws upon macro-societal (p. 12), medical (p. 16) and social structure (p. 67) discourses on the (pure) collective discourse level.

The collective-personal discourse level

This discourse level is the dominant one in Apache Odyssey, thus Decker views himself predominantly as a member of Apache culture where he also acts as an individual. Decker's tone is descriptive-narrative and he applies a huge variety of tones such as commentary and irony/sarcasm throughout the collective-personal discourse level. There are three sub-languages he uses, namely Anglo-American terms, Apache terms and unusual/sophisticated terms—all three sub-languages represent facets of his knowledge, hence facets of his identity. On this discourse level he establishes the two worlds' of 'I' and 'we', thus presenting himself as a full member of Apache society but also as an individual with his own mind. Decker structures his collective-personal discourse level the following way: He either starts with a biographical statement—'I' as an individual—or he begins with stating a general fact—'we' as a member of the Apache world or he speaks as an expert. In the middle part there are plain descriptions and explanations or sum ups and references to today or back-references to a personal event. The end is structured just like the beginning, either with a biographical statement or a general fact. By looking at this structure, we can see that Decker tries to link the past with the present, weaving an all-integrating whole. Discourses he draws upon are mainly macro-societal ones such as societal structure, religious and culture discourse.

The personal discourse level

Significant others, his education and work, near-death experiences and personal encounters with certain part of Apache culture, for instance tobacco, are topics presented on the personal discourse level. Decker's tone is mainly descriptive-narrative, as he evaluates his actions and experiences and at times he legitimises himself. As the expert on his life he talks to 'you' the audience, i.e. the reader (pp. 20–21, 63). Decker is also the interpreter for the reader when he translates Apache sayings and terms into American English (pp. 26, 29). Metaphors and instances of humour characterise the personal discourse level too. Again Decker establishes the two 'worlds' of 'I' and 'we' as he does in the collective-personal discourse level. The structure of this discourse level is simple in that respect that Decker tells a story and gives summaries in the middle part or the end of the story. Thus, he shows his ability to reflect on his personal life, which is a sign for a reflected identity.

The intra-personal discourse level

This discourse level occurs three times and is structured as a climax of self-reflection. Throughout that discourse level Decker's tone is reflective, as he evaluates end explains. He draws upon no other mode of discourse as this discourse level deals only with himself—his most inner part—alone. This discourse level occurs first when Decker writes about his inner reflection he was ten years old. At that age Decker writes he had "no contemplation" (p. 36), had no concept of past and future and he thought in contrasting terms such as "hard" and "beautiful" (p. 35). When Decker was at the age of thirteen he contemplated about his life "many a night" (p. 73) and now had a concept of past and distant future. Furthermore, Decker develops principles he lives by, namely being an example and never exercising any kind of violence. Again the language used consists of contrasting words such as "hell", "bleakest", "sorrow", "pain" and "happiness", "joy", "survival" (p. 73). Strong verbs, for instance "stopped", "prevailed", "fail" and "determined" are applied. So, this time was a crucial time for identity formation and orientation. In addition, religious and scientific language is found in the second occurrence of the intra-personal discourse level—influences on his identity formation. When Decker was in his twenties he reflected on his life "almost each day" (p. 95). Now in his language we find terms such as "complexity" and "confusion" (p. 95). In contrast, Decker uses mathematic metaphors "There were too many variables to contend with" (p. 95), which can be viewed as an attempt to take control over his life. Clearly, here is a climax regarding the frequency of contemplating about Decker's life. In addition, we see how this intra-personal discourse level changes throughout the process, thus identity work is taking place.

Identity Issues in the Four Discourse Levels—A Summary

Let us look at the topics addressed on each discourse level, so we might get a picture of how Decker's identity is mapped out. On the (pure) collective discourse level he writes about being an Apache, being a saviour of the Apache world, being an Apache warrior and also being a victim of the harsh life. He contrasts that with 'the other', that is the government and White world.

The topics on the collective-personal level are 'me and my people' in the positive and negative light and 'the harsh life of me and my people'.

Values and norms such as discipline, respect for animals, proper behaviour towards women, honesty, gratitude and work ethic are issues on the personal discourse level. His spiritual well-being—being a believer—is also a topic addressed.

The intra-personal discourse level deals with attitude towards life and mental orientation, namely having a future and success in life.

Coherence of Discourse Transition, Coherent Identity

Berger and Luckmann say that "Language bridges the different zones within the reality of life and integrates them into a meaningful whole" (1966:54). So, the question addressed to the text is: How does Decker come from one episode to the next, either within the same discourse level or among the other discourse levels? The 'bridging content' or discourse transitions can be a) geography/location, b) time, c) social structure and culture, d) activities, e) religion/rites and f) significant others.

On the (pure) collective discourse level it is geography/location, which is the dominant discourse transition, followed by social structure and culture. Religion/rites is the main 'bridging tool' for a coherent discourse/identity on the personal discourse level. Religion/rites, social structure and culture as well as activity are the discourse transitions which link the collective with the personal discourses level. On the personal discourse level it is geography/location and—from the time on when Decker has moved to his adoptive family—time, which are the 'bridging tools' for a coherent discourse. So, for Decker it is geography/location, which is the linkage to all other discourses/parts of identity.

So, geography/location is the constant for all three[4] discourse levels, thus geography/location can be perceived as *the* identity core of Decker. Social structure and culture as a bridging tool is mainly used on the collective discourse level, which is mainly descriptive and serves an overarching function. Activity—next to geography/location—is the dominant discourse transition on the collective-personal level. Involvement of people and their actions integrate parts into a meaningful whole. Kaufmann (2005) says that identity (formation) is only possible through action. This explains the dominant use of activity as a bridging tool. The most used discourse transition on the collective-personal discourse level is religion/rites. It integrates the individual into society and makes this connection strong and long lasting. Significant others is a discourse transition which has a 'sandwich-position' between the collective-personal and personal discourse level—it is on those levels that this type of transition is applied to and serves a bridging function. Time is predominantly used to link the various discourses on the personal discourse level. This works in

---

4 I speak of three and not four discourse levels as there is no discourse transition in the intra-personal discourse level

accordance to time being the basic concept of ordering one's life and producing a coherent identity. When Decker enters into the 'White World' and moves away with his adoptive family he loses geography/location and social structure and culture as a bridging toll—time is the only discourse transition left for him to produce a coherent discourse/identity from then on.

Guadalupe and Identity

Now let us illustrate our findings with an example (quote pp. 37–40):

On page 16 Decker writes "In some ways, growing up as an Apache wasn't any different from anyone else's upbringing. However, one difference was understanding your language, your songs, and prayers." Here, Decker writes that language, songs and prayers are elementary components of his identity.

The Guadalupe story plays on the personal discourse level. Decker starts with a perfect narrative first sentence. A metaphor he uses—as it is characteristic for this discourse level—is the personification of the tractor. Furthermore, we find a commentary about his father. There is a sum up in the middle part about Santa Claus and Uncle Billy. This is followed by an 'identity-narrative'—a narrative which shows his attitude towards discipline. Then he is our expert when he explains the importance of the Yaqui Deer Dance. Decker changes the topic by using geography/location as discourse transition and comes to another 'identity-narrative', in which he talks about how he learnt to behave appropriately towards women. He sums up and ends his story by talking about his competence in the Spanish language.

We also find in this story Decker's elementary identity components: language, as in learning the Spanish language; songs, as he writes about his music class; and prayer, as he explains the religious meaning of the Yaqui Deer Dance.

Final Remarks

This written autobiography by Don Decker can be perceived as a discourse that has intertexuality, interdiscursivity, recontextualisation and orders of discourse as general discourse features. In this paper I have suggested a view of discourse as identity by outlining the four discourse levels inherent in Apache

Odyssey. Furthermore, I have elaborated identity issues addressed on the four discourse levels and indicated which 'bridging tools' are used to produce a coherent discourse. Finally, I have attempted to show how these findings work on a micro-level basis.

References

BERGER, P. & LUCKMANN, TH. (1966). *The Construction of Reality: A Treatise in the Sociology of Knowledge*. London: Penguin Books.
CHILTON, P. & SCHÄFFNER, CH. (2002). *Politics as Text and Talk: Analytic Approaches to Political Discourse*. Amsterdam: Benjamins.
ELIAS, N. (1996). *Was ist Soziologie?* Weinheim: Juventa.
FAIRCLOUGH, N. (1989). *Language and Power*. London, New York: Longman.
FAIRCLOUGH, N. (1995). *Critical Discourse Analysis. The Critical Study of Language*. Harlow: Longman
FAIRCLOUGH, N. (2003). *Analysing Discourse. Textual Analysis for Social Research*. London: Routledge.
KAUFMANN, J.-CL. (2005): *Die Erfindung des Ich. Eine Theorie der Identität*. Konstanz: UVK Verlagsgesellschaft mbH.

Appendix

Figure: Don Decker's recontextualisation

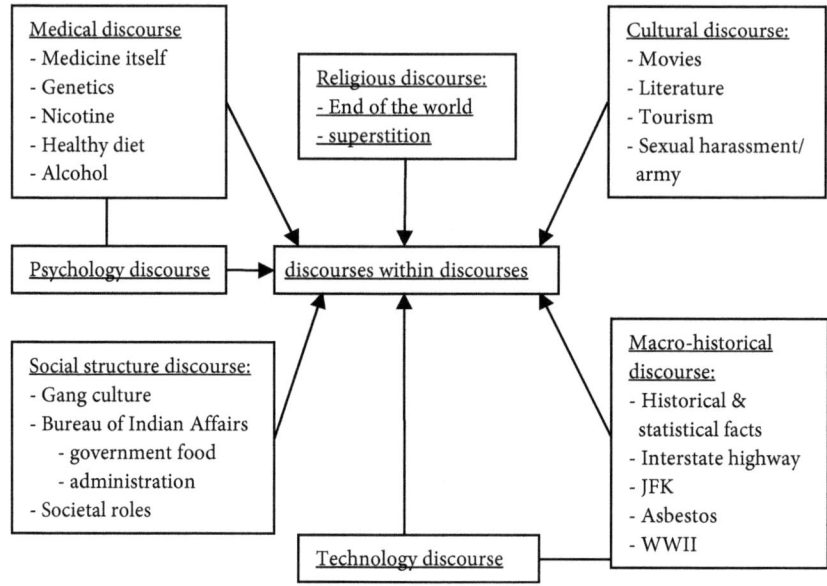

BÄRBEL TREICHEL

Identity Work, Narrative Analysis, and Biographical Processes. A Sociolinguistic Approach to Identity Constructions in an Apache Autobiography

1 Narrative Analysis and Autobiography

When linguists analyze narrative, they are usually concerned with storytelling in everyday life. Much of the research on storytelling was carried out in the 1970s and 1980s and is theoretically anchored mainly in text linguistics (van Dijk, 1980; Brinker, 1990; Gülich & Raible, 1977), psycholinguistics (Rumelhart, 1975; Chafe, 1990; Mandler & Johnson, 1977) and sociolinguistics (Labov, 1972; Bruner, 1990; Linde, 1987). There has been a renaissance of narrative analysis in interactional sociolinguistics more recently since it has a strong interest in social identity constructions by means of narrative (Bamberg, 2007; Bamberg, de Fina & Schiffrin, 2007).

Among the major criteria to distinguish narrative from other communicative genres is its display of rather clear boundaries which set it off from the communicative background. Discourse markers delimit the genre activity. Other defining criteria are its temporal organization following the particular event structure to be related and that its content is worth telling. Gülich and Raible (1977) point out that narrative is primarily an oral genre. When narrative occurs in literary texts, its oral character is staged through the creation of a story telling frame, and the narration itself resembles much the oral version of story telling.

In most of the data underlying research on narrative, the production of a narrative is only an episodic event within a larger communicative context. It is therefore useful to say that its content must be remarkable in the sense that it is exceptional or surprising and thus worth being related. Other researchers attribute a social function to narrative in everyday life in that it picks up the unusual and contributes to renormalizing experience within cultural expectations (Bruner, 1990; Linde, 1987).

This article looks at the written life historical account of a San Carlos Apache, Don Decker. His narrative is composed as an autobiography, and it is different in at least two respects from what linguistic narrative analysis usually looks at: a) It is written down and designed as a written text and b) it presents the story of a large segment of life. As compared to sporadic story telling within other kinds of communication, autobiographical narrative of the kind to be looked at in this article is a more comprehensive genre. It shares the plot structure as outlined by Ricoeur (1981). In its episodic dimension, it is repeated experience in time, in its configurational dimension, it is a meaningful whole that also says something about the gist of a lived-through life. Although narrators tell a sequence of episodes which all individually follow the episodic scheme of narration, the segments are at the same time contributing to the overall configuration or plot, and they have to be analysed as such. As Dilthey (1970) points out, the biography as a scheme of orientation is an organizing category in its own right, and it contributes to the plot structure of larger autobiographical accounts. The narrative of an entire life course is more than a sequence of individual narratives. The concatenation of individual stories as presented in the autobiography informs the development of identity and contributes to the biographical gestalt.

In order to better appreciate the autobiography at hand, it is therefore worthwhile to also look at biography and identity from a biography analytical perspective, where relevant categories to account for entire biographies have been developed. A major proponent of sociological biography analysis, Fritz Schütze has theoretically anchored his work in the interpretive sociology and symbolic interactionism of the Chicago tradition. Among his major contributions to analyzing biographies is the identification of the more general biographical patterns which operate across biographies and make them comparable on a metatheoretical level. Among these larger biographical patterns, which he termed *process structures of the life course*, are biographical action schemes, trajectories of suffering and processes of biographical transformation (Schütze, 2008a,b; for an overview cf. Riemann, 2006). Schütze has also pointed out that the different process structures of the life course are reflected in different features of the linguistic rendering of experience: It makes a difference whether one talks about an intentional biographical action plan and how to carry it through, whether one speaks about biographical suffering within a trajectory of outer forces operating upon one's biography or whether one talks about biographical transformation with all its elements of uncertainty.

Don Decker's autobiography is a narrative of biographical transformation. The author proceeds from the Apache world to the Anglo American world, and his adoption by an Anglo American Family institutionally enables this transition. Living on the San Carlos Reservation in his youth, the author shares the fate of a collective trajectory of suffering. He experiences extreme poverty, violence and lack of educational opportunities. His adoption allows him to develop personally and educationally. He ends up as a teacher and counselor who holds a college degree, and he is also quite successful as a folk musician.

What is true for processes of biographical transformation in general also applies to the transformation process Don Decker goes through. Such processes are complex and at times chaotic. Biographical transformation releases creativity, it changes individual orientations and may lead to a new outlook on life. Transformation may be experienced as an exciting increase in competencies and capabilities; it may as well be felt as something threatening. At least there is no well defined path transformation follows, and just as transformation may be irritating for individuals going through such a process, analysts may at times be irritated as well in face of such transformation narratives. Referring to the chaotic elements in his life, Don Decker states at a particular moment in time: *My world began to crash down upon me for the reasons that I couldn't understand* (p. 82).

Linearizing events and categorizing experiences is often difficult in narratives of biographical transformation. Also, we do not have a textual pattern at our disposal, which easily grasps transformation and makes it accessible to audiences. For analyzing narratives of biographical transformation, it is all the more necessary to see the entire narrative as a gestalt and interpret segments according to their contribution to the entire process and story.

2 Social and Biographical Identity

The issue of identity constructions is ideal for cooperation between linguists and sociologists. While sociologists say that identity is a matter of linguistic construction, linguists say that the linguistic presentation of the self depends on identity assumptions. As we are concerned here with an entire autobiography, it is worthwhile to mention that it is not so much social identity, which is at issue here, but *biographical identity*. In his autobiographical account, Don Decker seeks to develop a picture of biographical development and uniqueness, and he reflects upon himself as an individual who acts and talks in real life situations. A discussion follows on the distinction between social and biographical identity which I think is necessary to make when analyzing whole autobiographies.

2.1 Social Identity

When linguists pick up conceptualizations of identity, they usually go back to Erving Goffman and his notion of social identity (1963, 1967). For Goffman, social identity is an expectable structure that depends on categorization activities which members of societies perform vis-à-vis each other. Categorization activities are rather far reaching, in that they contain assumptions about such things as profession, status and gender as well as assumptions about moral character. If you are a such and such, you are very likely to act in a particular way and have a particular set of attitudes, and you are very likely to have such and such a character. It is also part of his theorizing on social identity to point out that social interaction is indeed rather fragile and that social categories are much less clear cut and unambiguous than we have a tendency to assume. There is a lot of communication out of character, as he shows in all of his books, particularly in "The Presentation of Self in Everyday Life" (1959) and in "Forms of Talk" (1981). The ascription of and self-identification with social categories identifies individuals as members of particular we-collectivities and differentiates them from others which they do not belong to.

Social identity as a category has received much attention in recent studies in interactional sociolinguistics. Researchers again mention the centrality of language in the ascription of and self-identification with social categories. They stress the embeddedness of the individual in social interaction and in discursive traditions, so that social identity is not something the individual possesses or carries with him- or herself as part of some sort of equipment, but social identity is generated, renewed and transformed in interaction with others, and these processes are largely communicative in nature. It is also inadequate to assume that social identities are merely represented in discourse; processes of linguistic performance, enactment and embodiment are central to social identity constructions as they occur in discursive interaction. As discursive interaction is fragile, social categorization in discursive interaction is fragile (cf. de Fina, Schiffrin & Bamberg, 2006).

Schiffrin (2006), for example, explicitly bases her analysis of reference in conversation on Goffman's category of social identity. In a similar vein, Ribeiro (2006) discusses the moment-to-moment display of social identities in conversation using Goffman's concept of footing (Goffman, 1981). She uses the category *identity work* to refer to social and discourse identities as *performed social identities*, a term taken from Erickson & Shultz (1982). In her work on group identity, de Fina (2003, 2006) combines analyses of stylistic choices and performance devices, such as the use of reported speech and other kinds of linguistic variation, with membership categorization analyses from the tradition of ethnomethodological conversation analysis (Sacks, 1995; Antaki & Widdicombe, 1998). She shows how Mexican undocumented workers cooperate in the construction of ethnic identity as a form of social identity in that they produce narratives which contain reference to themselves as being Hispanic and to their group relations with others.

Researchers being concerned with the more personal self-concept of their informants, often termed *personal identity*, and less with the presentational aspects of social identity, often start from the linguistic tradition of narrative analysis following Ricoeur (1981, 1983/1984, 1985/1988), Mishler (1999, 2006) and Bruner (1990). Schiff & Noy (2006) for example say that the narrative analysis of life stories sheds light on the whole complexity of the *subjective understandings* the individual employs to make sense of the self and the world. Narrative, in their view, is the prominent mode of personal identity formation, because through narrative the individual takes part in a shared horizon of meaning. With reference to individual sense-making practices by means of narrative Schiff & Noy (2006) use the term *narrative sense-making* (from Bruner, 1990). As they put it, "narrative identity, in the most concrete fashion, is part person, part situation, and part culture and entails relations between these three levels of analysis" (Schiff & Noy, 2006, p. 401).

The category of personal identity is designed to refer to the more authentic self conception of an individual, and his or her participation in a culturally shared tradition of narrative practice is an important factor as this self conception develops. It is also more common for biography analysts to use this category, since there is an interest in the more authentic self conception of narrators as they tell their stories.

2.2 Biographical Identity

As Anselm Strauss puts it, "identity is connected with the fateful appraisals made of oneself—by oneself and by others" (1997, p. 11).

While social identity is more concerned with the otherness of individuals, biographical identity is more or less a matter of consistent sameness. Biographical identity has to do with what we think who we are. Different from the presentation of self in everyday life, which may be rather episodic and varied, biographical identity refers to a more comprehensive, individualistic and authentic self-perspective. Biographical identity develops when the individual compares ascribed categories with self-identifications and with his or her individual life course in order to develop a conception of biographical uniqueness (Schütze, 2008a, b).

George Herbert Mead was the first to consider the productive tension between pictures of the self and images reflected by others in the process of developing a consistent notion of the self. He looked at processes of understanding which the individual has to go through, and he found that *reflexivity* plays an important role in negotiating different versions of the self.

I know of no other form of behavior than the linguistic in which the individual is an object to himself, and, so far as I can see, the individual is not a self in the reflexive sense unless he is an object to himself. It is this fact that gives a critical importance to communication, since this is a type of behavior in which the individual does so respond to himself.
(Mead, 1934, p. 142)

Personal identity in the sense of Mead is a product of interactional and dialogical processes within society and of the processes of understanding which the individual him- or herself performs in order to negotiate between different perspectives. It is largely by means of the linguistically symbolic system that the individual can make himself an object of reflection, and that the individual can reflect about him- or herself from the standpoint of the other.

Biography analysis has contributed the category of *biographical identity* to identity studies by means of introducing the *life history and life course experience* of an individual into the theorizing on identity. There is a theoretical difference between personal identity as conceived of by Mead and biographical identity as seen from the perspective of biography analysis. Biographical identity develops between the ascription of social categories, self-identifications and individual life courses. It is a self-reflexive process that negotiates between different perspectives of the self in search for a consistent version of itself as a biographical entity that exists and interacts in real life situations (Schütze, 2008a,b).

To summarize, constructions of biographical identity depend on
- Pictures of the self and images reflected by others
- Individual life courses
- Longer lasting social and biographical processes
- Social interaction
- The linguistic symbol system and communicative genres
- Reflexivity

3 Narrative Analysis and Biographical Transformation

In the analysis to follow, Don Decker's autobiography is considered as a narrative of an individual man who goes through his life course presenting an authentic picture of his personhood in search of biographical uniqueness. In other words, he is talking about biographical identity. As an entire biography is at issue, methods of narrative analysis and biography analysis are applied in order to find out something about the major mechanisms operating in his life. Don Decker tells a story of biographical transformation, and the linguistic rendering of biographical transformation will be the focus of analysis.

At a very prominent point in his autobiography, Don Decker tells the story of his adoption. The adoption is the turning point in Don Decker's biography. The segment to be looked at (pp. 83–85) captures the very episode of transition when Don Decker passes from the Apache world to the Anglo American world after being adopted. Functional elements are identified following Labov's (1972) scheme of narrative structure (*abstract, orientation, complicating action, evaluation, result or resolution, coda*), which may involve complex chainings and embeddings of the functional elements mentioned. The analysis to follow provides an example of such narrative chaining and embedding. It is an instance of the linearizing and configuring activity a narrator telling the story of his life following the organizing scheme of a biography is usually engaged in. Since there is no prefabricated genre for talking about transformation, certain difficulties in unfolding the segment are to be expected. Don Decker somehow has to develop his own way of presenting the issue, and he does so by means of telling two stories which are embedded within each other. Also, there is a focus on inner feelings and development, since Don Decker, when telling the story of his adoption, elaborates on his emotional attitudes and concerns. I have structured the passage using Labov's categories of functional segments. Also, to facilitate reading, I have indented the second narrative and highlighted particular phrases through bold print.

Main story line

Orientation
In spring of 1962, I stayed with the young Anglo family most of the time except to visit my grandparents every once in a while.

Complication
The young couple who already had children of their own (Brad and Dawn Ann, who later became a wealthy model in New York City) **confronted me one day and wanted to know if I would like to be adopted.**

Evaluation
I just couldn't believe that I was at that point where I was to make a commitment for adoption.

    I didn't want to be adopted by the white family and I was afraid they had plans to take me away from my grandparents. **I talked with my grandparents about the young couple's proposal for adoption.** My grandfather wasn't sure what he wanted for me. He did tell me that he was getting older and he could no longer take care of me due to his falling eyesight. My grandmother had gotten bedridden due to arthritis for the past few years, so she was relegated to staying in bed most of her life. Besides, I had gotten too accustomed to living with the young couple and their children in Globe. I didn't see any reason in turning back at this time.

    My grandparents weren't really sure and my grandfather said he would give me an answer very soon.

    All this was occurring during my sophomore year in high school.

Embedded story: Grandfather dies

Orientation
One day when I was in Mr. Joslin's biology class at Globe High, one of the student worker has brought a message to the teacher. It was an early afternoon. I was called out to the hallway, where the chorus teacher stood with a drawn face. It was not a pleasant situation from all appearances.

Complication
The chorus teacher told me that my grandfather had suffered a stroke and he was still alive at the San Carlos government hospital. I was excused from class that afternoon and was taken to the bedside of my grandfather, the ace road builder of northern Arizona. He laid there very still under the oxygen tent with his mouth wide open and he appeared to be asleep. I was crying very hard at this time because I knew he was dying and this would be the last time I would see him.

Coda of main story line
One of the things that really bothered me was that he never gave his permission for me to be adopted by the white family in Globe. He never did.

Resolution
I came that afternoon to the hospital to see him in hopes that he would somehow give me an answer. I talked to him and somehow I could tell he was listening to me. I told him that I loved him and that I hated to see him this way. I also asked him if it was alright to be adopted by the couple. He lay there very quietly without movement. I left him in the hospital that afternoon and went back to Globe with my choral teacher and his wife.

The next day, while at school, my choral teacher came to my classroom bringing the ultimate news to me—the death of my grandfather who had raised me ever since I was two years old.

Evaluation
I first cried and then bawled like hell down the hallways of the high school. I could not believe that life could betray me at this point in my life.

Development
The choral teacher and his wife were very supportive of me during this time, and so were the members of the First Christian Church in Globe. The funeral was held at the old wooden shack where I lived for many years in Gilson Wash. They brought his body back in the afternoon for an all night wake. I looked in the casket and saw my grandfather Irving.

Evaluation
It was the end of an era for this man who had brought so many people into the world. I looked at his face real close, the make-up was caked on his lips and somehow he didn't look natural to me with his Wall Street blue suit and neck tie. He should have worn his old blue work shirt and faded Levis for this final journey. He was really dead and I couldn't believe that he was gone. My grandmother Ivy was there with me as well. She was really heartbroken for seeing Johnson leave this earth. Many people from Globe came to the funeral. I saw my grandfather one last time before they closed the casket.

Coda
I look very much like my grandfather today and I am also beginning to see the very first stages of my grandfather's baldness. Grandpa was one of the few Apache men who were bald. He was a rarity of his time.

Main story line continued
Abstract of next larger experiential gestalt
After my grandfather's death, my life went into a drastic transition stage from my reservation days to an odyssey that was to lead me beyond the railroad tracks of the Southern Pacific and the cool running waters of the San Carlos River to the new horizons of a new life away from the reservation.

Resolution (of episode before) & Orientation of new episode
I was adopted by my high school chorus teacher and his wife in 1962 and my name was changed from Don Denny to Don Decker, after my new parents, Donald and Barbara Decker of central Illinois. I was now part of a new family which gave me a new start in life. **This was the biggest break in my life** as I

went on to my new family, which included a new 4 year-old brother (Brad) and a 6 year-old sister (Dawn).

Don Decker categorizes the biographical impact of his adoption as *a drastic transition stage* and the *biggest break in my life*. Just as Labov suggested when considering narrative functions, he becomes "deeply involved in rehearsing or even reliving events of his past" (1972, p. 354) and, taking into account the emotionality of his story, he "seems to undergo a partial reliving of that experience" (1972, p. 355).

Embedded within Don Decker's adoption story is another story, which relates how his grandfather dies. The death of his grandfather is presented as a fully fledged narrative with orientation, complication, resolution, development, evaluation and coda parts. The interconnection between the two narratives lies in the search for permission and advice from the grandfather as to the proposal for adoption. From a very young age on Don Decker lived with his grandparents. As he states in the coda of his main story: *One of the things that really bothered me was that he never gave his permission for me to be adopted by the white family in Globe. He never did.* Don Decker's grandfather died before he could finally comment upon the adoption proposal, a fact that causes severe moral trouble for the protagonist.

Because of the biographical impact of the adoption and the moral conflict connected to it, Don Decker carefully considers both, the story of adoption and the story of his grandfather dying too early. He goes into the details of their episodic development, presenting the concatenation of events, the occurrence of inner reactions, as well as the multiperspectivity of attitudes connected to it. A discussion of how the adoption may be seen by various proponents is given in the evaluation part of the main narrative. The grandfather points at his and his wife's old age and decaying health, Don himself mentions his staying with the Anglo-American family for so long. However, an explicit answer from his grandfather was still about to come, had he not died too soon.

The adoption is presented as an accountable action in the sense of Harvey Sacks, who states that accounts are systematic devices in communicative exchanges which provide for clarification, often in response to the—at times implicit—question *why*. It is Don Decker himself who asks himself why the adoption was to take place. He reviews the development of the event structure and his inner motives in order to reach clarification as to how it all came about.

Part of his inner conflict involves his leaving the Apache culture, determining where his cultural roots are, and transferring to the White Anglo American majority culture, where he gets access to education and finally develops a professional career. Among the reasons why he offers an account is that he wants clarification as to whether he may have been disloyal to his cultural origins and family and whether his passing into the alternative culture occurred too early.

The fact that there is a need to present an account is announced in the way the adoption episode is announced: *The young couple [...]* ***confronted*** *me one day and wanted to know if I would like to be adopted.* The first account follows in the evaluation segment. It is part of the account, that Don Decker seeks permission from his grandparents, that his grandparents suffer from bad health, and that he has stayed with the Anglo American family for quite some time.

The second account is the embedded narrative about Don Decker's grandfather's dying. It is presented as the answer to the question as to how the adoption came about and whether there is disloyalty involved against his family of origin.

Don Decker's narrative is far from being a chronicle which simply captures the factual skeleton of a life. He is involved in narrative sense making, and his accounting activities are an indicator of the authenticity of his efforts. Also, it is evident in the small segment looked at, that autobiographical narration has the entire biography as a frame of reference: Don Decker cannot talk about the adoption without looking at where he came from and where he will be ending up. To put it differently, when talking about the adoption, he does identity work in the sense of reaching an understanding as to his identity development, and he is concerned with biographical identity.

I now turn to another segment from Don Decker's autobiography (pp. 73–74), which is inspired by biographical identity work. Again, identity work occurs in the shape of an account, that is, an authentic search for clarification answering the question *why*, which Don Decker himself asks as to his life course. The segment is structured as an argumentation which centers around the fundamental claim that there is a need for Don Decker to change his life. The account is predominantly descriptive, dealing with the various facets of Apache life.

The segment is about what went through his mind when he decided that *a change had to take place before the wrath of hell consumed me in San Carlos.*

Here, Don Decker directly addresses the issue of biographical transformation. What follows is an account that discusses biographical identity and cultural roots. In terms of its linearization within the entire autobiographical text, it comes before the adoption episode. Again, it is useful to look at what issues Don Decker picks up in his account to learn what his inner motives are. I have included topical headings to facilitate reading.

Argumentation

Claim

Sometime during the summer of 1958, while sitting on the railroad tracks running through San Carlos, **I was determined to change my future.** At the young age of thirteen, I began to realize that I had some control of what I wanted of my life—in the distant future. After experiencing what I have lived through so far, **I knew that a change had to take place** before the wrath of hell consumed me in San Carlos.

Account

External Social Frames
Community & Care
Being raised by my grandparents, who had no formal education to speak of, did instill in me some precepts to live by. They were quick to point out the importance for **providing for the welfare of everyone**, including non-relatives who were a part of this small Indian community. Living by good example was a good measure of well-being and not how much money you had in your pocket. For this reason, even on the bleakest days in San Carlos, there was enough food for everyone. This meant giving up some of our own food for those who had none.

Poverty
Yes, there were days when there was no food at home and basic meals meant beans and potatoes. Free food furnished by the government usually consisted of canned ham nobody liked and honey that was as thick as motor oil.

Conclusion

I spent many a night looking at the San Carlos skies wondering about a better tomorrow, one possibly filled with happiness and joy.

Inner Identity

Distance to Apache adults

In the first 13 years of my life in San Carlos, I had seen too much sorrow and pain in the faces of Apaches. It seemed like everything was done at a snail's pace and I began to see the **idiosyncrasies of grown adults** who were determined to see others fail. As an observer from a detached perspective, I began to see holes through my dreams and wishes. However, nothing stopped me or prevented me from succeeding to ensure my survival and happiness.

As a youngster, I always avoided **physical violence** to settle differences with my buddies.

Christianity and Apache traditional beliefs

My dreams were confounded by value conflicts.

Attending the holy roller churches usually instilled fear in me. It was as if HE was watching every move I was making, and the Christian upbringing I had was in serious conflict with my own Apache traditional beliefs, such as using eagle feathers and cattail pollen to pray with. Going to hell became an alien concept to me as I got older. Perhaps the dark winds of the Apache witchcraft could be considered hell. However, being around Apache medicine men created a feeling of well-being. **It seemed as though Apache spiritual paths made you more at ease, more whole.** There wasn't any shouting here about the world ending. To dish out Christianity was to live in constant anxiety.

Somewhere, I rode the fence to get a better bearing on my values.

I was being pulled in all sorts of directions. My grandmother was a devout Christian while my grandfather had a traditional background. He never paid attention to the Christian doctrine. Oh he'd listen to the Mormon missionaries when they came on their Schwinn bicycles.

Family roots

Johnson Irving, or my 'she-choo' (grandfather), lived a hard life, having worked all his life, one filled with some pretty good experiences. He never tried to pass judgment on anyone nor did he involve himself with the bickering that seemed to divide many of the people on the reservation. He basically minded his own business. **His legacy lives on today in Payson**, where many of his blood relatives made something of themselves with a brand new casino, after having lived in deplorable conditions for many years. Johnson's brother, George Campbell, who is also long deceased, should receive credit for the successes of the Tonto Apaches in Payson. Descendants of his family, who are all members of the jil'she'ii'eh or the scrub oak/manzanita bush people, run that reservation.

In the segment at hand, Don Decker talks about the need for a severe change in his life course, and in the account to follow he goes into the details as to why this is the case.

In the account, Don Decker combines descriptions of social frames with reflections about inner attitudes: There is extreme poverty on the reservation, but also community and care. When poverty becomes an issue, the account changes in tone—it turns into something like a confession: *Yes, there were days when there was no food at home*. It is first of all the poverty on the reservation which suggests that he should take the initiative and change his life.

Just like as described in Feldman et al. (1990), Don Decker connects inner reflections with references to landscapes, as in his announcement of transformation:

Sometime during the summer of 1958, while sitting on the railroad tracks running through San Carlos, I was determined to change my future.

and in his conclusion:

I spent many a night looking at the San Carlos skies wondering about a better tomorrow.

Landscapes of consciousness occur in the context of talking about transformation. They are a textual means to address inner attitudes, and, taken together with their embedding within transformation talk, I take them as an indicator of identity work here.

In the second part of the account, Don Decker locates himself within particular social frames. He expresses closeness and distance as to particular cultural phenomena in the Apache community: He does not identify much with many Apache adults and he is against violence. As far as religious beliefs are concerned, he feels more at ease with the traditional Apache belief system. But when he comes to his family roots, his position is straightforward: He is full of admiration for his grandfather's contribution to the Apache community; he led a hard life, and he has always been an example to everyone for his honesty.

All these issues are organized in topically focused individual paragraphs. There are style switches as to the tone of presentation when he talks about poverty and when he talks about his grandfather. As for his grandfather, he has something very fundamental to say, and it is his grandfather who binds him to the Apache world.

In this segment, Don Decker informs about his intention to change the conditions of his life. He does so without neglecting a careful exploration of his deeper motives. And he seems to have the tacit assumption, that changing the outer conditions of his life means inner change as well. The ambivalence in his account comes from his authentic effort to search the deeper motives of his actions, and it is driven by his authentic intention to be loyal to his cultural roots. Also, there is a certain fear of internal change.

After the transformation segment as discussed above, Don Decker's life course takes a different path. When describing matters in categories of biography analysis, his life course from now on takes the shape of a *biographical action scheme*: Don Decker actively plans for a change in his life, which first of all means that he has to organize a professional career for himself in order to escape the collective trajectory of Apache society.

His first initiatives to plan a professional career are very rudimentary, though, and still very much connected to what is in reach within the Apache world. At issue are for example to become a carpenter, a Greyhound bus driver or a cowboy. His major impetus is to escape poverty at first, so he starts working as a day laborer doing the dangerous but better paid work.

It is among the difficulties in his life course, that he does not have any serious biographical advisers to assist him in this period of life, where he pursues his wish to escape poverty. This condition drastically changes when he meets his chorus teacher and future adoptive father. One of the many things the chorus teacher does for him is to offer resistance at first: When Don Decker is disobedient, his chorus teacher says *I'm not taking this from you* (p. 81).

Meeting the chorus teacher *affected the outcome of my life* (p. 80), as Don Decker says. He tells about decisive changes in the way he leads his life: He spends much time with the family of the chorus teacher and gradually starts to live with his family. They prepare him a room of his own. He goes to school and attends chorus classes. He receives support for his musical talent and takes part in a musical production at his school. Also, he earns some money and opens his first bank account. Beside these changes in the external conditions of his life, he also talks about changes in his sensory perceptions. When he spends more time with the white family, he feels that he didn't like his clothes smelling like mesquite smoke anymore, as they did when he lived with his grandparents. Also, he mentions a few *sincere relationships*, as he says, with Anglo girls in Globe. Biographical transformation often goes hand in hand with a breakdown of orientations: *My world began to crash down upon me for the reasons that I couldn't understand* (p. 82) as Don Decker says within the same context.

4 On the Position of the Transformation Narrative Within the Entire Autobiographical Text: A Bipartite Narrative

It is argued in this article that Don Decker's autobiography is a story of biographical transformation. Transformation is centered around the adoption, which is treated as an accountable action and accompanied by a variety of structural features representing identity work in the sense of biographical identity work.

The adoption episode also has a particular role to play within the design of the autobiographical text as a whole. It works as kind of a relais between the Apache world story and the Anglo American world story. These two stories differ from each other very much in structural design; one could argue that they even represent different communicative genres (in the sense of Swales, 1990; Martin & Rose, 2008). While life in the Anglo American world after the adoption is told as a straight narrative, the Apache world text does not follow a story script. Reference to the Apache world is presented mainly as a sequence of descriptions of social frames and routines in connection with episodic accounts of individual events. For illustration, I would like to quote and comment upon just a few examples from the Apache world descriptions.

Poverty and the simple way of life in Apache land are among the recurrent themes in Don Decker's descriptions:
- *The primitiveness of Apache land was a continuation of our old ways* (p. 14). A paragraph is then devoted to its spiritual world, to medicine men and to nomadic life.
- *A typical Apache diet consisted mainly of acorns, potatoes, beef jerky, beans, flour, sugar and coffee* (p. 19)
- *Each year my grandparents and I would go to Thatcher, Arizona, 60 miles east of San Carlos, to pick cotton for the Daleys* (p. 34).

There is also crime, violence and massive alcohol consumption:
- *When we returned to the reservation in San Carlos after the picking season, we found our cabin tent had been completely gutted* (p. 36).
- *Stealing in San Carlos was a sometime event for most of us youngsters* (p. 52).
- *I don't recall anyone drinking alcohol responsibly in San Carlos. I don't believe there was such a thing back in those days of massive consumption. It was usually a quick slam* (p. 66).

Young people in Apache land did not have much to do as pastime activities:
- *The summers in San Carlos were unbearable. Spending time at the river swimming and fishing was an excellent pastime* (p. 42).
- *Carving names on the railroad ties and trestles was another favorite pastime* (p. 29).

Some of the routines were more exciting than others:
- *One interesting event that occurred each year on the reservation was the annual cattle sale by the tribal cattle rangers* (p. 18).

There were a number of interesting people living in San Carlos and a number of remarkable cultural features in Apache life:
- *There were truly many fine people in San Carlos* (p. 55).
- *Humor has its special place in the Apache culture…White people always were the brunt of Apache jokes, especially when Apaches impersonate white people* (pp. 66–67).

Education was not continuously available:
- *While living in Tucson with my mother in 1956, I attended public school for a few weeks* (p. 41)

Some paragraphs have a summarizing function pointing out the meaning of Don Decker's life in Apache land for his biography as a whole:
- *Growing up in poverty in San Carlos in my formative years had its benefits in later years* (p. 17).

Individual paragraphs are devoted to these and other topics, each unfolded in a mainly descriptive mode. Don Decker comes to the conclusion that *Life in San Carlos was no bowl of cherries. It seemed like the devil himself had cast all of the world's misfortune on that community* (p. 60).

Don Decker's account of his earlier life in Apache land consists mainly of a sequence of descriptive paragraphs informing about social frames and routines and an episodic style of relating particular events. Although one learns a lot about his particular biography, his biography is not presented within a temporally unfolding narrative scheme. When comparing the sequence of generalizing descriptions of life in Apache land with the transformation narrative and the narrative of the time thereafter, its modes of presentation appear to be very different. The Anglo American story is a story of development in time, with the narrator as the major proponent. To put it differently, the account after the transformation is an autobiographical narrative in the true sense of the term. It is composed of a sequence of episodes which temporally and logically follow each other and which are connected within the unifying frame of a meaningful biography.

This change in communicative styles—if not communicative genres—is not a random choice made by the author. It has its origin in the very fact that Don Decker' story is a story of biographical transformation. Being able to tell something as a story means to be able to see it as a gestalt. For Don Decker, the concatenation of events in the narrative part can be linearized and meaningfully organized within a plot structure. This is different in the description part before the transformation. It is among the central features of transformation processes that there is a change in major orientations and attitudes. When looking back on his life course, Don Decker, as the man he is today, is unable to tell his experiences from the time before the transformation as a narrative gestalt.

He can only do so in a generalizing mode presenting descriptions of social frames and routines. This is the tribute he has paid to having changed as a person. Biographical identity, as it hopefully could be shown from this discussion, is a strong category, and it even has an influence on text organization.

5 Linguistic Identity Work in the Apache Autobiography

I first came across the category *identity work* or *biographical work* in sociological biography analysis. Schütze (1994) used the term with reference to the productive search for identity development that may occur in particular biographies. When I was first using *identity work* for my own analyses, I learned that it does not sound entirely idiomatic to speakers of English.

Face work however is a well known and accepted category. It goes back to Erving Goffman's theorizing on social identity and on the presentation of self in public encounters. Face work occurs, when an individual is engaged in social interaction and actively advocating a particular self presentation or social identity. Ribeiro (2006) talks about *"doing identity work"* (p. 50). She has an ethnomethodological perspective on *social identity* and looks at how identity is interactionally performed in social exchanges. Also, she draws from Goffman's work on footing, that is, the ever-shifting alignments between speakers as indicated by contextualization cues. *Social identity work* as a category is of widespread use in studies in ethnomethodological conversation analysis with approaches from a social psychological (Antaki & Widdicombe, 1998) and from a linguistic perspective (Auer, 2007). Social identity work there refers to social categorization as an active achievement by members in communicative interaction. Social identity work can also entail implicit acts of identification (Günthner, 2007). In their classical linguistic analysis of politeness phenomena, Brown and Levinson (1978) make use of Goffman's notion of face, and in this respect they argue from an interactional standpoint as well: Their differentiation between positive and negative face and the respective linguistic politeness phenomena of positive and negative politeness are based on the assumption that the public self-image, that every member wants for himself, depends on basic claims to territories and self-determination (*negative face*) and on the positive consistent self-image (*positive face*). Interactants are accomplices in face work in that they generally acknowledge their mutual interests to maintain face, and they employ strategies to maintain each other's face. While negative face can be supported by avoidance strategies or indirectness, positive face requires that interactants reassure each other their appreciation, and they do so even though they at times commit face threatening acts. In social science contexts, *biographical work* is used following Corbin and Strauss (1988) to grasp how patients accommodate to their illness, that is, how they understand the disease, what actions they take to gain control over the life course facing disease, and how they recreate a meaningful outlook on life. Ricoeur (1981), in a totally different endeavor, talks about "discourse as a work" (p. 136), referring to the configurational aspects of any sequence longer than the sentence as a matter of composition and style.

While authors like Goffman, Ribeiro, Antaki and Widdicombe, Auer, and Brown and Levinson are concerned with the presentational aspects of the self in interactional encounters, that is, social identity, Corbin and Strauss and Schütze focus on individual processes of self understanding, that is, biographical identity. When compared to face work, these processes of self understanding provide a more authentic perspective on the person performing that kind of work.

As Schütze (1994) points out, there are particular linguistic means by which biographical identity work is expressed in larger autobiographical accounts. In conclusion of this particle, I will briefly discuss instances of such biographically focused identity work in Don Decker's autobiography. That it is performed in search for an authentic self image is among the central features of biographical work. It is not the fabricated account to be presented in social encounters that is at issue here, but a coherent biographical self perspective. Don Decker goes through his life course, considering how he sees himself and is seen by others, and he comes up with an account of biographical uniqueness. To say it in accordance with George Herbert Mead: When doing biographical work, Don Decker has to respond to himself from the perspective of an interactional "other". In order to become a self in the reflexive sense, he tells the story of his life, and he includes his reflections.

Language with its system of semantic categories, discursive structures and with its communicative genres plays an important role in gaining such kinds of insights into our selves. Language helps us to point out how we are connected to particular we-groups, how we are unique, what our position in the life course is, how we are connected to society, what our major orientations are, what our competencies are, where we are likely to be successful or fail, what our goals in life are and what old and new strategies we can apply to reach those.

The category of identity work—or to be more concrete: biographical identity work—highlights the active side of biographical identity. As linguists, we can contribute to researching the accounting practices people apply individually and in interaction in order to come up with notions of the more consistent self. Since reflexivity plays a role in constructions of identity, many of the linguistic activities of formulation and reformulation, of argumentation, of weighing up of alternative views, of contextualizing, and of narration proper with its opportunities to evaluate and to take stock can be seen as instances of identity work. Disfluent accounts make us aware of episodes where identity is not a matter of clear cut categories and cardinal claims. And although Don Decker's narrative is a written text that has gone through editing, it has kept its instances of identity work. It is multi-layered in its texture and complex in its content.

Biographical work becomes necessary in situations of crisis: Don Decker was part of a stigmatized social collectivity and he lived under the permanent danger of social exclusion. One very salient moment in his stigmatization experience is when he was on his way to a new school and called off the bus. For some unknown reasons he could not be included in the group of students who was going to attend a distant boarding school. He realizes that he is not granted education. As a competent adolescent he has to think over his chances in life and actively engage in developing a biographical action scheme to escape such detrimental circumstances.

He explicitly turns his attention to his biography and he engages in deep reflection. That he goes through the various sides of his Apache biography is part of a contextualization activity, where he integrates aspects of his social identity into his biography. He does not deny his Apache identity, but he reaches an understanding as to what staying in Apache land would have meant for his biography. He owes much to his Apache origin, and much of his account is devoted to what life was like in Apache land. But it is also clear to him that he has to escape the reservation since otherwise there would be no chance for him to develop. I would finally like to briefly focus on some of the features of biographical work as linguisticly expressed in his account.

As described in the foregoing analysis, the autobiography is composed of two major parts, a mainly descriptive account of the various facets of life in Apache land and a mainly narrative part of the adoption and the lifetime thereafter. When discussed in terms of narrative sense making, this discrepancy in form reflects an experiential rupture. While Don Decker, at the moment of writing down his autobiography, has a clear grasp of his biography after the adoption as a narrative gestalt, this is not so for his life before this decisive event. It has been argued that Don Decker went through a process of biographical transformation, and that the narrative ordering of his life story from the adoption on is an indicator of his current system of orientations, while he feels some sort of estrangement toward his earlier biography, which obviously cannot be told as a story or somehow integrated within the autobiographical gestalt.

The fact that the descriptions of life in Apache land stand apart from the narrative of life from the adoption on is taken as an indicator of the authenticity of Don Decker's writing. He is not trying to produce a fabricated account, where a connection between these two larger experiential episodes may have been constructed. In Don Decker's autobiography orientational conflicts are not covered but spelled out. Also, chances to rationalize are not picked up. Don Decker is not simply claiming that social migration occurred because of the extreme poverty in the San Carlos Reservation, and he does not simply tell his life in the Anglo American world as a success story. There is much reflection going on as to what he owes to Apache and to Anglo American culture respectively, although he does have some difficulty finding access to his earlier life. In many parts of the text, the account, therefore, shifts from either narrative or description to argumentation, and argumentation is not applied for reasons of justification—another indicator of authentic biographical identity work. When Don Decker comes to formulate conclusive evaluations, he does not do so from scratch. It is only after detailed and at times ambivalent accounts that he presents a category or evaluation summarizing his experience. The embedded narrative structure of the adoption episode proper is an instance where an authentic search for meaning is reflected in the story structure.

Don Decker's autobiography tells the story of a very impressive life course, and it is at the same time a document of authentic biographical identity work.

References

ANTAKI, CHARLES & WIDDICOMBE, SUSAN (Eds.) (1998). *Identities in talk*. London: Sage.

AUER, PETER (Ed.) (2007). *Style and social identities. Alternative approaches to linguistic heterogeneity*. Berlin: Mouton de Gruyter.

BAMBERG, MICHAEL (Ed.) (2007). *Narrative. State of the art*. Amsterdam: John Benjamins.

BAMBERG, MICHAEL, DE FINA, ANNA & SCHIFFRIN, DEBORAH (Eds.) (2007). *Selves and identities in narrative discourse*. Amsterdam: John Benjamins.

BRINKER, KLAUS (1992). *Linguistische Textanalyse. Eine Einführung in Grundbegriffe und Methoden*. Berlin: Erich Schmidt.

BROWN, PENELOPE & LEVINSON, STEPHEN (1978). "Universals in language usage. Politeness phenomena". In: ESTHER GOODY (Ed.). *Questions and Politeness. Strategies in Social Interaction*. Cambridge University Press.

BRUNER, JEROME S. (1990). *Acts of meaning*. Cambridge, MA: Harvard University Press.

CHAFE, WALLACE (1990). "Some things that narratives tell us about the mind". In: BRUCE K. BRITTON & ANTHONY D. PELLEGRINI (Eds.). *Narrative Thought and Narrative Language*. Hillsdale, NJ: Lawrence Erlbaum. pp. 79–98.

CORBIN, JULIET & STRAUSS, ANSELM (1988). *Unending work and care. Managing chronic illness at home*. San Francisco: Jossey-Bass.

DE FINA, ANNA (2003). *Identity in narrative. A study of immigrant discourse*. Amsterdam: John Benjamins.

DE FINA, ANNA (2006). "Group identity, narrative and self-representations". In: ANNA DE FINA, DEBORAH SCHIFFRIN & MICHAEL BAMBERG (Eds.). *Discourse and Identity*. Cambridge: Cambridge University Press. pp. 351–375.

DE FINA, ANNA, SCHIFFRIN, DEBORAH & BAMBERG, MICHAEL (Eds.). *Discourse and identity*. Cambridge, New York: Cambridge University Press 2006.

DILTHEY, WILHELM (1970). *Der Aufbau der geschichtlichen Welt in den Geisteswissenschaften*. Frankfurt: Suhrkamp.

ERICKSON, FREDERICK & SHULTZ, JEFFREY (1982). *The counselor as gatekeeper. Social interaction in interviews*. New York: Academic Press.

FELDMAN, CAROL FLEISHER, BRUNER, JEROME S., RENDERER, BOBBIE & SPITZER, SALLY (1990). "Narrative comprehension". In: BRUCE K. BRITTON & ANTHONY D. PELLEGRINI (Eds.). *Narrative Thought and Narrative Language*. Hillsdale, NJ: Lawrence Erlbaum. pp. 1–78.

GOFFMAN, ERVING (1959). *The presentation of self in everyday life*. New York: Doubleday.

GOFFMAN, ERVING (1963). *Stigma. Notes on the management of spoiled identity*. Englewood Cliffs, NJ: Prentice Hall.

GOFFMAN, ERVING (1977). "The arrangement between the sexes". In: *Theory and Society* 4, pp. 301–331.
GOFFMAN, ERVING (1981). *Forms of Talk*. Philadelphia: University of Pennsylvania Press.
GÜLICH, ELISABETH & RAIBLE, WOLFGANG (1977). *Linguistische Textmodelle*. München: Fink.
GÜNTHNER, SUSANNE (2007). "The construction of otherness in reported dialogues as a resource for identity work". In: PETER AUER (Ed.). *Style and Social Identities. Alternative Approaches to Linguistic Heterogeneity*. Berlin: Mouton de Gruyter. pp. 419–443.
LABOV, WILLIAM (1972). *Language in the inner city: Studies in the Black English vernacular*. Philadelpia: University of Pennsylvania Press.
LINDE, CHARLOTTE (1987). "Explanatory systems in oral life stories". In: DOROTHY HOLLAND & NAOMI QUINN (Eds.). *Cultural models in language and thought*. Cambridge: Cambridge University Press. pp. 343–366.
MANDLER, J. & JOHNSON, N. (1977). "Remembrance of things parsed. Story structure and recall". In: *Cognitive Psychology* 9. pp. 111–151.
MARTIN, J.R. & ROSE, DAVID (2008). *Genre relations. Mapping culture*. London: Equinox.
MEAD, GEORGE HERBERT (1934). *Mind, self and society. From the standpoint of a social behaviorist*. University of Chicago.
MISHLER, ELLIOT G. (2006). "Narrative and identity. The double arrow of time". In: ANNA DE FINA, DEBORAH SCHIFFRIN & MICHAEL BAMBERG (Eds.). *Discourse and Identity*. Cambridge, New York: Cambridge University Press. pp. 30–47.
MISHLER, ELLIOT G. (1999). *Storylines. Craftartists' narratives of identity*. Cambridge: Harvard University Press.
RIBEIRO, BRANCA TELLES (2006). "Footing, positioning, voice. Are we talking about the same things?" In: ANNA DE FINA, DEBORAH SCHIFFRIN & MICHAEL BAMBERG (Eds.). *Discourse and Identity*. Cambridge: Cambridge University Press. pp. 48–82.
RICŒUR, PAUL. (1981). *Hermeneutics and the human sciences. Essays on language, action and interpretation*. Cambridge: Cambridge University Press.
RICŒUR, PAUL (1984). *Time and narrative* (Vol. 1). The University of Chicago Press. (originally published 1983)
RICŒUR, PAUL (1988). *Time and narrative* (Vol. 3). The University of Chicago Press. (originally published 1985)
RIEMANN, GERHARD (2006). "A joint project against the backdrop of a research tradition: An introduction to 'Doing Biographical Research'". In: *Historical Social Research* 31. pp. 6–28.
RUMELHART, DAVID E. (1975). "Notes on a schema for stories". In: D. G. BOBROW & A. COLLINS (Eds.). *Representation and Understanding. Studies in Cognitive Science*. New York: Akademic Press. pp. 211–236.
SACKS, HARVEY (1995). *Lectures on conversation* (Vols I & II). Ed. by Gail Jefferson. Oxford: Blackwell.

SCHIFF, BRIAN & NOY, CHAIM (2006). "Making it personal. Shared meanings in the narratives of Holocaust survivors". In: *Anna de Fina, Deborah Schiffrin, Michael Bamberg* (Eds.). *Discourse and Identity*. Cambridge, New York: Cambridge University Press. pp. 398–425.

SCHIFFRIN, DEBORAH (2006). "From linguistic reference to social identity". In: ANNA DE FINA, DEBORAH SCHIFFRIN, MICHAEL BAMBERG (Eds.). *Discourse and Identity*. Cambridge, New York: Cambridge University Press. pp. 103–131.

SCHÜTZE, FRITZ (1994). "Das Paradoxe in Felix' Leben als Ausdruck eines 'wilden' Wandlungsprozesses". In: HANS-CHRISTOPH KOLLER & RAINER KOKEMOHR (Eds.). *Lebensgeschichte als Text. Zur biographischen Artikulation problematischer Bildungsprozesse*. Weinheim. Deutscher Studien Verlag. pp. 13–60.

SCHÜTZE, FRITZ (2008a). "Biography analysis on the empirical base of autobiographical narratives. How to analyse autobiographical narrative interviews. Part 1" In: *European Studies* 1&2. pp. 153–242.

SCHÜTZE, FRITZ (2008b). "Biography analysis on the empirical base of autobiographical narratives. How to analyse autobiographical narrative interviews. Part 2". In: *European Studies* 3&4. pp. 5–77.

STRAUSS, ANSELM (1997). *Mirrors and Masks. The Search for Identity*. New Brunswick, London: Transaction Publishers. (originally published 1959).

SWALES, JOHN (1990). *Genre analysis. English in academic and research settings*. Cambridge University Press.

VAN DIJK, TEUN A. (1980). *Text and context. Explorations in the semantics and pragmatics of discourse*. London: Longman.

FRITZ SCHÜTZE

Biographical Process Structures and Biographical Work in a Life of Cultural Marginality and Hybridity: Don Decker's Autobiographical Account

1   Introduction: The Concepts of Marginality and Hybridity and Their Application on the Don Decker Text[1]

In social and cultural sciences we can witness a long tradition of fascination with persons who have incorporated two or more ethnic or national cultures in the course of their life histories. A great part of the fascination stems from the ambiguity of the biographical situation of those persons. On the one hand, some authors of social and cultural sciences outline that these persons feel as, and are seen as, biographically enriched by the capacity for different cultural outlooks and different cultural traditions and practices. On the other hand, some authors of social and cultural sciences also underline the suffering of those persons being torn between two or more different cultural and community-based sets of obligations that each requires full and undivided loyalty. In addition, some authors of social and cultural sciences draw the picture of the well-versed cosmopolitan person, who can stand the difficulties of complex situations and their multi-task requirements; while other authors stress the awkwardness of life-situations in a strange social and cultural environment, where one feels less than fully competent to understand how to handle the complex tasks of communicating, interacting, and cooperating in a situationally adequate way. Furthermore, some authors of social and cultural sciences focus on the high-status stranger admired because of his or her competency in mastering and moving within various national or ethnic cultures, including that of the autochthonous onlookers; while other authors stress the difficulties

---

[1]   I have to thank Gerhard Riemann, Nuremberg, Andra Sadoun, San Francisco, and Anja Schroeder-Wildhagen, Magdeburg, for correcting and improving my clumsy English language writing and for sensitizing me to unclear formulations in a first version of this text and to ambivalent phenomena in Don Decker's autobiographical document.

of the stigmatized stranger, who is assessed by the autochthonous onlookers as culturally and socially incompetent and undistinguished. Finally, some authors of social and cultural sciences underline the creative impact of the admired and perhaps somewhat enigmatic stranger coming from another socio-cultural world and bringing new potential for cultural learning and even enlightenment to autochthonous societies; while for others, there is discussion of the predicament of the essentially alien stranger, who is seen by the majority of autochthonous members of society as a danger bringing turmoil to their everyday life.

For this flock of persons being socioculturally in-between, social and cultural sciences have in use the old concept of the marginal man (Park 1967 and Stonequist 1937/1961), who is defined as existing in-between two cultures, and the more recent concept of cultural hybridity (Homi Bhabha 1994) that basically conveys the same meaning, but might pinpoint the specific potential of those persons for cultural creativity somewhat more than the old concept, although Park also stressed the creativity potential of the marginal man. The two concepts transport both the brighter and darker qualities of assessment, and the various features of meaning that, put together, deliver an overall ambivalent picture, although the concept of marginal man might stress the darker qualities a bit more.

The autobiographer Don Decker is an exponent of cultural marginality or cultural hybridity, although the scale of his life course turns out to be much more in the direction of the favourable assessment positions just alluded to. We can learn from his autobiographical text how living in two very different cultures has a central impact on biography, complicating the life course, and must be managed by lots of biographical work. This is even more the case, when one comes from a culture and community deprived of cultural reputation and political and economic power, i.e. the San Carlos Apache Reservation[2]

---

2   In order to orient myself with regard to the geographical areas and the history of Southern Arizona and Central Illinois where Don Decker /Denny has spent his life up to now I used the English language version of the "Wikipedia" online encyclopedia. The same holds true for my attempts to get background information about pop music, rock music and folk music during the Fifties and Sixties in the US.—In the following chapter I will not quote these very useful Wikipedia articles explicitly; it is always obvious from the textual context of my contribution that I used them.—The background information from the Wikipedia articles is important for assessing the conditions of Don Decker's / Don Denny's various life situations. For example, it is important to know that the small town of Globe close to the San Carlos Apache reservation is a town with

175 km east of Phoenix, Arizona, and 193 km north of Tucson, Arizona, and compares it to the high-reputation culture of Main Stream USA and its communities of political and economic power, especially in university towns of Illinois and Indiana.

In the following chapter dealing with the hybrid, "dual-quality" life course of Don Decker (before his adoption by a young Anglo couple: Don Denny), I will preferably use the term "marginality", since Don Decker's formative years from birth through late adolescence have been spent within, or at least near to the San Carlos Apache Reservation, and under its very harsh life conditions. His mother tongue is Apache; he had to learn the English language as a second language. He had the enormously difficult task of acquiring the competence of White Anglo-American culture and language not only from the cultural and linguistic standpoint of Apache culture and language, but also from the underprivileged and marginalized position of a reservation child enduring the life condition of extreme poverty under paternalistic control (and, to be fair, of protection, too) of the Bureau of Indian Affairs of the US government. Don Decker's life course is in a double sense marginal: It is a life in-between two cultures and languages, and was started not only at the bottom of the stratification ladder of wider American society, but also in a social position of the excluded ethnic and cultural margin of the wider US society. (Actually it is even threefold marginality: Don Denny / Decker is the offspring of an Apache family of the Camp Verde Reservation in the north of Arizona that his grandfather had left. As group of strangers his family is especially poor and despised by their neighbours.)—But preferring the term "marginality" doesn't mean ignoring the enormous creative power of cultural hybridity in Don Decker's life history. That complex and dramatic life history finally leads him to the rich inner state of cultural bi-valence of even tri-valence (Antonina Kloskowska 1996/2001: chapter 6)—taking into account that he also learned the Spanish language and acquired aspects of Mexican culture, while at a Spanish-stream elementary school near Phoenix that he attended for a while together with Mexican children). His rich life course also lets him arrive at a personal state of competence in autonomous art production, and at a professional state of competence as a certified art teacher and educational counsellor, dealing with all questions of Native American college education.

---

mainly Anglo / white inhabitants in order to understand that Don Denny had to fight against stigmatization and social exclusion.

Many individuals in a structural situation of underprivileged cultural marginality (i.e., coming from another cultural and linguistic community alien to the main culture and language of the recipient wider society) initially—by some sort of naturally motivated vision—attempt to reach an educational state of enculturation, where they can command a "more-than-perfect" competency in the target culture, and that means that they would like to undergo a biographical identity conversion or alternation (Berger and Luckmann 1967: 143–150), which might have to do with much social networking and identification work. Later they realise that their super-focusing on the identification with the dominant target culture has some negative aspects, and that the real wealth of their life is the double-cultural competency and the experiences (quite often of severe suffering) connected with crossing the cultural borders and living in an ambivalent frontier situation. Being both a stranger and more or less competent in both cultures, and having all the rich but difficult biographical experiences connected with the journey from one socio-cultural community to the other can be the real essence of the creative lifestyle of a cultural stranger, although in the target-culture community she or he is still recognizable as a stranger by linguistic accent, by physical features, or by uncommon socio-cultural habits.

In later life, some of those migrants to another socio-cultural community return to their home community and turn back to their former cultural affiliation. In addition, they might attempt to become spokesmen, mediators or even teachers of their culture of origin. This can only be successful if they can retain the memory and awareness of their former difficult journey to the target cultural community and their ambivalent experiences with biographical travels through its social networks, and if they also realize that because of the long years of absence and their different biographical experiences "out there" and because of the missing of the experiences of "growing older together at home", they are at a distance to their culture of origin. Their interaction partners and clients, with whom they presently have to deal, clearly feel and realize that double cultural and biographical distance[3]. Therefore, marginal men, even if they have not lost the full competence of socio-cultural life at home, run into difficulties of losing and missing trust in interaction, and into difficulties of

---

3   As Alfred Schütz (1964b) has succinctly demonstrated in his famous article on "The Homecomer". See also Maurenbrecher (1986), especially the chapter on "homecoming" to Turkey for vacation.

their over-reaction to it: i. e. of self-righteousness and over-rigidity, if they present themselves as core trusties of their home culture, i.e. as priest, medicine men/women or wise alderman/alderwomen, since that would be felt by many members of their community of origin as inauthentic.[4] Instead, even in taking leading roles as spokesmen, counsellors, teachers, and politicians of their people, they find much more personal acceptance in presenting themselves as travellers, home-comers, and half-strangers, who are able to compare phenomena at home with those in foreign or strange other worlds, and to look at their own home culture from a distance with "other eyes" (Schütz 1964 a, b: "The Stranger" and "The Homecomer").

In order to arrive at such a sophisticated stance and attitude to be able to see oneself as a creative stranger who is competent in two or even more cultures, but at the same time at a distance to them, the biographical work of looking back on one's own biography is necessary. This results in some biographical "self-mirroring" and self-realization, which is basically accomplished by autobiographical narration and other presentational basic activities connected with it, especially description and argumentation. Producing one's own autobiography as a carefully considered and composed written document, and using one's own literary writing power for accomplishing this task, is experienced by such a person to be the most intensive and the most circumspect way of self-mirroring and self-realization[5]. In case the author is gifted in literary writing

---

[4] This irrritation of the autochthonous onlookers about the marginal man, who has bi-national or bi-ethnic parents and/or is a homecomer from a life within a foreign we-community and who emphatically identifies with his cultural or national we-community of origin doesn't apply so much to the role of politicians, although even the politician of marginal personality has to fight the mistrust of the autochthonous onlookers, as, e.g., can be seen in the cases of Èamon de Devalera (1892–1972, the third president of Ireland, and Barack Obama (2004).

[5] Common sociological thinking is that literatizing one's biographical experiences reduces the text validity of the written autobiographical document. Text validity means the quality of the autobiographical text to express authentic biographical experiences in the course of the life history of the autobiographer as well as the sequence and simultaneity of biographical process structures (like biographical action schemes or biographical trajectories of suffering). This goes against common sociological thinking, but I would like to insist that the capacity to literary writing remarkably enhances the biographical text validity of the product of autobiographical writing. The capacity to artistic writing entices the autobiographer to embark on a deep search for authentic biographical experiences. Impressive examples for this phenomenon are, e. g., the German autobiography "Anton Reiser" by Karl Phillip Moritz (1785–1790) and the "Autobiographies" of R. S. Thomas (translated from the Welsh, 1997). Contrariwise, the famous autobiographical document "The Jack-Roller. A delinquent boy's own story", edited by Clifford Shaw (1930) disguises important biographical processes which the autobiographer Stanley had to go through. This doesn't mean that "The Jack-Roller" is not an enlightening socio-biographical document. But it is analytically much more difficult to arrive at analytical insights into authentic biographical experiences of the biography incumbent Stanley than working on the texts of Moritz and Thomas. In addition, the capacity of literary writing enables the author to express a much wider gamut of experiences, and the concomitant orientations and emotions. —Don Decker's autobiographical document has a

and at the same time serious and circumspect in following up the task of trustworthy biographical reconstruction of his or her own life experiences, the product will be an autobiography of remarkable text validity that expresses self-experienced social and biographical processes with high experiential authenticity. This is remarkably the case with the author Don Decker.

2 The Two-Stage Autobiographical Document of the Author

The autobiographical document of Don Decker (whose family name had been Denny before his adoption) is divided into two parts.

The first part, spanning two thirds of the whole document, is basically a concrete and abstract description of his life situation as child and adolescent on the territory of the San Carlos Apache Reservation in the arid South East area of Arizona (p. 2–73). The first part of the autobiographical document doesn't tell about the temporal unfolding of the autobiographer's biographical development in a straightforward and explicit narrative way, although (at a second glance) it is possible to learn about the important stages of Don Denny's life as child and adolescent. It rather makes a vivid and loving descriptive drawing of the social and cultural "nesting" and framing of Don Denny's life. The more or less hidden background structure of this description is the program of a quasi-social-scientific, systematic "ethnography" in the style of social anthropology. But at the same time this style of rendering is artistically literatized in a language of personal observation dealing with the common experiences of one's former we-community from the point of view of the child and adolescent who would like to learn about the mysteries of the we-community which he is born into[6].

The first part of the autobiographical document deals with the audacity and the final military defeat of the Apache nation that was finally confined within the borders of the Arizona and New Mexico Indian reservations. It also depicts Apache religion and culture, especially singing, dancing and rituals, on the one hand, and the revival religiosity of Pentecostal Protestantism and its fight

---

remarkable literary quality.

6   This is very similar to the writing perspective of R.S. Thomas (1997)

against, and its co-existence with, the problem of collective alcoholism on the reservation territory. It also characterizes the life situation of social exclusion and extreme poverty amongst the indigenous inhabitants, who must always live on welfare checks. And last but not least it describes the very different milieus of the government elementary school for Indian kids on the reservation territory and of the Junior High School and High School in the nearby town of Globe, where the Indian adolescents are outsiders.—The more abstract features of the quasi-anthropological description are empirically grounded by many episodic narratives, mostly experienced by the child Don Denny himself. The perspective of the textual presentation is quite often shaped by the interested, affectionate and partially also amazed observation of Don Denny as child and adolescent.

Don Denny lives on the territory of the Indian reservation alone with his old grandparents, who are representatives of the two main cultural sources of community life on the reservation: the Apache religious rituals and Apache cultural life style that is at least partially represented by his grandfather, and the Protestant revival religiosity that is at least partially represented by his stepgrandmother, although she later becomes a famous indigenous healer, too. (The mother of Don Denny is just sixteen years older than her son; she lives far away in Northern Arizona. Don Denny rarely visits her; he doesn't believe what his mother tells about the identity of his father, although—visiting her— he meets an older man, an invalid Vietnam veteran, whom she lives with and about whom she claims that he would be his father. We don't learn if this man is an Apache; it seems to be not improbable, since in another section of his autobiographical text the autobiographer tells about the engagement and bloodshed of many Apaches in the Vietnam War.—p. 81, 65.)

Of course it is not possible to do a normal straightforward type of narrative analysis of the first part of Don Decker's / Denny's autobiographical document as we know it from the analysis of autobiographical narrative interviews (Schütze 2008) Instead, it is feasible to ask about the impact of the cultural and social features on the unfolding of Don Denny's biographical identity. These features are analytically depicted—although affectionately painted and embellished in a literatized style—by the autobiographer[7] in the cognitive style of

---

7   In the following analysis I will use the term "autobiographer" for the author or narrator of the

social anthropology (an academic discipline that he knows quite well). It is not so difficult to fulfil the analytical task of biographical reconstruction from a basically descriptive ethnographic text put into a we-language, since the autobiographer inserts some "I language" expressions of biographical turning points and biographical work of the child and adolescent Don Denny into the written text document.

The second part of Don Decker's (Denny's) autobiographical document is a straightforward autobiographical narrative—not so much different from extempore oral autobiographical texts (p. 73–101). The linkage to oral autobiographical story telling is obvious, for example, in the clearly expressed sequence of narrative units of presentation, in the expression of partial discrepancies as competing or clashing trends of biographical unfolding and even in the use of repairs of "mistaken rendering", especially by means of background constructions (Schütze 2008: 42–50). Nevertheless the second part of the autobiographical document is similarly literatized and artistic as the first part of the autobiographical document is.

The second part starts with telling about the beginning of Don Denny's thinking about himself and his future life course while he is sitting at the Southern Pacific Railroad tracks that mentally direct him to the world of cultural development and biographical possibilities outside of the confines of the reservation. The straightforward autobiographical narration starts with the following sentences:

Sometimes during the summer of 1958, while sitting on the railroad tracks running through San Carlos, I was determined to change my future. At the young age of thirteen, I began to realize that I had some control of

---

written autobiographical document. But more often I will use the names "Don Denny" or "Don Decker". These names refer to the actor or—technically speaking—story carrier within a certain event constellation of the narrated life history. Quite often a discrepancy between the perspective of the actor, respective story carrier, and the narrator can be witnessed. One possibility of bridging such a discrepancy is to use irony. For example, the autobiographer Don Decker tells about how the drunken Don Decker staggered on a Chicago stage during a big folk festival in order to play and sing a folk song (p. 69). But, alas, he was so drunk, that he forgot the refrain. The autobiographer puts an ironical perspective on this event, whereas the actor, respective story carrier, got extremely angry and attempted to legitimize his drinking by his long waiting before the performance. In addition, there is the (admittedly clumsy) term "biography incumbent" that refers to the "natural history" of the autobiographer's identity unfolding.—For these analytical differences see Schütze 2008: 212–225.

what I wanted of my life—in the distant future. After experiencing what I had lived through so far, I knew that a change had to take place before the wrath of hell consumed me in San Carlos. (p. 73, par. 5)

It is remarkable that his straightforward autobiographical story telling starts with depicting the onset of Don Denny's reflective stance of adolescent life. It is known that the capacity for autobiographical story telling as most elementary activity of biographical work (dealing with one's own personal identity— Schütze 2008: 66–71) starts with personal reflection in puberty and adolescence—perhaps in connection with the feeling that one's body becomes strange[8]. The very fact, that the autobiographer starts with a detailed and straightforward autobiographical narration exactly at that time point within the document when he focuses on his first steps of biographical work, is one of the striking empirical evidences for the high text validity of Don Decker's / Denny's autobiographical document. The term "text validity" as used here refers to the authentic and unrestrained expression of autobiographical experiences, biographical process structures and autobiographical self-theorizing.

The straightforward autobiographical rendering can be analysed basically in the same way as this can be done with the textual presentation of extempore oral autobiographical narratives. In order to accomplish the task of segmenting the text into narrative units and supra-segmental macro-units, one can focus on the continuations and discontinuations of narrative rendering that deal with biographical episodes, events and phases or with parts or wholes of biographical process structures. Important signs of discontinuation are, e.g., the sudden rise of the level of detailing, episodic narration with depiction of the dramatic features of a situation, and the specific recollection of biographical time. In order to accomplish the delineation of autobiographical process structures, one can attempt to find and analyse supra-segmental markers, that abound in written autobiographies and—similar to extempore story telling—often symbolize or even formulate biographical process structures and their pivotal features and phases. In order to analyse the biographical work

---

8   Through this experience of the "estranged body" the adolescent human being develops the perspective and relationship of excentric positionality ("exzentrische Positionalität") towards oneself (Plessner 1928/1975). Excentric positionality is the basic condition for developing the capacity of autobiographical story telling in adolescence. Now the young person acquires the ability to focus on her or his change of identity (as biography incumbent: maintaining oneself both as identical and changing), which was not possible before (Stötzel 1998).

of the biography incumbent one can focus on the biographical commentaries and biographical self-theorizing of the informant—features that are as common in written autobiographical texts as in extempore story telling.

The text fragment quoted above shows most of the features which have been just mentioned. The text fragment is the introduction to a complex narrative unit that ends much later; at the same time it contains a first kernel sentence of the narrative unit: *"I was determined to change my future."* This kernel sentence expresses the beginning of a complex biographical action scheme entailing the intention to escape from the potentials of the unfolding of a trajectory of suffering and losing control lurking on the reservation territory and to search for and accomplish a biographical change. The segment ends with: *"Taking a pair of boots off from a drunken firefighter was like bartering with a mad and enraged bear in the forest."* (p. 77, par. 3). The succeeding narrative unit starts with a marker of discontinuity in conjunction with a new kernel sentence: *"In 1957 or 1958 I was selected to attend a work camp..."*: In the introduction to the complex narrative unit just finished before (and quoted above) one can surmise the dim idea that Don Denny felt that he had to leave the reservation territory and to enter the Anglo world. The detailing sub-segment following the introductory kernel sentence, then, is an inner argumentation about the acceptance or non-acceptance of the two main cultural resources and influences of life within the confines of the reservation (traditional Apache culture and Protestant revival religiosity) and on the future possibilities to fight the dangers of being trapped by the collective trajectory of social exclusion, stigmatization and developmental paralysis. It spans from *"... I knew that a change had to take place before the wrath of hell consumed me in San Carlos."* until *"There are very few orators* [of Protestant and traditional Apache culture—F.S.] *left in San Carlos today"* (p. 75, par. 2).

It might be helpful for the reader to have an overview of the definitions of the four basic biographical process structures which we have derived from the analysis of numerous autobiographical texts, especially extempore autobiographical narratives collected by means of autobiographical narrative interviewing (Schütze 2008: 183–191; Treichel 2004). These four basic concepts of biography analysis are systematically used in the following analysis:

1. **biographical action schemes:** a person attempts to actively shape the course of her or his life;
2. **trajectories of suffering:** the afflicted person is not capable of actively shaping her or his own life any more, since she or he can only react to overwhelming outer events; in the course of her or his suffering the afflicted person becomes strange to her- or himself;
3. **institutional expectation patterns:** the person is following up an institutionally shaped and normatively defined course of life, e.g. a career in an educational organization or the family life cycle that opens up and forms family life in the first part of adulthood; as well as
4. **creative metamorphoses of biographical identity:** a new important inner development is starting within the course of one's own biography, that might be enigmatic and irritating in the beginning since it is new and that initially hinders the unfolding of pertinent competencies of the biography incumbent; therefore she or he must find out what the very quality of the enigmatic new development might be.

For the textual analysis of *both* parts of the autobiographical document of Don Decker / Denny the text phenomena of explicit biographical change and of biographical work were central. These text phenomena express the gradual or dramatic change of the unfolding of Don Denny's, respective Don Decker's, biographical identity. Sometimes identical with supra-segmental markers, the text phenomena of explicit biographical change and of biographical work helped to discover the biographical process structures which Don Denny / Decker underwent in the course of his life history.—However, only a few explicit formulations of autobiographical reflection can be found in the autobiographical document which we are discussing. Of course, there are a lot of hidden expressions of biographical work, on the one hand, and the lack of them at places where one would normally expect such expressions (for example regarding the distortion or even loosening of the relationship with his adoptive parents during Don Decker's university studies in Charleston, Illinois, and in Indianapolis), on the other.—The fact of the scarcity of explicit formulations of biographical reflection in the autobiographical document might hint to the fact that Don Decker has still to do at least some biographical work at the time when he finished his autobiography (in 1997)—biographical work which is emotionally difficult to accomplish against the background of the suffering—which is characteristic of the life course of culturally marginal and hybrid personalities. (In the meantime, after finishing his autobiographical document in 1997, he has probably accomplished much more biographical work. The fact that he offered this document for further analysis is a vivid sign of the intensity of his ongoing biographical work.)—Here is the list of the explicit formulations of autobiographical reflection in his autobiographical document:

- p. 17: mentioning of growing up in poverty and of persistence of values after leaving the reservation
- p. 19f: shame about grandparent's poor shack: "my values were slowly changing"
- p. 23: taking part in singing during puberty rites: "I have continued to reaffirm my Apache beliefs throughout the years since I left reservation …"
- p. 35f: with regard to living on the reservation: "This was different than sitting in a beautiful home on the hillside of the Camelback Mountains of Phoenix, where I might have stayed with the German family."
- p. 40: regarding teachers at elementary school: "I never had a bad experience with any of these teachers": they instilled discipline and showed how to survive
- p. 65: "I also believe that most of us who grew up in San Carlos during the harsh times of the 50ties and early 60ties experienced some type of post-traumatic stress disorder (PTSD). My alcoholism and even loss of my family in later years may have been the result of years of mental warfare in San Carlos."[9]
- p. 73: "I began to realize that I had some control of what I wanted of my life."—Change of general text register from abstract description

---

9   This is one of the few remarks "off record" about later difficulties in the life of Don Decker. Obviously in later days he was separated from his former wife. He mentions her at the very end of his autobiographical text and in its dedication. It is clear that in 1997 he is not married to her any more, but he doesn't tell about a divorce or—in more detail about—his own alcoholism that may have led to this divorce. By the same token, it is clear that after Don Decker's return to Southern Arizona the dynamics of the double trajectory of suffering conditioned by his former life in poverty and social exclusion on the reservation and perhaps also conditioned by the life situation of too great expectations while living as a cultural-conversion immigrant, has started again. This might have been provoked by certain difficult life situations after his successful academic gradation and successful return to Southern Arizona.—The resuming difficulties with himself are part of the natural history of the identity unfolding and change of the biography incumbent.

with anecdotic stories in the style of a memoir to straightforward autobiographical narration proper
- p. 80: first biographical mentor and counsellor is Orion Dillon, the Apache surveyor in the work camp episode so important for Don Denny's biographical development
- p. 84: feeling no reasons for a return to San Carlos reservation when living with his Anglo "pre-adoption parents" in Globe near the Anglo high school
- p. 85: "it bothered me that grandfather never gave permission for adoption"
- p. 86: life of transition and odyssey (one of the central commentaries regarding the life history as a cultural hybrid)
- p. 88: "In the last 9 months of my high school career I more than made up for all the lost time at Globe High back in Arizona." (claim for moratorium)
- p. 89: Regarding the lifestyle of Midwest farmers of Don Decker's extended adoption family: "Their kinship values match those of American Indians. It is for this reason that I felt never any different when I was adopted into the white farm family."
- p. 90: coming across and living with the chorus teacher (the adoptive father) and his family: an "encounter which changed the whole world for me. ... I accepted the adoption without question."
- p. 97: first dim planning to become a bi-cultural teacher and mediator on American Indian reservations; planning to return to his first university in Charleston, Illinois, in order to follow up his biographical action scheme of becoming a bi-cultural teacher
- p. 100: Commentary of having needed four extra years for his academic career; his assessment that the peers would have been ten years ahead of him; making plausible the necessity of a significant biographical moratorium regarding his life course of coming from a culture of poverty and exclusion and being under the difficult biographical and social condition of identity change of a hybrid personality
- p. 101 Commenting on returning to the area of San Carlos reservation as a "full circle": this is the metaphor of "dialectical learning" in the sense of Heinrich von Kleist's "Über das Marionettentheater" [On the Marionette Theatre]: It conveys Don Decker's idea of not having be-

trayed one's culture of origin, of having seriously learned the ways of both cultures, having arrived at the level of full bi-culturality and hybridity and having matured in the course of a Perceval-type of long and irritating journey with several enigmatic stages, which he, Don Decker, would be too naive to grasp in their complex meaning at first glance ("chasing rainbows")
- p. 101: Assessing the community and private life on the reservation as still being primitive (pp. 14, par. 2; 101): this might allude to a personal stance of functioning as a mediator of the educational standards of Anglo culture towards Indian adolescents and of a liaison worker between both cultures helping young Indians to find their way in-between the two cultures.

There are various topical possibilities to deal with Don Decker's autobiographical document. It would be intriguing to study in-depth the author's techniques of writing up his autobiography. It would be interesting to scrutinize his provisions for authenticity, for quasi-ethnographic adequacy and for literary vividness in his autobiographical writing. It would be worthwhile to compare his text document as dependable empirical data with other autobiographical productions—be they in a written or in a oral form, be they produced with an artistic writer's attitude or just with the pragmatic attitude of an everyday informant (like Stanley in the "Jack-Roller"—Shaw 1930/1966). But right now it seems to be more important to (a) demonstrate how the analysis of a single written biographical text can be accomplished and (b) to find out about the basic features, creative potentials and difficulties of Don Decker's life history as a hybrid one with many experiences of crossing cultural borders. This might even be of greater interest for the autobiographer himself, who works hard on finding out about the problems and chances of cultural hybridity and of the pertinent biographical work.

3   First Part of Autobiography (up to p. 73): Manifestation of the
     Hidden Aspect of the Author's Personal Biography,
     When he Describes the Features of his Collective Identity
     as an Apache Indian

The author Don Decker was born in 1944 in Phoenix Indian Hospital. In his first eighteen years of life he carried the name of Don Denny (p. 11 and 30). In 1962 he was adopted by one of his school teachers and his wife, a white American couple, and his name was changed to Don Decker (p. 86). Of course, this was a drastic change for him. Most of the first 18 years of his life as Don Denny, the autobiographer doesn't tell chronologically. Instead, he gives an abstract description in the style of an ethnologist of what life was like on the San Carlos Apache reservation, when he was a child and adolescent. Nevertheless, the quasi-ethnological description is interspersed with personal anecdotes that have autobiographical underpinnings. From those anecdotes, it is possible to relate the following biographical events and processes of the child and adolescent Don Denny.

Don Denny was the child of a very young Apache mother (15 years of age), who herself, along with four siblings, had been put by her parents into the Phoenix Indian School, a government boarding school for Indians, when the grandfather "found it too hard to care for all his children" (p. 13, par. 4). This set the situation for at least part of the family offspring, i.e. for five children, of being put away and not loved enough. At least this had probably been the experience of his mother, and she again, still being a student, gave her son away into a German-American foster home.—Of course, there are several understandable reasons for Don Denny's grandparents to put five children into the Indian culture school: First of all, Don Denny's grandfather was at the time a migrant road worker, and was extremely poor. In addition, at the Phoenix Indian School it could be expected (at least by traditionally-oriented parents), that the children would learn how to preserve indigenous Indian culture (p. 48, par. 1). On the other hand, the autobiographer states that Don Denny's grandfather had found it too hard to care for all his children, and this conveys the understanding that Don Denny knew quite early that his mother had felt abandoned by her parents.

The first two years of his life Don Denny lived in a quite affluent German American foster home. (At least the autobiographer surmises this affluence in retrospect and compares it with the extreme poverty of the next 16 years of his life on an Indian reservation.—p. 35f) But the fact of Don's being handed over to his grandparents not by the foster mother but by a "German teenaged babysitter" (p. 13f) might be understood as an empirical sign of emotional abandonment, at least to a certain degree, of Don Denny by his former German foster family. (On the other hand, it could also mean exactly the opposite: that the foster parents had felt conflicted, and emotionally could not stand to hand the child back over to Denny's grandparents. This opposite interpretation fits with the autobiographer's assumption that he most likely cried all the way back to Globe—a town 142 km east of Phoenix.—p. 14, par. 1)

At that point, Don Denny was taken in and cared for by his grandparents. What reason they had for taking over the care of for their grandchild is not clear in the text. The grandparents might have felt responsible for Don Denny, since they had abandoned their daughter, Don's mother, by putting her into the Indian boarding school, which could also be seen as a place to learn the Indian tradition, but which obviously did not turn out for Don's mother to be a good place to grow up. We additionally know that Don's grandfather had by then put an end to his migrant life as a road worker, and instead, worked in a copper mine in Miami, Arizona, near Globe. Two years later he, his wife and Don Denny moved to the San Carlos Apache Reservation 175 kilometres east of Phoenix, where he had transported by truck a primitive hut to. Now the condition and moving mechanism of the unfolding of a trajectory of personal abandonment in Don Denny's early life was under control, the trajectory itself had been stopped.

In the following roughly fifteen years, living on the San Carlos Apache Reservation, or nearby, when his grandparents occasionally worked as harvesters on local farms, Don Denny underwent a double cultural learning process in the course of the socialisation process, essentially patterned by his grandparents and the reservation community: He was encultured by the Apache culture, including the Apache religion (addressing the images of ancestors, observing ghost dances, etc.), and he became acquainted with Protestant conversion religiosity. The first was encouraged by his grandfather, and the second by his grandmother.—Generally speaking, Don Denny was under the socialisation condition of learning two very different ways of looking at the world and handling it. In his adolescent years, Don became more familiar with the Indian religion. The cultural cleavage might sometimes have been quite difficult for him; but on the other hand he learned early on how to handle cultural situations of marginality or hybridity. The capacity to master situations of marginality and hybridity were certainly not just newly acquired when, as an adolescent of eighteen, he came under the influence of his future adoptive family and moved with his new parents to Illinois. Instead, he learned to handle marginal situations much earlier, as a child. This is certainly a favourable biographical condition for his later mastery of biographical journeying into White American culture. We can see that the autobiographer's developmental line of a hidden metamorphosis process of acquiring cultural bi-valence (Kloskowska 1996/2001: chapter 6) and becoming competent in conducting a culturally hybrid life took its beginning in his childhood. (pp. 15–20, 21f, 26f; 59–63)

The child Don Denny had to undergo and endure extremely poor living conditions. Even in the year 2011, 58.8 % of the population of San Carlos, Arizona, were still living under the poverty level (defined by a median household income of $13.412 per annum); 92.63 % of the 3716 inhabitants were Native Americans. Therefore, even in 2011 San Carlos was one of the poorest Native American communities in the U.S.. Don Denny lived with his two grandparents in the one-room shack already mentioned, without his own territory for personal retreat (pp. 19f, 24, 36, 83). He, too, was on the brink of becoming a personal victim of the collective trajectory of extreme poverty and socio-ethnic exclusion. As a child, he could observe this predicament looking at the daily lives of the adult inhabitants of the reservation, including his grandparents: Being dependent on collecting government pay checks, not being capable of autonomous budgeting, not being able to get rid of the periodic habit of collectively becoming drunk, always living at risk of being robbed, often journeying under deadly dangerous travelling conditions, suffering from health conditions caused by tailings from local copper and asbestos plants and poorly-announced mining blasts, and being frequently terrorized by the fierce aggressiveness of fellow Apaches who had been destabilized through delinquent behaviour, imprisonment, etc. (pp. 34–36, 41f, 72f). The poor living conditions and the concomitant socio-ethnic exclusion also had consequences on the level of collective self-confidence. In retrospect the author diagnoses a partial socio-cultural alienation, as could be seen when the children of the San Carlos Indian Reservation were watching Hollywood western films: The children always identified themselves with the white men and the US cavalry in the conflicts between American Indians and white settlers. The author comments: Children would always identify with the winner, but by the nature of this psychosocial mechanism, the Apache children would lose at least part of their collective self-esteem (p. 43, par. 3).

On the other hand, the author stresses his learning process of becoming competent in terms of rational agency within the orientation framework of a culture of poverty (Oscar Lewis 1961). The poor living conditions in the semi-desert of San Carlos taught him and his peers to become practitioners of practical rationality. He and his peers learned to organize the food supply from the desert flora and desert fauna by gathering acorns and hunting desert rats. They collected a certain type of semi-precious stone and also scraps of copper wire from the copper plant in Miami (pp. 31–34). In addition, he and his peers learned to trick more affluent inhabitants of San Carlos: For example, by wearing two different costumes one after the other on Halloween night, they were able to collect double the amount of goodies from the employees of the Bureau of Indian Affairs in San Carlos (p. 30f).—Learning the culture of poverty also includes becoming a circumspect, inventive adolescent community member with high networking capacity. For example, Don Denny took part in all types of adventurous peer activities, and he participated in religious ceremonies with social dancing and social smoking (pp. 25, 26–29). Furthermore, he got into the adolescent peer habit of name carving: He realized that Indian life and Indian kinship structure is very much related to the inhabited and surrounding land, and in order to underline this understanding, he used to carve his name on all types of natural and technical objects spread over the countryside, including very dangerous ones (pp. 14f). Last but not least, it should be stressed that Don Denny became competent in the Apache cultural habit of "bullshitting", an interaction which is a special type of joking relationship with the interacting counterpart: "Showing off" in an exaggerated fashion, and at the same time letting the interaction partner know that one's behaviour should not be taken too seriously (p. 29). Mutual "bullshitting" makes fun in social settings, and can sometimes be connected with attempting to receive something normally not attainable. For example: Don Denny, as a pre-adolescent boy, told the old Indian man who had a reputation for handing out tobacco to boys as a small gift, that his grandparents had given him permission to smoke. The old man was expecting a "good lie", and only after a good performance in lying did he hand out the tobacco to Don Denny and his peers (p. 28f).—The autobiographical text underlines that the culture of poverty connected with life on the San Carlos Apache reservation provided some incentive for learning and creativity in connection with handling a particularly difficult everyday life. This is very similar to narrative recollections of present day elderly Germans, who were children in World War II and immediately after it: How they managed to "organize" food and how they would inventively attempt to have fun and stage harmless adventures, even though they were surrounded by the disaster of war and the collective hunger predicament immediately after its end. In order to characterize the specific wit and circumspection of the poor children of the San Carlos Apache Reservation, the autobiographer uses the term and formulation that they were forced and invited to become "abstract thinkers" (p. 29, end of par. 1).

Don Denny's biographical situation existed in an ambivalent state, with its tendency toward creative learning within a culture of poverty as a hidden precondition and incentive for a biographical metamorphosis process which ultimately gained dynamic momentum; and also with a strong tendency toward collective and biographical destabilization within a collective predicament of extreme poverty, which was always on the threshold of deteriorating into a process of the collective trajectory (Schütze 1989) of demoralization of the Indian population of the San Carlos reservation. There were all the cleavages between the Apache population on the level of both adults and children lowering the level of public security (p. 53f), various conditions of deadly danger in everyday life (e.g. bad transportation opportunities and the brutality of marauding bands of uprooted Indians), tendencies toward collective alcoholism (including his grandparents in certain situations—pp. 41f, 65f, 67f, 75), and experiences of alienation through the activities and attitudes of some government and school officials. In retrospect the author diagnoses features of permanent exhaustion of the inhabitants of the San Carlos Reservation caused by the very necessity of always having to be on the alert, due to the multifarious dangers of everyday life (pp. 52–73). The author names the impact of this collective predicament with its tendency to deteriorate into the collective trajectory of demoralization with a very recent medical diagnostic category: "Post-Traumatic Stress Disorder" (PTSD—p. 65, par. 4).

On top of this trajectory potential for collective demoralization, the condition of an additional or second-degree collective trajectory was unfolding: Don Denny's family belonged to a group of collective and biographical outsiders (pp. 19f; 36, par. 4). The latter paragraph and the two last sentences of the paragraph before are a background construction that gives a probable explanation for the vandalism of the tent cabin of Don Denny's grandparents while they, with their grandson, worked as harvesters in another region quite distant from San Carlos. It surmises that the tent cabin was destroyed by adolescent boys from the neighbourhood, because they saw Don Denny's family as detested strangers on the reservation territory. This was the situation of all the offspring of Camp Verde Apaches, who had been forcefully displaced from the north of Arizona to the San Carlos area by US troops in the eighteen-eighties (p. 12) and who did not return to their former dwelling areas at the shores of the Rio Verde after the release from their enforced detention, which most of the northern Apaches accomplished between 1910 and 1920 (p. 12). And, hence, this also was the personal life situation of Don Denny: Feeling himself as a personal outsider, even among some of his peers, as somebody who was the offspring of an especially poor stranger family. For example, we can read that he was personally ashamed of the small "shed", "shack" or "cabin tent" of his grandfather Johnson Irving, which he and his grandparents had to live in (p. 19f, 36f). The neighbours seemed to have forgotten the historical circumstances of the suffering and audacity of the Camp Verde Apaches (p. 36, par. 4). In addition, there might have been another, or even a contrasting reason for the outsider status of the Irving family, although the autobiographer doesn't discuss this possibility: that the grand-grandfather of Don Denny, Henry Irving, had been a scout for the US Army in the Verde Valley in the mid-nineteenth century (p. 13, par. 4). Perhaps there was still a remote trace of traitor image connected with the Irving family within the collective recollection of the neighbours, and that would mean that exactly the contrary of a vanished collective memory of the neighbours that is claimed by the author as part of the reason for the outsider status of the Irving family (p. 36) would then have been effective.

When he was approaching his adolescent years, Don Denny found himself in the unfolding limbo situation of another personal trajectory: Facing school year 7, he was said to be referred to a government boarding school for Indians in Phoenix. While waiting with many other children on the bus which would take them to Phoenix Indian School—(p. 47–49; also see p. 13, par. 4), an unexpected event happened, which saved Don. Among parents with a traditional orientation towards native Indian culture, Phoenix Indian School was seen as a good assignment for their children; but for most of the other children it was an intimidating social reality, that both adolescents and adults on the reservation saw this school as a place for abandoned children and juvenile offenders. It seems to be quite plausible that the Bureau of Indian Affairs (BIA) had almost automatically selected Don Denny, as the child of an unmarried mother just 15 years older than her son, and as not living together with his mother. Looking at the very detailed narrative rendering of Don Denny's waiting on the Phoenix school bus and of his being disappointed and full of sadness, one can surmise that he was very scared and apprehensive of being processed by the powerful school administration as an abandoned child or a delinquent adolescent. That would be just like what had happened to his own mother, who had been put by her father into that same school with the obvious result of having gotten in lots of difficulty (especially through her premature pregnancy) while studying at Phoenix Indian School. Don might have feared that his beloved grandfather had abandoned him, too, as he seemed to have done with his mother. It is not clear what exactly happened while Don Denny was waiting on the bus, that could explain the unexpected intervention of the travel organizer of the BIA in charge, who put him off the bus. Perhaps the administration of the reservation had finally, in the last minute, realized that Don was not an abandoned child, since he was well cared-for by his grandparents. In addition, his grandparents might have protested against the referral decision of the BIA administration, especially since it can be surmised that they had feelings of guilt because of having made the big mistake of giving away their youngest daughter to that boarding school in Phoenix. (On the other hand—this is another possible explanation—the Phoenix Indian School was known as a good educational place providing a bi-cultural education with emphasis on Indian-culture socialization, and perhaps there was competition for the last free appointment places for students. We know that Don's grandparents were seen as outsiders for being Camp Verde Apaches not having gone home to the Camp Verde Reservation, and, possibly, even being the offspring of an army scout who had not kept the Apache traditions with sufficient loyalty and diligence. Therefore, Indian board members of the BIA might have conveyed the opinion that the Irving family, the family of Don Denny, did not deserve the referral of their offspring to a boarding school that was distinguished in imparting authentic Apache culture.—In any case, Don Denny was very relieved not to have been brought to the Phoenix Indian School, with the expectation of only being able to see his beloved grandparent just once a year during Christmas.

As mentioned already, there were certain intervals in Don Denny's life when the hidden metamorphosis principle of biographical development (Schütze 1994, 2001) manifested itself more and more powerfully. First of all, he learned to become a good cultural liaison worker. A precondition and, at the same time, a first strong manifestation of it was the acquisition of a second and third language in addition to his Apache mother tongue. At the age of ten, he learned the Spanish language in the very short time of four to six months, while he and his grandfather stayed in Guadalupe, near Phoenix, to work as daily wage harvesters. Since the great majority of children in the Guadalupe school were Mexican, the teaching medium was Spanish, and not English (p. 38, par. 2 and 4). In addition, Don Denny learned the intricacies of the English language very quickly (p. 38f). Not long after their return from Guadalupe to the San Carlos Reservation, he discovered that it was easy for him to connect and converse with Mexicans who were moving through the reservation, and were geographically disoriented and in urgent need of help in terms of food and water (p. 39, par. 2). Later, he became a good acquaintance of a Mexican family which had a small taco and tamale making business, and he also washed their car (73).—But Don Denny was a fast learner in all other school subjects, too: In addition to his sophisticated understanding of the form and function of the English language, he was especially good at mathematics and at comprehending the principles of physics (p. 24, par. 2; p. 40, par. 1). An additional source of momentum for Don Denny's biographical metamorphosis process as child and adolescent was his learning of musical instruments: First the harmonica, and later on the guitar (p. 39, par. 3; p. 64f). The autobiographer gives credit to his teachers at the elementary school on the reservation as having been very supportive of his personal development (p. 40, par. 1). In his autobiographical rendering lay some subtle arguments denying any possible accusations against the white and black teachers as having had a colonizing attitude toward their Indian students. Such accusations would seem to be imaginable, since Don Denny was attending a school run by the Bureau of Indian Affairs, an organisation that for long historical periods had controlled the native Indian population closely and had the reputation of pressing native students to assimilate into white American culture. Instead, the autobiographer stresses that he successfully gained insight into the White American and the Black American culture, in addition to his native Indian culture. Also according to the autobiographer, a Navajo teacher with a gentle demeanour additionally insured Don Denny that he, as a native Indian, could make his way into the world of sophisticated education.

Nevertheless, Don Denny experienced the BIA school itself, not the staff and faculty of devoted professional teachers, as a very harsh disciplinary institution. This line of differentiation by the autobiographer, although not drawn by means of these abstract categories, means that the experience of harsh discipline in school did not apply to the aspects of teaching as such, but to the aspects of enforcing and preserving the organizational and disciplinary order of the school by special supervisory staff officers. The autobiographer underlines that he himself experienced the processing of the students that was dictated by the everyday routines of supervisory staff officers of the BIA school, likening to treatment in an army barrack. He summarizes: "School was murder." (p. 45, par. 4). The students were shorn like sheep, they were washed in bulk under initially too-cold, and then too-hot shower water, and there was no privacy, as if they had been in a total institution like a prison. They were forced to eat whatever had been put on the table, and each of the table groups was only allowed to leave the dining hall when everybody at the table had finished his portion without any leftovers, and only then could they start to play outside.

Although this type of treatment was typical for many boarding schools of the Fifties in White America and Europe, too, and although most of the supervisory staff officers were probably Native Indians, some traces of systematic or "structural" racism against the native Indian population, at least the systematic and relentless attitude of getting the dirty native Indian children clean (p. 46, par. 3), could have been encapsulated in these organizational routines.—But Don Decker experienced the features of racism even more strongly at Globe Junior High School and High School, which he attended during his adolescent years, by means of a daily shuttle bus between San Carlos and Globe. Globe Junior High School and Globe High School were typical Anglo-American institutions, where the native Indian students were recognized and partially excluded as a minority ethnicity. (Globe, with roughly 7.500 inhabitants, is situated 142 km east of Phoenix and 35 km west of San Carlos. In the year 2000, 77.6 % of the inhabitants of Globe were white, 32.71 % were Latino of all races, only 3.1 % were native Indian. Probably the demographic situation of Globe did not change much between the nineteen-fifties and the year 2000 except in terms of the growth of the proportion of Latino inhabitants. Comparing his former *ethnic-exclusion* situation at Globe High School with his later *inclusion* situation at Charleston High School, Illinois, where nobody knew his native Indian background (after his adoption and the return of his adoptive family to Illinois), the author gives the following assessment of the contrast: "Suddenly, I had forgotten about undertones of racism, which I had barely overcome in Globe, Arizona." (p. 88, par. 2).

Don Denny reacted to the organizational atmosphere and the ethnic categorization and stigmatization of the elementary school in San Carlos and even more to the junior high school and high school in Globe as characterized by the closed mindset and tight control of an army barrack. In his antagonism toward this type of organizational atmosphere, he assumed a partial attitude of more or less mildly delinquent overreaction. He took part in some truancy from junior high school in Globe, in petty thefts in and around San Carlos elementary school, and in playfully chasing around the cantankerous watchman of the elementary school at night, etc. (p. 50—53). These moderate activities of delinquency were quite productive for his biographical development: They were the seeds of a personal protest habitus he later developed during his high school years in Globe, Arizona, and in Charleston, Illinois, and a learning ground for his later active participation in the civil society. He later took part in a work camp insurrection in southern Arizona because of bad camp nutrition; later at Eastern Illinois University he founded workshops addressing problems of native Indian education and was active in the civil rights movement; after the death of friends in action he became part of the anti-Vietnam-War movement; and as part of the Illinois National Guard after the shooting down of the protesting students of Kent State University, he was instrumental in defusing the fight between conservative students and Vietnam War protesters through a peaceful and clever intervention (pp. 79f, 99, 100).

As stated already, the religious life of Don Denny's childhood and adolescence was always characterized by the two traditions of Protestant revival religion, and traditional Apache religion with its spiritual relationship to deceased ancestors and to holy spirits found in certain natural surroundings. In his early adolescent years, Don Denny together with his grandmother regularly visited the church services of Pentecostal revival religion (Pope 1942), commonly called assemblies of the "Holy Rollers". The attendants of these assemblies would speak in tongues, dance in trance, and come to the altar in order to confess, to repent and to "accept the Lord's word". In the San Carlos area, their pastors and evangelists would normally be native Indians, and their services and sermons were in the Apache language. The Pentecostal groups were fighting against the obsessive alcoholism on the Indian reservations and were helping "backsliders" who had fallen back into alcoholism to return to a life of sobriety. In early adolescence Don Denny finally was somewhat brainwashed by this revivalist Protestantism, and therefore in danger of losing essential aspects of the Apache Indian religious culture, i. e. the spiritual community with its Apache ancestors and holy spirits. He was about to undergo a Baptist/Pentecostal conversion (pp. 59–63) and was already waiting for his re-baptism at a big three-day open-air event, when a hail storm destroyed the entire event, and he never actually got re-baptised. For him this was perhaps a sign from the native Indian religious spirits (p. 60–62). A little while later, Don Denny became friends with the son of a white Christian missionary from Nebraska, who had protected him against marauding native adolescent gangs at the time when Don attended church. In addition, he was very impressed by the cooperative attitude of the missionary father toward his sons (especially when he did not reprimand his sons after an accident involving his pick-up truck, caused by their carelessness), and therefore Don Denny became a "believer" and member of the missionary's church (p. 62–64).

As he grew a little older, Don Denny became more inwardly distant toward Protestant revival religion. He realized that this type of religion installed systematic fear in him: to be permanently endangered by the devil bringing misfortune to him and the many drunkards of San Carlos, and forcing him and them to go to hell (p. 59, 73). Gradually he emancipated himself from the permanent fear of "going to hell", and traditional Apache religion became more important to him again. He was supported in this by his grandfather, who had a special sense for Apache religious tradition, and who did not appreciate his wife's revival religiosity. The autobiographer acknowledges that his uncle, Abraham Logan, had a special influence on him, and on the frontispiece dedicates his autobiographical document to him as a "traditional doctor and spiritual counsellor" who lived near and maintained the Holy Grounds of San Carlos, and took care of "the Apache prayers" (p. 14, par. 2). Don Denny became more and more intrigued by the features of traditional Apache religion: The mediums of cattail pollen and eagle feathers for the Apache medicine men in getting into contact with the spiritual world (p. 14 and 74f), the ceremony of the Changing Women (p. 14) and the ceremony of the female puberty rite (p. 22–24), the "Ghans" as Mountain Spirit Dancers (p. 21f), and the essentially native Indian proceedings of funerals (p. 70–72).

The autobiographer conveys that Don experienced a value conflict in his later adolescence between revivalist Protestant religiosity and traditional Apache religion (p. 71, par. 2). This is surely true. But one also has to take into account that in San Carlos collective culture and in his own family, he experienced not only some hidden, but also some "seen, but unnoticed" syncretism, too. E.g., his grandmother, also called Poison Ivy, became a traditional healer with mystic power in the last years of her life, although she also kept her revivalist Protestant beliefs (p. 71, par. 2; 74, par. 3). It can be assessed that Don Denny experienced not only a conflict of religions (especially regarding the different attitudes of grandfather and grandmother), but also, through this syncretistic religious situation, a chance to experience various types of spiritual adventures. In later adolescence it became important for his biographical development to intellectually overcome the gruesome religious scenario of the end of the world and the relentless wrath of God, to cherish the feeling of well-being in the presence of Apache medicine men, to accept himself as a basically valuable human being, and to understand that there would be many additional possibilities for further development of his biographical identity beyond the narrow confines of the "repentance" world view of the notorious sinner. In addition, he felt that traditional Apache religion fostered adherence to the precept of mutual help among the members of the Apache community. Being intrigued by Apache religious activities was an important condition for the biographical process of metamorphosis that became more and more persistent in Don Denny's adolescent life (p. 74, par. 1–75, par. 2).

Another condition fostering the metamorphosis surely was Don's focus on music, and his learning to play musical instruments. He learned to play the harmonica in school (p. 39, par. 3), and from his new friend Brian, the son of the protestant missionary, he learned to play the guitar (p. 64f). In addition, overlooking the train tracks in front of Brian's house, Brian and Don Denny practised folk songs and rock songs. This was the kind of music which became extremely important later in Don Denny's life, when he became a semi-professional musician. Quite often he would also sit alone by the railroad tracks and meditate about the railway itself as a symbol for biographical and collective-historical development, a socio-technical instrument of transportation that allowed him to embark on a personal metamorphosis of undergoing totally new experiences and emancipating himself from the unchanging routine of life on the San Carlos Apache Reservation, via going into the Anglo world (pp. 57–59, 73, par. 5).

4 Second Part of Autobiography (starting on p. 73) With Explicit Autobiographical Rendering; Detailed Analysis of Don Denny's / Decker's Crossing the Ethno-Cultural Demarcation Line (up to p. 93)

The second part of the author's autobiography (p. 73, par. 5, to p. 101) is a straightforward narrative. It is an artistic production, too, with a lot of literary formulations, but it is not as much interspersed with abstract descriptions and argumentative reflection as the first part of the autobiographical document is (pp. 12 to 73, par. 4). The following reconstruction of Don Denny's or Don Decker's life history is based on a detailed structural description of each narrative unit of the narrative rendering. It does not reproduce the structural description of these narrative units though, but is rather focused on the supra-segmental connections of several narrative units that express larger phases of biographical process structures. These supra-segmental connections expressing phases of biographical process structures can be identified in terms of beginning and end by textual markers: Such markers indicate that something new is coming up right now in the course of narrative rendering and, later on, that the present context of narrative rendering is now getting closed.—The straightforward autobiographical narrative rendering of the Don Decker autobiographical document expresses a complex sequence of (actually eleven) phases of biographical process structures. The analytical reconstruction of them will be focused on Don Denny's / Decker's process of a conversion type of change of cultural and biographical identity that ends up in a two-fold severe biographical trajectory process (Riemann and Schütze 1991, Schütze

1992). The later phases of Don Decker's biography—the dynamics and phases of a double trajectory and the working through of the trajectory dynamics and the biographical action scheme of becoming a culturally bi-valent (Klowskowska 1996/2001: chapter 6) and bi-competent teacher of American Indian adolescents—will be shortly mentioned.

4.1 Adolescent Meditation how to Search for Metamorphosis Potentials of Biographical Development

When Don Denny was thirteen years old he started to reflect on his future while he used to sit at the railway tracks crossing the territory of the San Carlos Apache Reservation. By turning to this imaginative symbol he always felt invited to embark on a mental movement into unknown territories of future personal possibilities. He reflected on the values that his grandparents stood for: the well being of the whole family group and the welfare of the local community of native Indians. He realized that in the foreseeable future the local community of San Carlos would not experience a notable collective improvement and, therefore, wouldn't foster his own personal biographical unfolding—especially if it should be something really new and creative (p. 73, par. 5, to 77, par. 3).

The adolescent Don Denny also reflected on the cleavage between the religious beliefs and attitudes of Protestant revivalism with its stress on personal atonement, on the one hand, and native Indian religion with its emphasis on the well-being of family and local community, on the other. The first seemed to be represented by his grandmother, the second by his grandfather Johnson Irving and especially by his uncle Abraham Logan. He started to understand that the Pentecostal Christian ideas of sin and atonement were closely connected with a critical assessment of friends and neighbours as "sinners" and that he himself would surely be seen in the same way: His family and neighbourhood would not assume that he had a real chance of a new, creative biographical development (p. 73, par. 6—p. 75, par. 1). Therefore he concluded (still quite vaguely) that he had to get some personal distance from Protestant revivalism and to seek the community of traditional Apache religious men when they were singing their holy songs (p. 75, par.2).

In addition, adolescent Don Denny started to dream about occupational and educational career possibilities: he was diffusely, but strongly attracted by all vocations on the base of higher academic education. He did not like to become an artisan or a farmhand (p. 75f). He also discovered the importance of a stable income in order to manage a circumspect budgeting—something which was not possible for his grandparents who depended on welfare payments (p. 76f).—Generally speaking: Starting to imagine and reflect on one's personal future and its various occupational options and changing one's perspective on surrounding social and cultural collectivities and, by implication, quarrelling with their obligatory expectations regarding one's biographical identification with them are basic activities of biographical work—including collective identity work. Those mental activities can also be signs of pursuing dimly seen paths of a beginning biographical metamorphosis process.

During the long summer vacation of that year Don Denny had individualized biographical experiences (in a strenuous summer work camp for cutting wood in the Point of Pines area, a mountain region of eastern Arizona with ruins of ancient native cultures, roughly 100 km east of San Carlos. These experiences were pivotal for his biographical development because of the following reasons: He learned about hard manual work and the basic division of labour. In addition, he was trained how to do social movement in terms of collectively protesting against rigid powerful organizations and their representatives (here: the camp organizer who used to order too cheap and monotonous meals). In the surrounding area of the work camp he observed the archaeological excavations by scholars and university students from the University of Arizona in Tucson and the amenities of students' life. He turned against atrocities by his native Indian peers towards animals, and later on in his life this turned out to be Don Denny's / Decker's stable spiritual attitude towards all living nature. And, most important: He experienced and realized to be somebody special while being personally selected by a land surveyor (a man whom he admired) to help the latter in the geodetic marking of certain areas for planting new trees.

All of these experiences were fostering conditions for the crystallization of the potential for a biographical metamorphosis process with all its features of creativity: Don Denny got acquainted with "strange" social milieus and social worlds (the social milieu of university students and the social worlds of the social sciences of ethnology / anthropology and archaeology) that aroused his interest. He learned important parts of collective identity work, i.e. to fight against non-legitimized ordering devices of authoritarian organizations and to help to establish the social arrangement of social movements. And he learned the reflective use of elementary social categorization (manual work versus academic work) as orientation devices for the ordering of everyday life and biographical work.

But it was most important for the crystallisation of his potential for a powerful biographical metamorphosis process, that, when he was 14 years old and in the 8th grade, Don Denny got a first biographical quasi-mentor, the surveyor Orion Dillon mentioned above, who as an Apache intellectual functioned for Don Denny as coach and counsellor, although he possibly did not know that he would play this important biographical role for his young co-worker. Don Denny already knew him as coach and teacher from his training and counselling activities in a 4-H club that Don Denny had attended two years ago, and from those first encounters on Don Denny admired him as an intellectual role model (p. 47, par. 4; p. 76, par 2; p. 80). ("4-H clubs" are local branches of a large federal-government assisted American youth organization with voluntary coaches, counsellors and teachers who foster experiential learning and adolescent biographical development; "4-H" means: "head, heart, hands, and health" that should be used and personally developed by the adolescents.) Now, in Point of Pines, the surveyor even more so became a role model and counsellor for Don Denny—a role model and counsellor for his everyday work attitude, his personal presentation of self and his early steps of reflective biographical work. Don Denny got "mirrored" by his quasi-mentor (in the sense of George Herbert Mead's "me" pictures of significant interaction partners about oneself—Mead 1934: part III), and so he could see himself as a developing being of personal uniqueness and social worth. Generally speaking, this is the most basic learning step of biographical work (Schütze 2008: 66–71) (pp. 57–61).

4.2 Don Denny's First Clumsy Steps of Searching for his Metamorphosis Potential and, Therefore, Acquiring the Urban Anglo Life Style

In the summer vacation of 1959, when he was 15 years old, Don Denny spent time with his still quite young mother and his "stepfather" whom his mother referred to as his biological father, but the autobiographer still was not sure about the truth of her statement when writing down his autobiography almost forty years later (in 1997). Don Denny questioned his biological origin—perhaps this even strengthened his wish to enter the Anglo world and his search for biographical identity "out there". Don Denny' mother was living in Prescott, a colourful town of 34000 inhabitants with many "Wild West" buildings in the mountains 190 km north of Phoenix and the centre of the third largest metropolitan area of Arizona. Prescott was, and still is, a white town with 93% white inhabitants, 1.27 % Native Americans and 8.17 % Latinos of all races (data of 2010). This medium-sized town with country-style tourism was very fitting for the rural Apache Indian to enter the Anglo world. Don Denny learned from his very sophisticated quasi-cousin "Sugar Price" the combined role-set of the Anglo-urban personage types of bon vivant, pool gambler and musician (especially playing the guitar). His personal combination of all three of these personage types crystallized into entrance ticket of becoming "streetwise" in the urban Anglo world of amusement and entertainment (pp. 81, par. 2). Later on this attitude of presenting oneself as streetwise and making an easy-going impressive impact on one's social environment in the Anglo world became a trap for Don Denny's personal development.—We don't learn anything about a deepened relationship between his mother and him; one does not find any references in the text that his mother became a significant other and biographical counsellor to Don Denny.

After returning to San Carlos in fall of 1959 Don Denny had to enter high school in Globe. (Before that year he had attended junior high school in Globe for two years.) There are three reasons why his enrolment in Globe High School turned out to be quite difficult for him: First, as offspring of a non-educated family, he did not know about the functioning of the complex high school organization with his university-type of expectations regarding the self-organization of students. Second, coming from an utterly rural everyday life world (Schütz 1962) he still had to learn the everyday life organization of an urban environment that was epitomized by Globe High School, its teachers and most of its students. Third, as an adolescent coming from an American Indian culture and community, he had to get acquainted with the much more powerful Anglo culture and to win respect within the social networks of the Anglo population. Don Denny had many difficulties with this new situation, he often felt strained and was irritable. Here are some features of this strain: He did not know how to choose between different eligible courses offered by

Globe High School in advance. Since he came late, he was not able to enter some of those eligible courses which he liked most. In addition, it was quite difficult for him to do elementary social categorizing of the organization and the social world (Strauss 1993: chapters 9 and 10) of his high school and of his own personal abilities. In spite of his admiration of the world of knowledge and culture (as we could see in his cooperation with the surveyor Orion Dillon as his biographical quasi-mentor), he still kept his rural system of social categorization as his self-insuring elementary stock of knowledge (Schütz 1962) in which learning skills of manual work was much more fitting for him as a rural man than the acquisition of high-culture activities, which for him, in addition, seemed to be effeminate. This attitude of conventional social categorizing hindered him to embark on reflective circumspection regarding his own capabilities for biographical development: In the beginning of his high school days this fading out of awareness (Schütze 1989) worked especially against the self-realization of his obvious talent for, and interest in, music: He had already learned to play the harmonica and even more the guitar, and he had started to practice rock-n-roll and country music (p. 39, par. 2; 64f; 81, par. 2). Instead of picking an eligible music class he originally had chosen a craft shop class, which he fortunately could not enter, since it was too full. Therefore Don Denny had to sign up for the chorus class which he did not like at all in the beginning (p. 81, par. 4).

Concomitantly, the social relationship to his young chorus teacher, who was new at Globe High School turned out to be strained for quite a while. Don Denny used to be angry and disruptive in getting taught within the Chorus class and in practising chorus, which requires special attentiveness and harmony of emotional movements and activities. The chorus teacher, who later became the adoptive father of Don Denny, reacted with anger and organizational disciplinary steps to the frequent disruptions: He used to send Don Denny to the school board, where he was severely reprimanded and sent back into the class; by then, after coming back, both conflict partners had usually calmed down again (p. 81, par. 4).—Just to mention in passing: In the future, Don Denny's later adoptive father would systematically resort to this method of reprimanding; he always let the adolescent Don be disciplined by "organizational referral", whenever he would observe a systematic misbehaviour of his adoptive son. The autobiographer's narrative presentation does not convey the chorus teacher's attempt and self-perception, that he tried hard to talk and argue with his adoptive son and that he spent all the emotional energy that is necessary to cope with such a bitter and, at the same time, essentially pedagogical verbal exchange, as well as that he really tried to keep his composure (see, e.g., p. 88, par. 2).

Nevertheless, the chorus teacher found his way to the heart of Don Denny, although the autobiographer doesn't tell, how he accomplished this. (Looking at the autobiography's overall way of dealing with the relationship between Don Denny and his later adoptive father, one has to state that there is no serious attempt to make this important social relationship transparent: how it began, grew and probably deteriorated later on.) Anyway, Don Denny started to enjoy chorus; in addition, he started to stay in the house of the chorus teacher during the weekends. On the base of partially living in the family of his chorus teacher and of living under the condition that the chorus teacher would be publicly seen as his caretaker and as his guarantor of ethno-cultural acceptance, Don Denny got more and more accepted within the Anglo world. He experienced this change of his personal life situation as a total and categorical transformation of social environment. He started to successfully date Anglo girls.

Here again it is remarkable what the autobiographer does not mention: he does not dwell on Don Denny's friendships with new *male* Anglo friends (although he vaguely mentions one such friendship—p. 83, par. 2). Of course, in his full adolescence, in the age between 15 and 18 years, Don Denny was mainly interested in relationships to girls—as most male adolescents would be. But there might be one additional reason for focussing on relationships with girls, and especially with *white* girls. The proof of being accepted within and by the Anglo world was much stronger in having white girl friends than having white male friends, since parents tend to control the social relationships and the social space of their daughters more than those of their sons. Even more than 35 years later the autobiographer again and again dwells on the fact that he dated numerous Anglo girls (he had "*many sincere relationships*", but "*sex was still such a tabu*" for him): the daughter of a physician, Patty, other Anglo girls, June, Kathrin (p. 82, par.2–83, par. 3).—At least in his retrospective reconstruction—but it can be assumed that the following attitude also was *actually* dominant in Don Denny's adolescent life in Globe -, one of the main biographical concerns of Don Denny in the age between 15 and 18 was to get social and inter-ethnic acceptance within the circle of Anglo middle class families of Globe (p. 82f). During these three years one cannot witness any really deep and longer lasting friendship of Don Denny with a white girl to the extent that this girl would become a significant other to him. Instead, all these girl friends help him to become a member of the Anglo white middle-class community of Globe. And the chorus teacher and his wife assisted in it, too.

But in-between this finally very successful process to win acceptance across ethno-cultural borders within the bourgeois Anglo world of the town of Globe Don Denny had to experience an outside attempt to be excluded from the dating network of the middle-class Anglo community of Globe. The stepmother of Patty, one of the girls whom he dated, got in contact with the chorus teacher as the obvious care taker of Don Denny and requested that he should make sure that Don wouldn't date her stepdaughter Patty any more. The reason was: "*Patty's real mother had been killed within a head-on collision by a car load of drunk Apaches a few years prior my arrival in Globe.*" (p. 82, par. 3) At first glance the attempt to exclude Don Denny from the social space of her daughter might be an emotionally understandable turn of Patty's stepmother; at second glance one wonders, why Patty herself did not find it difficult to date a young Apache man. Does the stepmother attempt to find a good legitimizing formula for her prejudiced attitude towards Native Americans? Would she like to use the only really forceful argument to hinder her stepdaughter to stay in a relationship with the detested young Apache man? Would she attempt to win the symbolic position of Patty's "real" mother in order to get closer to her stepdaughter? We don't know for sure, but the very fact that later on Patty's stepmother "gradually accepted" Don Denny might be a hint, albeit a weak one, that she really was emotionally moved by the tragic traffic accident caused by the alleged problem of collective alcoholism of some native American communities.—Whatever the reasons for the intervention of Patty's stepmother, in his commentary the autobiographer uses i the higher predicate "overt expression of racism" in an ambivalent way:

This was an overt expression of racism that made me feel bad and sorrow for Patty. This was the time when I began to question my own feelings toward white people in the town of Globe. I thought that all of us Indians weren't alike though. My world began to crush down upon me for the reasons that I couldn't understand. (p. 82, par 3)

In the beginning of text passage just quoted it is not totally clear, who is the perpetrator and who is the victim of racism and exactly why Don Denny feels bad and sorrow for Patty. Of course, at first glance the subject of acting as a racist is Patty's stepmother and the object, the victim, is Don Denny since Patty's stepmother obviously extended her understandable bad feelings for the drunken group of Apaches who had killed Patty's mother, to the non-guilty Don Denny, just because he was an Apache: The mechanism of over-generalizing negative social categorization and the transfer of generalized hate connected with it is a typical feature of racial prejudice. But why, then, should Don Denny feel bad for Patty and not for himself? The reason of Don Denny's feeling bad for Patty could also be that he just had learned about the tragic lethal accident of Patty's mother. But then, if this compassion is the case for the mature autobiographer and even for the adolescent Don Denny—by the way: in the present text segment of the autobiography no textual hint for a discrepancy of perspective exists between the two—it would not be so easy to qualify the intervention of Patty's stepmother and her explanation for it as "overt expression of racism". Such a qualification would turn out to be especially difficult when taking into account that throughout his writing the autobiographer is normally very circumspect and fair in his assessments of other people. Again, still another question comes up: Could it be to the contrary, that Don Denny would see *Patty's mother and herself* as the victim of collective Apache racism exerted by the car load of drunken Apache men not being careful enough or even reacting aggressively, when somebody from another race is an obstacle on the road? This probably isn't the case either—especially if the autobiographer tells in his next sentence that immediately after the intervention of Patty's stepmother he started to question his feeling about the white people in Globe. (Of course here the assumption is: his feelings about white people in Globe had been positive before, and now, after the intervention of Patty's stepmother, his attitude towards the white people of Globe got more negative.) Therefore he must have had a misbehaviour of white people in mind and not of Native Americans.—To sum up: The reader has to realize that it remains open what is really meant and ascribed by the quoted passage. But exactly such an irritating textual ambiguity expresses the turmoil in the head of adolescent Don Denny taking his first clumsy steps on his way from the Apache we-group and Apache culture to the Anglo we-group and Anglo culture.

Such a turmoil of social categorization and feelings is typical of situations of an attempt to cross[10] the demarcation line between collective we-groups; it is typical for life situations of betwixt and between (Turner 1964) that require hybrid cultural orientations and life styles. This holds especially true for life situations situated between we-groups whose relationships are poisoned by prejudice or even racism practised and imposed by the more powerful group (in this case: the Anglo we-group). It is almost an of course, that Don Denny not only started to question his own feelings towards the excluding group of white people in Globe, but also began to distance himself from those parts of his own Apache in-group whose public behaviour and loss of control would help to legitimize prejudices of white people against "us". Social research (Miller and Park 1921/1969; Waniek 2006) has shown again and again that many immigrants tend to distance themselves from the "Caffone"[11] social type of their own immigrant group: those persons who appear to be unable to adapt to the culture of the receiving society; who seem to just concentrate on earning money and to avoid any type of high-cultured interests that require time and/or cost money, or who even misbehave in public (e.g., by heavy drinking), since they are socially and culturally dislocated or even demoralized (Shibu-

---

10 The crossing or transgression of the demarcation line between collective we-groups with their different cultures and the involved change of biographical identity can be almost identical with passing over from one ethnic or "racial" we-community to another or from one elementary social category to another as it has been intensively studied with regard to passing over the colour or "racial" line in the U.S. (Myrdal 1944) or from a male identity to a female identity (see the case of "Agnes" in Garfinkel 1967) or from one religious group to another (e.g., from being Jewish to being Christian in Nazi times in order to escape from the Holocaust—cf. Andrzej Szczypiorski's novel "Poczatek" (1986) which was published under the title "Die schöne Frau Seidenman" in Germany (1988)). But crossing such a line is clandestine by definition: The person must hide her or his former identity, which might be quite difficult in the beginning, since she or he must tacitly learn the ways, habits, styles and rules of the newly assumed collective identity and its culture while accomplishing the crossing or transgression and entrance into the new we-community. But cross-cultural transgression as it is accomplished by Don Denny—generally speaking—is not clandestine.—However, in the first time after his move from Globe to Charleston, Illinois, it is clandestine. Then Don Decker, the adopted Don Denny, with his changed social identity presents himself as a someone who was born as Anglo American; i.e., then his cross-cultural transgression partially implies features of (clandestine) passing-over.—It should only be mentioned in passing, that passing-over not always implies, although it quite often does, the intention to change the "real", inner, personal identity or the intention to acquire an "outer" social ascription of one's really felt "inner" identity (as in the case of sex, when the person assumes to have been sexually different and having belonged to the opposite sex category from the beginning of her or his life). In the case of not intending to change one's inner identity, the person passing over would hide her or his real identity some bit similar to an impostor, whereas cross-cultural transgression always implies the biographical intention to undergo at least a partial change of inner identity.

11 The Italian word "cafone" or "caffone" originally meant: poor peasant. However, in Italian it evolved to mean an uncouth, boorish, ill-mannered person. This type of immigrant—amongst others like the "colonist" and the "political idealist"—is addressed in Miller's and Park's study of European immigration into the US in the first decades of the 20th century. (The report was mainly written by William I. Thomas).

tani 2000: chapters X and XI) through harsh types of stigmatization exerted by the dominant cultural groups of the receiving society. Don Denny, a Native American and not an immigrant, was on his way into the Anglo-white society of the U.S., and therefore he would like to distance himself from utterly "misbehaving" or especially detested parts of his own native Indian we-group that are especially known and stigmatized for drunken behaviour. (The autobiographer mentioned the drinking behaviour of the San Carlos community several times, and he even referred to his beloved grandparents in this context.) But this emotional move created severe difficulties for him—because of the turmoil and discrepancies of (what could be called) the "collective-culture and collective-belonging layer" of his own biographical identity. Concomitantly, it let his imagined social and moral world break down, and this resulted in his severe personal disorientation for a certain period of time.

The respective last sentence of the above quote *("My world began to crush down upon me for the reasons that I couldn't understand.")* is a typical and unequivocal supra-segmental marker of a specific biographical trajectory of cross-cultural transgressing[12] borders between national or ethnic we-communities and the suffering connected with such a move between their collective identities. The disorientation of collective and individual identity and "identity suffering" are almost always the by-product of such a move from one collective we-group (with its own culture and its powerful inculcation of features of collective identity into the biographical identities of its members) to another collective we-group. The biographical process of transgressing from one collective we-group to another one is basically a mixture of (a) a biographical action scheme, since the process is at least partially intended by the person crossing ethno-cultural or national borders, and (b) a biographical metamorphosis process. The transgressing is at least partially connected with an essentially creative change of biographical identity of the person moving beyond such demarcation lines since the added, lost and changed layers of collective identity and its obligatory expectation patterns of culture are an important part of her or his individual biographical identity. But this mixture of bio-

---

12 The term "transgressing" is utilized here in its abstract and general understanding: "to pass beyond or go over (a limit or boundary)" and not in the special sense of violation (although the latter might sometimes be implied, too).—See Merriam Webster' Collegiate Dictionary, Tenth Edition. Other terms as "crossing", "stepping over", "going across", "going over", "moving", "travelling over", "traversing", "migrating", "immigrating", "assimilating" "converting", "passing", etc. are either too concrete, too special or too mundane or routine in their meaning,

graphical action scheme and biographical metamorphosis typical for crossing ethnic or national demarcation lines is almost always connected with a sometimes dominant and sometimes sub-dominant biographical trajectory process of suffering and losing control, since the transgression necessarily implies the loss of one's known and habitual everyday world and its expectation patterns (Schütz 1964 a). Hence, the inter-ethnic or cross-national transgression of borders builds up the potential of becoming dislocated, (Shibutani 2000: chapter XI) of becoming uprooted, of losing a transcendental world of sense-making (i.e. the higher-symbolic "finite provinces of meaning" that are connected with one's membership in an ethno-cultural or national we-community—Schütz 1962). It also implies the danger of losing one's sense for the structure and continuity of one's own personal identity. As mentioned above, the biographical trajectory of cross-cultural transgression is not always dominant in the specific, normally quite extracted, "immigration" phase of the specific life history, but it always implies the potential of becoming destructive in terms of losing one's sense for collective and biographical identity. This happens especially in times of difficulties in—and disappointments about—social relationships, which is always connected with sudden breaches of expectations regarding the behaviour of interaction partners.

4.3 First Success of Adaptation Within the Anglo World as Result of the Ethno-Cultural Transgression Process and Finding the Personal Metamorphosis Topic of Becoming Excellent in the Social World of Popular Music

The chorus teacher and his wife became involved as liaison workers for helping Don Denny to get accepted in the bourgeois Anglo world of his peers. They negotiated with Patty's stepmother to accept Don Denny as dating partner of Patty and as visitor in her house. By introducing him into their Anglo church community, letting him get acquainted with other important members of that church community or even letting him make friends with some of them, they could help him even more to get accepted in the Anglo middle class of Globe. Against this background, because of his own openness toward the Anglo world and his remarkable capacity to create networks with his peers, especially with girls of his age, and because of his attractiveness as music performer, Don Denny was able to overcome the barriers of ethnic (or racial) exclusion. Looking back, the autobiographer proudly assumes that his activities were part of the change of the negative attitude of the Globe middle class white community towards a better image of the Apache community and its culture (p. 82, par. 3). It later turned out in the life history of Don Denny / Don Decker that his work of inter-cultural mediation as it had started with first successful steps in his adolescence became an important part of his biographical agenda. At the same time it was an important condition for his own creative change of identity features, i.e. for his biographical metamorphosis process.

Don Denny became more and more involved in the Anglo family of his chorus teacher. In 1960 he got his own room in the back of his house, and at the first time of his life he had his own personal possibility of shaping his immediate environment and a territory of personal retreat. (The hut of his grandparents in San Carlos was a one-room shack.) In his biographical body work connected with this first forming of a private refuge he wanted to lose as much of his native Indian appearance as possible. So he brought as much clothes as possible from the hut of his grandparents to the house of the chorus-teacher family in order to let his clothes get rid of the smell of the mesquite wood which his grandparents used for cooking and heating in their little hut (p. 83, par. 2). For Don Denny, the smell of mesquite smoke was the most elementary symbol of being Native American. Getting rid of this smell was the central symbol of presenting himself as Anglo and of transgressing the demarcation line between the collective we-group of the Apache world and the white Anglo world; now he was utterly determined to turn Anglo-cultured. Connected with this bodily self-presentation was learning the chores of a typical middle-class Anglo household: how to clean the house, how to cook and how to prune fruit trees. He learned most of these skills from a business man who was a member of the Anglo church community, which the family of the chorus-teacher attended and which had accepted him as new member. (He spent a few weeks with this business man in his house when his wife visited her family back in the Midwest.) This business man also provided him with his first well-paid high-school job on a lumber yard, and this enticed him to open his own bank account and gain some financial autonomy (p. 83, par. 3).

The autobiographical text describes the multi-layered process of Don Denny's collective cultural identity change. This process took place on different levels: (a) on the level of social relationships and social networks (the relationship with the family of the chorus teacher, with the Anglo church community and their members, with numerous white girls), (b) on the level of body and house-related work, (c) on the level of paid jobs and of having one's own financial budget and (d) on the level of mastering the high school and its educational offers (with topics of musical education turning out to be most important). The four levels of change of collective identity appear in almost each of the pertinent narrative units of the autobiographical documentary in order to express the multi-layered complexity of Don Denny's transgression of the demarcation line between the collective we-group of the Apache world and the white Anglo world.—Anyway, especially by living within the house of his teacher and his wife, Don Denny learns the ways of everyday life, ways of thinking and ways of acting of educated middle-class White Americans.

The other medium that is pivotal for Don Denny's entering the middle class Anglo world was his growing personal engagement within the musical work of the chorus at Globe high school and of the music work of his Anglo church, where his chorus teacher was the director of the choir: First Don Denny was introduced into the cultural areas of classical music, religious music, country music, pop music and light-entertainment stage music (vaudeville music, the music of the Broadway musicals of the Fifties). He got personally enticed by collective music productions. Especially learning from the personalized relationship with his chorus teacher, Don Denny was then trained how to do musical arena productions. A social arena is a central performance place of a social world of special cultural or professional activities. It very often has the social form of a stage that devides the performers from the audience (Strauss 1993: chapter 10; Schütze and Schröder-Wildhagen 2012). The stage form of arena entails a centripetal focussation of the audience and non-performing activists on where the action of the social world of special cultural or professional activities is (Schütze 2002). Don Denny took actively part in re-staging two very widely known Broadway musicals of the late Fifties and early Sixties in Globe High School. One was "Li'l Abner" (Broadway production 1956; film 1959), a story of a simple-minded, but good natured and very handsome young Hillbilly man, who doesn't seem to be interested in young women, but this doesn't discourage young lady Daisy Mae. The other was "Bye Bye Birdie" (Broadway production 1960; film 1963). The story is modelled after Elvis Presley's recruitment into the US Army. Superstar Conrad Birdie will say good-bye to his fans by publicly kissing one of his young female fans. Therefore he visits a little village in the Midwest. Lots of complications follow.

In the first production Don Denny's San Carlos church friend, the son of the missionary, got the leading male singing role, in the second Don Denny himself. In addition he played the guitar (p 84., par. 1). Don Denny was probably very much enticed by performing on stage for a quite large audience. Of course this was an additional symbol of acceptance within the Anglo middle class world. It is quite remarkable (and the autobiographer underlines this) that the chorus teacher was so gifted, circumspect and energetic that he would bring quite recent complex productions of American popular music culture to rural southern Arizona. These productions were not pieces of restrained high-culture or church music, but they introduced Don Denny into the centre of US American refined entertainment music. The chorus teacher thereby opened his native American student a very attractive cultural bridge into the cultural lands of the white Anglo world.

In addition, the chorus teacher and his wife introduced Don Denny to the country music style of the then (and even later) quite famous singer duo Bud (Dashiell) and Travis (Edmonson) that was very much influenced by Northern Mexican Mariachi music. The duo showed a high mastery of the guitar, and they quite often sang in the Spanish language. The autobiographer tells us that Don Denny was very much attracted by this style of music and that it contributed a good deal to his later outlook and style as musical performer. He tells us that 13 years later he personally talked to Travis Edmonson on phone (p. 84, par. 1). Even though the autobiographer does not mention it, Travis Edmonson might also have been a role model for Don Denny in *other* areas of his creative work, since Edmonson had studied anthropology in Tucson, helped to produce a Yaqui-Spanish dictionary and became a honorary member of one of the Yaqui communities. With other words: he was a cultural mediation worker as Don Denny / Don Decker would later aim to become, too.

All of these processes of reflection and learning that had started with Don Denny sitting at the railway tracks of the San Carlos Apache Reservation belong to two different socio-biographical processes, although in Don Denny's life history they were quite often intertwined with each other:

- One is the process of undergoing a biographical metamorphosis. Biographical metamorphosis starts with some irritation that there are new features of one's own identity which are still sensed as something indistinct, but that they seem to creatively lead to something unknown. Don Denny knows that he has creative capacities which he cannot develop on the territory of the San Carlos Apache reservation. He feels that he has to search outside the boundaries of the reservation. But in the beginning he doesn't know what and where to search for. Especially this feature is typical for a process of biographical metamorphosis. Many of these processes involve journeys in unknown cultural territories and carry a host of new and strange experiences with them. The new personal experiences of such cultural journeys can be especially intensive, if and when one transgresses the demarcation line between two collective we-groups and their different cultures.
- This leads to a second socio-biographical process: the transgression of the demarcation line between the former collective we-group which one had lived in up till now and the new collective we-group which one would like to live in in the future. This necessarily involves a lot of dramatic personal experiences of losing the "fit" and security of one's former everyday expectations and of being confronted with totally new phenomena that do not fit one's old everyday expectations which one has brought along into the new life situation (Schütz 1964a). This is what happens with Don Denny, when he gradually leaves the Apache world and its culture. The socio-biographical process of cross-cultural transgression is necessarily connected with the conversion or alternation (Berger and Luckmann 1966: 144–150) of at least part of one's collective identity and the culture of that collective identity. But it doesn't necessarily imply that the alternation or conversion would be a creative metamorphosis process. It could also be just an adaptation, an assimilation, a loss of a former collective identity and its culture and the acquisition of conventional features of the targeted collective identity and its culture. Especially if the "cultural migrant" attempts to hide and subdue her or his former collective identity and tries to be absolutely perfect in the target culture, she or he is at risk of losing the metamorphosis

potential that is mostly conditioned by the steps of crossing the demarcation line between two collective we-groups.

Don Denny's journey into the white Anglo culture was not an act of betraying his indigenous we-community and culture. In order to follow the dimly felt metamorphosis principle in the development of his biographical identity Don Denny had to step over the demarcation line between two collective we-groups. Of course there was always the danger of just passive adaptation to the Anglo world and its culture. But in concentrating on various musical styles, on the arrangements of musical performance and its arena structures and on his own role as a central performer of pieces of popular music he entered the course of a full-blown biographical metamorphosis. Concentrating on various musical styles and on musical staging became an important accelerator of Don Denny's biographical metamorphosis. On the other hand, learning the staging or arena structure of producing popular Anglo music and learning to become a central performer in it also endangered Don Denny's biographical future. Being a central performer could be misunderstood by him to be "in the heart" of the audience and to be even "more than identical" with the Anglo audience by exaggerating his identification with the Anglo audience. The stage and arena structure of Anglo musical production and performance was always on the brink of becoming a personal addiction; it could cause Don Denny to forget everything else, whatever was important in his former and his present life (for example: his indigenous biographical background, his ordinary school work, his work of getting deeply involved in significant social relationships, of doing circumspect biographical work).

4.4 Adoption as Ethno-Cultural Conversion and its Problem for Biographical Work

From fall of 1959 up to spring of 1962 Don Denny's visits to his grandparents (over a travel distance of 35 kilometres one-way) gradually diminished. Of course he had his own room in the house of the chorus teacher since 1960. Therefore he did not return permanently from Globe High School to San Carlos; his home was in Globe now. Sometimes the family of the chorus teacher joined him on his visits to his grandparents. For them it was obvious that their grandson had found a new family context and had turned Anglo cultured.—Somewhere in spring of 1962 Don Denny was suddenly confronted with the plan of his Anglo family to adopt him (p. 84f). Of course, this was a moral problem of familial and cultural conversion (or alternation[13]) for him. It involved the question whether or not this would mean betraying his grandparents, his ethno-cultural community and his own biographical continuity. He talked about the issue mainly with his grandfather (only in the second instance with his grandmother, since she was just his step-grandmother), and his grandfather promised to think about the issue and to respond soon. In the conversation with his grandson, the grandfather Johnson Irving was very fair and circumspect[14]. Don Denny's grandfather scrutinized the pros and cons: He felt that because of their age and bad health (his bad eyesight and a heavy arthritis of his wife) he and his wife were less and less able to take care of Don. Perhaps the grandfather felt some disappointment since he might have expected that their grandson would stay with him and his wife when they were very old and helpless. But he would not allude to it at all (and the autobiographer would not mention this possibility), but—to the contrary—he would explicitly talk about the possibilities of care which he could still offer to his grandson. (And the autobiographer doesn't mention the hidden background issue of a possible reversal of the obligation for care.) It is for sure that Don Denny's grandfather saw the dramatic life-historical chance for his grandson to get academically educated, to enter into a professional occupation and to be better off. On the other hand, this would mean leaving the we-community and the culture of his indigenous ancestors behind. What would this mean for the spiritual welfare of his grandson?

---

13 "Alternation" is the general term of Berger and Luckmann for a near-total transformation of identity: "We will concentrate here on the extreme case; in which there is a near-total transformation; that is, in which the individual 'switches worlds'. ...Alternation requires processes of re-socialization. These processes resemble primary socialization, because they have radically to reassign reality accents and, consequently, must replicate to a considerable degree the strongly affective identification with the socializing personell that was characteristic of childhood." (Berger and Luckmann 1966: 144). Alternations with a strong religious accent are called "religious conversion" by the authors. They are seen by them as the historical prototypes of all other types of alternation (p. 145f).

14 Grandfather Johnson Irving showed a similar circumspect and restrained attitude toward the question of an alienating adoption of his grandson Don Denny, as old Silas Marner in George Eliot's novel "Silas Marner" (Edinburgh and London 1861) did towards the issue of an alienating adoption of his foster daughter Eppie. But Don Denny acted differently as compared with Eppie, who immediately and without any further consideration refused the invitation from her biological father and gentry gentleman Mr. Godfrey Cass to get adopted by him.—On the other hand, one has to admit, that Eppie did not have any social relationship with her biological father at all—to the contrary, he had abandoned Eppie's mother—, whereas the family of the chorus-teacher family had cared for Don Denny for more than two years already.

Don Denny himself felt contradictory impulses: On the hand, he saw the danger to lose his grandparents by being taken away from them, when the chorus-teacher family would move to other parts of the U. S.; on the other hand, the autobiographer writes: "*... I had gotten too accustomed to living with the young couple and their children in Globe. I didn't see any reason in turning back in this time*" (p. 84 par. 2). This quote seems to be a realistic description of Don Denny's inner attitudes: The adoption issue seemed to be emotionally difficult for him, but the quote doesn't reveal a dynamic inner argumentative conversation immediately provoked by the adoption offer and the deliberation of his grandfather. The close analysis of the sections of the autobiographical text commencing with the start of autobiographical narration proper (when Don Denny was sitting at the San Carlos railway tracks and began to reason about his own personal future) has shown that Don Denny had successfully accomplished the crossing over the demarcation line between the two we-communities already, he had turned Anglo-cultured in a biographical conversion or alteration process and he felt that he had to do all of this in order to follow up his inner principle of biographical metamorphosis. Therefore he did not have to think a lot about the issue of a partial loss of his identity when the Anglo family made the offer to adopt him.—It is also clear that neither the chorus teacher and his wife nor Don Denny himself had any sophisticated concept of the creativity of cultural hybridity (in contrast to the author of the autobiography who has such a concept to a certain degree), since at that time the adoption solution as a matter of course was not questioned by both of them. The autobiographer does not tell us about any thoughts of adolescent Don Denny why the chorus teacher and his wife had made their quite generous offer of adoption. The chorus teacher and his wife obviously liked to help Don Denny to pursue and accomplish an academic career, since they had enjoyed his participation in their family life. They might have also taken the following points into account: Since they planned to return to their mid-west home area after a while, it might have been much easier and much more protective for Don Denny / Decker to accompany them as their legal family member. Last but not least, in the future Don Denny / Decker could become a partner in the musical arena work of the chorus teacher. Don Denny was quite attractive as young musician partner in terms of his capacity to perform as a guitar player and singer.—Anyway, for the biographical orientation of Don Denny himself and for that one of his host family the biographical process structure of a successful institutional expectation pattern in the form of an academic educational career and the connected spirit of the "nomos" of an orderly main-stream society with its career institutions were utterly dominant. It helped to fade out of awareness all the deeper problems of parting form significant others and of undergoing changes of identity (Schütze 2008).

But a few days later Don Denny was confronted with the biographically deeply embedded moral problem of not having gotten the final license by his grandfather Johnson Irving to undergo the adoption procedure, since before any final answer to Don Denny's question his grandfather got a stroke and died without getting back the capacity of clear thinking and speaking (p. 84f). Don Denny would have liked his grandfather to understand and accept the momentum of his inner biographical metamorphosis process that simply required the transgression of the demarcation line between the two we-communities. According to Don Denny he, the grandfather, should have understood that his grandson had undergone an irreversible change of biographical identity already and that the adoption just technically helped his grandson to follow up his academic and / or musical career. Now, the grandfather could not give his blessing any more. He could not concede any more, that the adoption did not signify Don Denny's distancing from his grandparents. Don Denny was now confronted with the general ethical problem of marginal or hybrid personalities to be forced to part from old significant others and to appear disloyal to old biographical caretakers and to social networks of old we-communities.

After the burial of his grandfather Don Denny became officially adopted and became Don Decker. The adoptive father was not so much older (perhaps sixteen years[15]) than his adoptive son. The autobiographer doesn't call the

---

15 The autobiographer mentions that his chorus teacher Donald Decker in 1959, when Don Denny himself was 15 years old, was 21 years old (p. 81, par. 4). On the next page the author mentions that his "young wife ... was no more than 27 years old" (p. 82, par. 1). In 1959 their two children—it is said—had been 1 and 3 years old (p. 86, par. 2). This would have meant that the chorus teacher got his first child in the adolescent age of 18 years. Taking into account that he had undergone a university education, the autobiographer's age ascription to Donald Decker doesn't seem to be plausible—especially if one takes into account that he stresses the young age of Donald Decker's wife Barbara, who, hence—according to the age ascription of the autobiographer—, would actually have been six years older than her husband. This would surely have been a remarkable deviation from the standard expectation towards the age difference of couples in Western societies, and, therefore, the autobiographer would probably have commented on this.—In sum: it seems to be more probable that here is a mistake in the autobiographical manuscript; perhaps the chorus teacher was 31 years old and not 21, when he met the 15 year old Don Denny the first time. The social relationship between the chorus teacher and his adoptive son is not free from tensions. Therefore a correct assessment of the age difference between "father and son" seems to be important.

adoption *"his decision"*; instead, he is formulating it as a passive undergoing (p. 86, par. 2). Later on he gives the commentary: *"I accepted the adoption without question"*—even conveying the possibility that his adoption was provided by god). Such formulations are empirical evidence that adolescent Don Denny / Decker did not do a lot of biographical work in order to take over the responsibility for personally accepting the offer of adoption. Don Decker's writing up of his autobiography with all its various and complex perspectives, that takes place 35 years after the depicted events connected to his adoption in 1962, is one of his first powerful means for retrospectively making himself accountable for his long-standing biographical attempt, forced by the metamorphosis dynamics of his life history, to cross the ethno-cultural demarcation line that— more or less naturally, although luckily– ended up in his adoption by the Decker family. Even after the legal adoption process, Don Decker had to permanently cope with guilt feelings of not having gotten the license from his late grandfather to undergo the adoption process (p. 85, lines 9 and 10 from above).

In later phases of his biography, the guilt feeling of not having gotten the license for adoption of his grandfather became a driving force for Don Decker to return to the cultures and social networks of indigenous we-communities of south-eastern Arizona. E.g., in the "here and now" of his autobiographical writing he identifies himself with his grandfather's baldness that is regarded as rare in indigenous men, and he mentions with satisfaction the growing similarity of his bodily appearance with that one of his grandfather (p. 85, 3 last lines). The autobiographer envisions his return to south-eastern Arizona as academic Indian counsellor for the Eastern Arizona Junior College in Thatcher, Arizona, as "full circle" (p. 101).—Of course, on the level of suprasegmental markers of autobiographical rendering the autobiographer uses the language of conversion in order to biographically categorize his adoption: *"After my grandfather's death, my life went into a drastic transition stage from my reservation days to an odyssey that was to lead me beyond the railroad tracks of Southern Pacific … to the new horizons of a life away from the reservation"* (p. 86, par. 1). At the same time the conversion language of "drastic transition" is a language of biographical metamorphosis, especially with formulations as: "beyond the railroad tracks" and "new horizons".

4.5 Playing the Role of the Covert Convert and Perfectly Encultured Stranger

In spring or summer of 1962 Don Decker's adoptive parents Donald and Barbara Decker decided to return to their home town Charleston, Illinois. Three years before, they had moved to Arizona in order to fight the asthma of their two little children. They had probably for quite some time taken care to prepare their adoptive son Don for this move, since they had visited together with him their old home area of central-eastern rural Illinois for the Christmas holidays before, had introduced him to their family and relatives and had eventually talked with him about their move to Illinois in the summer of 1962. Barbara Decker even provided her adoptive son with a biographical interpretation formula for his part in the move to rural Illinois. "*She actually said that this move would give me a clean slate to start with after living in Globe and in San Carlos for the first part of my life*" (p. 86, par. 3). "Clean slate" means a totally new beginning with an empty record. But Don Decker could have understood this utterance as an announcement that now his former biographical experiences would be radically eradicated. Probably for Don Decker the formulation "clean slate" self-theoretically implied "the assumption that now his former biographical experiences would become more and more irrelevant. Such an self-attitude of enforced biographical fading-out" (Schütze 1989, 1992) would denigrate the imprint of the first 18 years of Don Denny's / Decker's life history and would declare as irrelevant how his biographical identity was shaped during this time. The assumption and attitude of biographical fading out entails the risk of future biographical difficulties, since nobody can get rid of the "shaping force and heritage" of her or his biographical processes and the implied unfolding of biographical identity. (Exactly if one likes to defocus biographical processes they become powerful in the back of one's self-awareness.)

Don Decker was very sad of leaving his friends in Globe High School and the San Carlos Reservation behind, especially his very ill grandmother, since she had been a central religious significant other for him for many years of childhood. He departed with his adoptive family to the small town of Charleston, Illinois, the home town of his adoptive parents (66f). Charleston is a rural town of about 22000 inhabitants in East-Central Illinois. Main employer is the Eastern Illinois University with roughly 12000 students. (Very soon Don Denny got familiar with his new extended rural family network of local farmers, which at first glance reminded him a bit of the extended rural family network at his former home in San Carlos. Don Decker very easily learned to speak Illinois "Farmanese" (p. 89, par. 2), and he practised the same type of free-time entertainment with his new cousins and friends (many of them had a farming background), as he had done in Southern Arizona (e.g., playing pool—p. 89, par. 2). He was similarly at ease in doing successful networking with his new peers in the local high school, especially in order to have dates with girls. Therefore he very soon felt totally integrated within the local youth culture. Don Decker was able to dwell on personal experiences of, and capacities for, social relating and networking that he had already learned in Southern Arizona.

But by concentrating on the activities of networking as super-perfect cross-cultural "immigrant", Don Decker faded out of his awareness how he culturally and personally differed from members of the Illinois farmer culture and the local youth culture. He also underestimated the otherness of his own *biographical* development, which was very much shaped within an poor indigenous family and we-community, as compared with the typical well-to-do rural and small town Illinois biographical developments of his new peers. Don Decker tended to fade out of his awareness his former biography and cultural experiences and to denigrate cultural and biographical differences between him and his new peers in order to be "at home" in his new social environment. As a culturally hybrid person he narrowly focused on his new social relationships and on attempts to "be like them". Generally speaking, this super-focussing on social relationships is a dangerous cultural and biographical tendency of being in the existential situation of a marginal or hybrid personality. Having entered the path of successful or even perfect transgression of ethno-cultural borders, one feels the necessity to undergo an identity conversion and to accomplish a seemingly total adaptation to the target we-community and its culture. Instead, the sense for finding one's own biographical way can be severely diminished or even lost, since such a super-perfect transgressor of ethno-cultural borders would like to become even more "like them" than her or his new role models and targets of emulation would like to be and could be. And the super-perfect transgressor would tend to neglect her or his own biographical resources, which can be found in her or his life history before the conversion.

Don Decker again participated in the Li'l Abner musical production of Charleston High School, conducted by his adoptive father (p. 88, par. 2, middle of p.). This event probably contributed to his becoming well known (in the whole school community) as a gifted guitar player. He also recommenced to play pop music with his new peers in school. Last but not least he got in contact with the folk music scene of the local university. His mastery of the guitar was appreciated by the semi-professional university students (p. 88, par. 2; 90–92). In Charleston Don Decker could therefore continue his biographical development as a creative musician; this can be categorized as a full-blown extension of the metamorphosis process as a creative musician that he had embarked on in Southern Arizona. But at the same time he also risked to be too narrowly focused on his social encounters. Some of them might have been even some bit "premature": for example his relationships with the folk music students of the local university (p. 88f). Of course Don Decker could make use of these contacts and musical co-operations in order to demonstrate that he was ahead of most of his school mates in some areas of personal development and cultural education. On the other hand, it implied the risk that the critical sense for the timely unfolding of his biographical identity and timely development of his creative capacities would get lost.

The autobiographer underlines that Don Decker *"truly had a clean slate to start with, and no one knew about my past"* (p. 88, par. 2). The autobiographer explains this assessment with Don Decker's experience that he was not confronted with any type of racial prejudice, since nobody—as the autobiographer stresses—had been informed about his indigenous American background or recognised it by his outer appearance. (And in their overwhelming majority the people in central Illinois including the students of Eastern Illinois University, who were at home in the immediate geographical surrounding[16], probably did not know how a real American Indian man would look like, since the last Indians had been expelled from Illinois in the 1830ties.) The autobiographer states: *"I had been accepted by everyone in the community"* (p. 88, par. 2). But, of course, living under the condition of such a clandestine passing the border line between the two cultures, Don Decker had

---

16 Eastern Illinois University is just a "master university" that doesn't run doctoral programmes and as state school offers citizens of the State of Illinois a considerable reduction of fees. In dictionary articles about this university it is said that students would come from the immediate geographical surrounding of Charleston.

to present himself as a covered convert and perfectly encultured stranger, who was forced to culturally and biographically adapt very fast and to defocus and hide the 18 years of his former life. And this could cause remarkable difficulties for his future biographical work and self-presentation of his personal identity. (Some years later, when he is in university a second time and also when he performs in folk music contexts, Don Decker actually presents his former collective identity as indigenous American; but first he does this in a very schematic and abstract and therefore non-biographical and unproductive way.—p. 91, line 7f; p. 99, par. 2) Of course, Don Decker's adoptive mother Barbara Decker wanted to help Don with her biographical formula of the "*clean slate*", that would imply the self-presentation strategy of the covert convert. She and probably her husband, too, wanted to protect her adoptive son Don especially against any type of social and racial prejudices. They did not have the biographical experience to see the difficult side effects of this strategy of presenting oneself.

4.6 Start of the Primary Trajectory of the Perfectly Encultured Stranger; Secondary Trajectory of Difficulties of School Career and/or Academic Achievement

Soon after his arrival at Charleston, in his last year at Charleston High School, Don Decker started to have severe difficulties in concentrating and in making the grade—difficulties which had to do with his tendency to spend all his time on establishing and maintaining his social contacts within his general high school peer group as well as within the special pop and folk music scenes. The autobiographer uses a supra-segmental marker of the biographical process structure of trajectory: "*I spent much of my high school days goofing off (meaning: to evade work and responsibility—F.S.). Suddenly, I was having too good of a time.*" (p. 88, middle of par. 2). The biographical process structure of trajectory of suffering and losing control is characterized by a form of relationship to one's life course in which one can only react to powerful outer events and—at least for some areas of life—loses the ability to actively shape one's life course. Even the capacity for managing one's daily life and its responsibilities diminishes. This can also apply to the capacities for fulfilling the duties of an educational career or work career, i.e. to be conform with the institutional expectation patterns of the "regulated life course" (Schütze 2008: 189f).

The autobiographical document mentions, that Don Decker's high school counsellor intervened in the course of the unfolding trajectory of school difficulties and that his dramatic one-shot admonition was strong enough to bring Don Decker successfully back on track to fulfil the school requirements; he accomplished the last year of high school career without any significant new difficulties, and he finally graduated without difficulties in 1963 (p. 88, last 3 lines of par. 2; p. 90, par. 2). But there was still the problem of narrowly focusing on peer networks and on the attractions of pop and country music with its staging and arena structure. Don Decker always attempted to become an excellent musical performer in order to get (even "more than") complete acceptance within the Anglo world. This implied the de-focussing of inner biographical developments and quiet types of school learning. When the autobiographer remembers his high school graduation, he formulates the following introductory supra-segmental marker for an upcoming metamorphosis process: "*After high school graduation in 1963, I had several things waiting for me*" (p. 90, par. 2). But after having inserted this introductory metamorphosis marker he just tells about his getting drafted by the army (into selective service and the Illinois National Guard) and his—finally quite unsuccessful—career in the social worlds of pop and country music. He skips his enrolment in Eastern Illinois University. Of course his university studies, too, were part of his possibly upcoming biographical metamorphosis process with "things waiting for him", even if a career within the social worlds of pop and country music was more attractive for Don Decker by that time; therefore the reader expects that the manuscript would also dwell on his university studies as an important "thing waiting for Don Decker". Instead, the author just mentions that Don Decker *had the plan* to study there; this explains his option for "Selective Service" in the course of the drafting process (p. 90, par. 2).

The autobiographer only mentions later on and in passing (when he tells that Don Decker delivered a brand new Cadillac from Chicago to Tucson for a prominent dentist and appeared with this impressive car in San Carlos) that he had dropped out of Eastern Illinois University (p. 93, par. 1). And he alludes to this event in a very indirect way—some bit similar to a small background construction (Schütze 2008: 42–50) known from oral extempore narration in order to keep the dominant line of narrative presentation trustworthy. Of course, appearing in San Carlos with a car, which he had to deliver to a person in Tucson, was a welcome chance to visit old friends. But the very fact that it was a luxury car that didn't belong to him and that would be presented in poor San Carlos, implied the potential for engaging in illegitimate showing-off or "bullshitting", and actually this happened: "*I told… how I went out to seek my fortunes in the tall buildings of Chicago*" (p. 93, par. 1). In his admirable attitude to reconstruct the truth of his life for the reader and himself—and this is basically to find out about the biographical process structures which he had experienced—the autobiographer felt responsible to be frank and open about this "bullshitting". It was even more outrageous and self-humiliating than a standard showing off with a luxurious car that one doesn't own, since Don Decker had just dropped out of university (and in terms of economic success his career as pop and country musician was a disaster, too). And this implied that Don Decker felt like an impostor pretending to be a successful professional or businessman. In order to make the symbolically quite complex scenery of intended imposture transparent, the autobiographer had to put in a text piece of additional information about his dropping out of his university. This additional information was even more pivotal, since the author wanted to make sure that the reader did not misunderstand Don Decker's "Anglo type" of bullshitting as identical with the artistic conversational play of Apache culture which he had dwelled on in the first part of his autobiographical text.)

Originally the autobiographer did not *like* to insert the additional piece of information about his failure of university studies, since even in the times of writing up of his autobiography 30 years later he feels ashamed and hurt that his first attempt of embarking on an educational career at a university had been unsuccessful. His hesitance to mention his lack of success is beautifully expressed by a first vague or even in-correct formulation and a secondary correction of the former: "*I still hadn't gotten my college degree either. As a matter of fact I just had flunked out of Eastern*" (p. 93, par. 1). On the other hand, he is forced—by the narrative drives to go into details and to close the forms, known from the analysis of oral autobiographical narration (Schütze 2008)—to intersperse the quoted additional information piece as a background construction into the course of narration, since otherwise the dominant line of narrative presentation would not be trustworthy and plausible any more. (Not plausible, too, since the autobiographer has announced that he would also deal with the topic of university studies, but up till now he has never started to tell about it in the course of the narrative supra-segment that is dealing with his announced process of metamorphosis after high school graduation—a supra-segment that actually expresses a full-blown, but faded-out process of a trajectory of suffering and losing control.)

In sum: In the narrative supra-segment starting with Don Decker's difficulties to concentrate on his school work in Charleston High School and ending with Don Decker's "bullshitting" in San Carlos three years later (p. 88, par. 2: *"I spent much of my high school days goofing off."*; p. 93, par. 1: *"It was fun driving that Cadillac across the country and into San Carlos."*), we can witness typical features of the textual expression of the general biographical process structure of trajectory. The trajectory of difficulties of concentration and academic achievement started in the first months of Don Decker's last year of high school in Charleston, Illinois, (i.e., in the fall of 1962), and even in the summer of 1966, when Don Decker visited San Carlos in a luxurious Cadillac, its detrimental dynamics was not controlled. The problem centre of this trajectory was that Don Decker was always distracted by the lure of doing social contacting in peer networks and of entering the arena structure of the social worlds of pop and folk music. He had lots of difficulties to concentrate on the quiet topics of academic learning. His high school counsellor could help him to control the difficulty for a while, but he could not enforce him to eradicate it thoroughly. Without the close control that Don Decker had profited from in high school, the problem grew worse in university life with all its amenities of a liberal life style and incentives for contacting and visiting the arenas of pop and folk music, and for years Don Decker could not control it successfully. For a long time a successful control of the secondary trajectory of difficulties of concentration and academic achievement was not possible, since the primary trajectory was permanently feeding into it: the trajectory of the perfectly encultured stranger, who had allegedly undergone a total ethno-cultural conversion. Don Decker and probably his adoptive family, too, were not aware of its dynamics—at least in the beginning. It was a long way for Don Decker to realize that the concept of a total ethno-cultural conversion would not work. Only after he had understood the illusionary quality of such a project, he could also overcome the secondary trajectories: the difficulties of a lack of academic concentration and achievement. (Nevertheless, the secondary trajectory of study problems had developed its own powerful dynamics and trap mechanisms beyond those ones of the trajectory of the perfectly encultured stranger, and Don Decker had to find specific antidotes against it, too, for example in the form of a detailed and circumspect planning of the logistics of the upcoming studies and in the form of daily work discipline.—p. 98f).

The unfolding of both trajectories had a detrimental impact on the social relationship between Don Decker and his adoptive family. Donald Decker, Don Decker's adoptive father, requested other teachers to reprimand his son. The autobiographer comments: "*Much to my surprise, my Dad was the driving force in having other teachers discipline me*" (p. 88, 2nd last line of par. 2). Donald Decker and his wife Barbara must have felt that they were not able any more to control their adoptive son's drive to do social relating in his peer groups and to engage in the various music scenes, although they knew that he would get lost in those contact activities One reason might have been that Don Decker's adoptive parents were not so much older than their adoptive son himself (probably 16 and 12 years older), and that very fact might have hindered them to take the stance of parental authority. In addition, even in Globe High School (a few years before that time) Donald Decker used the educational strategy to let his student Don (and other disobedient students) to be disciplined by "organizational referral", whenever he had discovered something which he regarded as his misbehaviour. This means, that Donald Decker probably hated a personal authoritarian and disciplinary stance towards his students including his adoptive son. Therefore, it seems plausible that Donald and Barbara Decker had great personal difficulties to stand in the way of Don Decker's exaggerated social contacting and arena behaviour.

But, on the other hand, in their educational interventions Don Decker's adoptive parents did not have a fair chance against the devastating power of the trajectory of the perfectly encultured stranger. First of all, they themselves had provided Don Decker with the basic biographical concept of "clean slate" for a person who wants to transgress ethno-cultural borders in order to bridge the abyss of cultural and personal strangeness and to circumvent the danger of being categorized (or even stigmatized) as an ethnically or culturally detested stranger. But this concept is basically wrong, since it lures the cultural immigrant into the attempt to be the perfect convert, who would be impeccable in her or his cultural competencies of the target culture (and therefore highly appreciated or even loved by his new we-community). Such impeccable competences of the target culture normally are not possible. In addition, the biographical concept of the "clean slate" fades out of one's awareness and even one's recollection the biographical processes and experiences of the first part of one's life history before the transgression of the ethno-cultural border. And these biographical processes brought competences and vulnerability dispositions with them, that are still powerful in the life situation of being a "cultural immigration"—especially in case they are faded out of awareness. Donald and Barbara Decker are not morally responsible for having offered the wrong biographical concept of "clean slate", since they just wanted to help the pleasant Don Denny to escape from the prejudices and utter poverty of life on the San Carlos Apache Reservation, and it seemed to be plausible that he would start "incognito" in Illinois again. In addition, in the Sixties of the 20th century the concepts of "starting anew", of "conversion" and of "cultural assimilation" were dominant in discussions regarding any type of immigration and ethno-cultural crossing of borders in an American society that still believed in the melting pot of cultures. Barbara and Donald Decker did not have personal biographical experiences of immigration, which would put these dominant concepts of the American Dream in question. And even if they would have known about the trajectory dynamics of the perfectly encultured stranger, the question still remains whether or not transgressing ethno-cultural borders would mostly or always entail phases of such a biographical trajectory.

On the other hand, the systematic educational strategy of Donald Decker to let his adoptive son be disciplined by "organizational referral" was a sign of severe communication anomy within the social relationship between Don Decker and his adoptive family.—The organizational referral strategy of education would not entice Donald Decker and his wife Barbara to have personal educational talks with his adoptive son, however difficult and even how hopeless they might be. (Those talks would have been especially bitter, since Donald Decker had introduced his adoptive son into the arena structure of popular music making with its specific lures—especially the expectation to become a famous performer). The growing communication anomy between Don Decker and his adoptive parents is one of the growing signs of estrangement between the two parties. The adoptive family might have felt somewhat abandoned and betrayed by Don Decker's narrow focus on social contacting in the peer group and on his personal engagements within the arena structures of pop and folk music.—It is remarkable, that the autobiographer doesn't talk about his adoptive father and adoptive mother any more after the finishing of the text segment dealing with Don Decker's high school graduation (p. 90, par. 2).—But at the same time Don Decker attempted to keep at least some bit of a good social relationship with the extended Decker family in Charleston and in other nearby places of rural Illinois (pp. 89–90). It was, as if Don Decker wanted to let his adoptive family indirectly know, that his links to them would be still very important for him.

By successfully doing folk and rock music Don Decker kept some aspects of his metamorphosis process within the social worlds of performing music. But this was connected with extensive networking that estranged him from his adoptive family and forced him to neglect his university studies. Perhaps one could speak of a precarious equilibrium between the metamorphosis and the trajectory principle of his biography in high school and the first time after high school graduation, but later the double-faced unfolding principle of his primary and secondary trajectory became dominant (p. 90f). Surely Don Decker was not clear about the direction of his educational career, which could have been a normal type of college education in order to become a professional in the educational field (which he accomplished later on, but the autobiographer doesn't tell about this first attempt lasting three years), on the one hand, or embarking on the course of becoming a professional musician, on the other. Probably Don Decker tried both options at the same time with some dominant focus on a career of a performing rock or folk musician. But this also meant severe orientation diffusion in his biographical outlook and phenomena of neglect of the work to be done. The orientation diffusion was surely connected with lots of self-doubt and lack of confidence and the related suffering—especially if one takes into account the powerful mechanisms of Don Decker's main trajectory of the perfectly encultured stranger that was hidden to himself. Part of the hidden dynamics of the trajectory of the perfectly encultured stranger is to burden the trajectory incumbent with utterly unrealistic expectations of personal perfection and total social acceptance, which he or she can never fulfil.

After some while the secondary trajectory of academic concentration and achievement difficulties became dominant in Don Decker's student life: a) Three years after his enrolment in Eastern Illinois State University he dropped out (p. 93, par. 1; 98, par. 3 bottom). b) He was drunk at a crucial semi-professional performance as folk musician in Chicago during an important festival and made himself an object of joke or even stigmatization in a central arena situation (p. 90f). The autobiographer critically looks back at himself, the young Don Decker, in this scene as irresponsible, non-dependable and non-accountable: His drunken behaviour is envisioned as the situational outcome of some sort of biographical regression resulting from difficulties of crossing the ethno-cultural border. In writing about this biographically pivotal situation, the author probably remembers the scenes of collective intoxication within the San Carlos Reservation (p. 41f, bottom; p. 59, par. 3; p. 63, par. 2; p. 65–69)—especially when one takes into account that for the sake of a most glamorous presentation young Don Decker was mistakenly presented to the audience as Geronimo's, the great Apache war hero's, grand grandson. (c) After years of participating in a quite successful amateur rock-n-roll band Don Decker gave up his position as a guitar player without giving any reasons (p. 92, par. 2). The autobiographer doesn't tell about the event constellation of Don Decker's quitting and he doesn't attempt to give any explanation; in an oral extempore autobiographical rendering the listener would expect a detailed narrative account of quitting such a biographically important function and a reflection about its reason. Giving up his position in the rock band might have had to do with Don Decker's parting from Charleston (although he applied at the art school in Indianapolis only one year later). But it might also have to do with his diffusion of perception and attention as an ethno-cultural immigrant, who was very much affected by the hidden biographical trajectory of the perfectly encultured stranger. And this would mean the burden of narrowly focusing on permanent tasks of social relating to old and new social networks and types of experiences and engagements involved in it (in the sense of Thomas' and Znaniecki's bohemian type of adaptation—Thomas and Znaniecki 1918/1927).

Anyway: The narrator fades out of his awareness and recollection his probably severe sorrow about parting from the band partners as his significant others and his possible moral difficulties with this step. Is this fading-out again the impact of a severe suffering caused by the double biographical trajectory of the perfectly encultured stranger and of the difficulties in academic concentration and achievement—a suffering that might be too painful to remember and not to lose one's composure? Is it again the imprint of communication anomy—this time regarding his social relationships with the rock band and/or with the members in it?—To sum up: The autobiographer would like to present a clear-cut metamorphosis narrative about the gifted ethno-cultural immigrant who has accomplished the transgression of the borders between the two we-communities. Admittedly, it is remarkable what Don Decker did achieve: a high school diploma, his enrolment in university and a creative metamorphosis development within two social worlds of popular music. But it is obvious, that for a long while the two biographical trajectories hindered a real success on two possible career ladders: the occupational ladder of an academic professional and that one of a creative performer of popular music.

The fact that Don Decker was in the trap of this double trajectory is most conspicuous for the reader of the autobiography when he reads about Don Decker's visit to San Carlos in a brand-new Cadillac to be delivered to Tucson from a dentist of Chicago (p. 92f): Here Don Decker acts as an impostor faking a successful university graduate on his way to a promising position in a Chicago company. The scene expresses the further unfolding of the double trajectory in form of a decisive transformation towards personal inauthenticity and immoral showing off by "faked" "bullshitting" his former neighbours and co-members of the Apache we-community. It is faked, because it is not the playful "bullshitting" game of Apache culture, where every interaction partner knows the real life situation of the other "bullshitting" participant. Nobody knows about the factual disastrous life situation of Don Decker just having flunked his university studies.

5   Some Short Remarks on the Further Unfolding of Don Decker's Life History

The impact of the combined biographical trajectories of the perfectly encultured stranger and of difficulties in academic concentration and achievement got stronger and stronger. First Don Decker attempted to stop the dynamics of the secondary trajectory of difficulties in academic concentration and achievement by entering the art school of Indiana University. This did not work, since Don Decker had to earn money during the day, and in the evenings and during the weekends he still performed in the arenas of rock music. Both types of activities absorbed his energy; so he could not concentrate on fine art work and produce a portfolio. As a result he had to quit the art school. Don Decker returned to Illinois in order—as the autobiographer underlines—to be at least *in the near* of his abandoned career as university student; but more important might have been the aspect—however, the autobiographer doesn't talk about it—that Don Decker cut himself from his easygoing relationships to the luring social arrangements of cultural arenas and performance staging in the social worlds of pop and folk music that were provided for and offered by the big city of Indianapolis.

Back in rural Illinois, Don Decker did hard and exhausting house construction work (p. 97f) in order to keep his material level of living. As far as his material and bodily well-being is concerned, this is the lowest point of the unfolding of the two trajectories of having difficulties in academic concentration and achievement and of being alienated from any type of self-realization by following the role model of the perfectly encultured stranger. Then, in the course of his exhausting house construction work Don Decker had a bad accident and severely hurt one of his hands. He had to quit the construction work and finally sold his still partially unpaid car in order to escape from the debts trap (p. 98, par. 2). In addition, with selling the car he got a step further into the direction of retreating from the arena and staging structure of American pop music. Without a car it became difficult for him to do complex networking and contact work in the social worlds of pop music that had always been a dangerous addiction for him. Giving away his car, which had always served as a means to do all sorts of social networking and to engage in various types of music arenas, is one of the essential turning points in Don Decker's life course. It started to arrest at least parts of the energy-absorbing and self-alienating impact of the hidden main trajectory of following the role model of the perfectly encultured stranger.

This partial disconnection from the lures of the social worlds of pop music was the basic condition for Don Decker's resumption or new envisioning of a biographical action scheme of becoming a teacher. The autobiographer doesn't write about this plan of his professionalisation explicitly, although a short time before he has mentioned that Don Decker had started to think about a biographical action scheme of becoming a teacher on the reservation of San Carlos; but this reasoning about his future was argumentatively discouraged by his entourage of colleagues and friends at the work place (p. 97, par. 2). Therefore in the beginning the biographical action scheme of resuming his academic education might have been no more than a biographical action scheme of escaping from a trajectory trap. At least the autobiographer uses a formulation which is a typical verbal marking of an action scheme of escaping a trajectory: "After flunking out two times, I was determined to tough it out" (p. 98, par. 3). Unlike before, Don Decker was now very modest and circumspect in his biographical planning and arranging: He provided for preparatory extra community college education in philosophy and in English in order to raise the necessary grade point average for getting readmitted at Eastern Illinois University (p. 98, par. 3). Finally Don Decker could resume and successfully finish his university education (probably majoring in art history and art—99f).

During the last two years of his studies at Eastern Illinois University Don Decker started to do some biographical work in explaining to himself that, compared to the other graduates of his high school graduation group of 1963, he had needed three years of extra time, a moratorium, in order to be able to personally develop and to reach a social and mental state of being at home in Anglo America (p. 99, par. 1; p. 100, par. 2). Compared to former times, he now, in his two last years of university studies, practised the virtue of personal modesty: Being an older student he could not successfully compare himself with his peers who had graduated with him from Charleston High school and had gotten their university diplomas already (p. 99, 1st lines of par. 2). In addition, in a modest and circumspect way he harnessed his capacity of doing art, but he gave up his intermittent habit of cashing in on his being a Native American, that he had originally invented for his performances of folk music. He got rid of his habit to utilize Indian symbols and topics in his paintings all the time (p. 99, middle of par. 2). In addition, he abandoned his strategy of seeking a mental shelter against the dangers of producing individualized art and its exposition to critique by sneaking under the hiding shield of the abstract collective category of American Indian culture, which mistakenly seems to make unnecessary individualized attempts to one's own creative artistic forming.

Don Decker finally reached the point of biographical maturation, where he accepted to be a really hybrid or marginal personality, who took his way back and forth in transgressing ethno-cultural borders. He became able to be productive in the Anglo-Saxon art culture on its own terms and on his personal terms. He became circumspect enough to fight against the non-authentic abstraction processes (Waniek 2006) of total identification with one's former culture/ethnic group or with one's present one.—In sum: Don Decker realized his biographical action scheme of getting a university degree and becoming a teacher, and, at the same time, he resumed the biographical process of biographical metamorphosis (a) by doing creative art work and by undergoing the process of being critically evaluated by his teachers (p. 99, par. 2) as well as (b) by doing successful liaison work between supporters of the Vietnam war and war protesters at a big protest meeting at his university (the quarrel about the flag on top or at half staff—p.100, par. 2); here he could finally use his double cultural competence as a hybrid personality in a pivotal and even witty personal intervention with lots of situational and scenic understanding and personal courage.

Don Decker got married—probably to an Anglo woman—during his last time in university and still in university he got a son: Finally, even in terms of Indian cultural criteria, he arrived at White America by becoming part of the basic social structure of kinship relationships (p. 100, par. 3; 101). After graduating from university Don Decker embarked on the career line as a high school art teacher in Anglo America (close to San Louis). Three years later he took a position as study counsellor for native students in a junior college at Thatcher, Arizona, in the very near of San Carlos Reservation (p. 100). Taking this position was not just the realization of an biographical action scheme of becoming a professional, but in addition it was a biographical move of harvesting the fruits of a difficult and extremely extended "wild" biographical metamorphosis process (Schütze 1994) the difficulties of which are almost impossible to circumvent when crossing ethno-cultural demarcation lines, especially when this way was complicated by a biographical trajectory of the perfectly encultured stranger. Finally, Don Decker had successfully found a hybrid path of cultural translation and a marginal way of identity development, which, albeit of all its suffering, furnished a creative metamorphosis process. Now, as a student counsellor he was finally able to harvest the fruits of his "wild" metamorphosis process and to utilize them for the counselling and assistance of his Indian students in their hybrid life situations and life courses: "*I took all of that experience and attempted to mould it into something I could utilize out in Indian country.*" (p. 101).

But at the time of writing his autobiographical document (1997) Don Decker's biographical work is not very explicit yet. He has arrived at a biographical stage that is shaped by the personal virtue of modesty after "having chased rainbows". He can modestly assess that his "ambitions were validated finally" (p. 101). But, on the other hand, he doesn't comment very much about all the intellectual, emotional and moral difficulties of the persons involved in his life history and the shortcomings of significant others (as his adoptive parents and his teachers in Illinois, who had a lot of difficulties to understand situations and biographical processes of cultural marginality). He doesn't dwell on his own partial abandonment of his significant others (on the problem of his temporary lack of personal dependability and personal loyalty as well as on the possible features of temporary moral opportunism—two shortcomings, which seem to be almost unavoidable on a biographical course of cultural conversion). He doesn't comment on his perpetual lack of getting biographical counselling as well as on his vain desire and attempt to become somebody else. He doesn't reflect on his former attempt to erase his own biographical and cultural past. He doesn't reflect about his former non-acceptance of his cultural hybridity and marginality and about the psycho-social difficulties involved in this non-acceptance: At first he had the illusion to become an educated and music-cultured white American, and later on he might have had the equally unrealistic plan to become the essentially authentic or even the proverbial or "token" Apache who is protecting his traditional culture. He does not reflect about his attitude to aggrandize himself in the urban bohemian culture—by trying to be come a great pop musician. He does not reflect his addiction (conditioned by the hidden, but powerful trajectory of the perfectly encultured stranger) to do all possible sorts of networking and social relating, and to take detours that might not have been necessary at all. We do not learn from Don Decker's possible reflective insights into the above list of all these problems that seem to be essential and almost unavoidable in hybrid biographical processes, but somehow he must finally and sufficiently have mastered them in his life practice.

6 Systematic Life Constellations and Difficulties of the Two Dominant Biographical Process Structures in the Life Course of Don Decker—Metamorphosis of Creative Learning in Hybrid Life Situations and Trajectory of Self-Alienation

The two systematic life constellations in the life course of Don Denny / Decker are very much connected with dominant biographical process structures in his life history:

1. The systematic life constellation of social marginality and of the culture of poverty is connected with the permanent intersection of a personal trajectory of Don Denny and his grandparents of extreme poverty and social exclusion including experiences of stigmatization, on the one hand, and of a biographical metamorphosis of adventurous learning in the "prairie" situation and community situation of the reservation with its features of a culture of poverty.
2. The systematic life constellation of Don Decker's cultural hybridity while undergoing an identity change within the Anglo world is very much connected with the permanent intersection of the two biographical process structures of metamorphosis towards cultural hybridity and creativity, on the one hand, and of a trajectory of the perfectly encultured stranger and the concomitant self-alienation, on the other.

The two life constellations exert two ambivalent logics of a conduct of life ("Lebensführung" in the sense of Max Weber 1920) on the life course of Don Decker (and probably many others in comparable life situations). The systematic ambivalences of these two logics of conducting one's life are expressed in the permanent intersection of two different biographical process structures competing with each other. The two logics of the conduct of life of Don Denny / Decker and others in similar life situations are of a comparable quality of exerting a powerful influence on daily life orientations and on the overall life courses as Max Weber's logic of the conduct of life of Protestant ethics does on the biographical life orientations and on the practical everyday behaviour (Weber 1920). The comparability even applies to comparable *paradoxical outcomes* of these orientations: the fact that religious-ascetic ethics would cause unexpected moral difficulties of living in the daily framework of secular wealth and that the concept of total conversion and of the perfectly assimilated stranger would cause a life condition of permanent self-alienation in the everyday world of the target culture.

6.1 The Life Constellation and Biographical Difficulties of Social Marginality and the Culture of Poverty:

As a child Don Denny lived within the confines of an American Indian reservation with its typical features of cultural exclusion and social marginality, on the one hand, but of governmental protection and care, on the other, too. Life on the reservation territory was characterized by features of administrative and institutional processing which turned out to be quite benign in school, but it was marked by some elements of structural racism, especially in the field of school hygiene, too. In addition, most of the inhabitants of the reservation— including Don Denny's grandparents—had to fight against the discouraging and paralysing impact of the life condition of welfare support: One had to wait for the monthly pay cheque, that was always too small, and the shopkeeper of the local trading post would let himself get reimbursed first for the piled-up debts, before one could buy anything anew. Financial autonomy and careful bookkeeping were not possible under such conditions. There were periodic instances of collective alcoholism instead—including some heavy drinking periods of Don Denny's grandparents. Hence, life conditions on the reservation territory nurtured some mechanisms of collective trajectory. Collective trajectory (Schütze 1989) is a state of collective affairs in which the collective events of the affected we-community are conditioned by overwhelming outside powers and cannot be successfully shaped by agency of its individual and interacting members. In San Carlos some of the features of collective trajectory were: a life in permanent unemployment due to a long distance from the labour market and from advanced educational opportunities, a reduced quality of health due to the long distance to differentiated medical care institutions as well as the mutual envy, the lack of security and the habit of personal brutality in neighbourhood relationships. Being as individual more intensely and /or multifariously affected by these mechanisms of collective trajectory could also elicit severe individual trajectories (Riemann and Schütze 1991) that dramatically reduce the ability of individual trajectory incumbents to intentionally shape their life courses and everyday life situations; instead, they can only conditionally react to overwhelming outer forces invading their lives more or less unexpectedly. If Don Denny had stayed in San Carlos or Globe his potential for a creative biographical metamorphosis process in the course of academic education and/or in the course of an education and career as music performer would have been destroyed.

But, as the autobiographer shows clearly, life on the reservation territory also offered chances to practise a culture of poverty (Oscar Lewis 1961) with a lot of creative possibilities for sensible everyday activities, for keeping oneself not only alive, but even active and proud, for supporting the others and keeping solidarity, for having collective and private fun and for developing one's local culture. The classical picture of persons afflicted by permanent unemployment is as follows: They are immobilized or even paralysed in their everyday activities, they have lost their sense for time and daily order, and they are totally passive and depressed in their outlook towards their future life. The classical picture of the biographical impact of unemployment has been painted by Jahoda, Lazarsfeld and Zeisel (1933/1975) in their Marienthal study or in more recent biography analyses of life situations and life histories impacted by unemployment. But this classical picture of the impact of unemployment on life histories, on biographical outlooks on the future and on everyday life doesn't fit with the lives of Don Denny's grandfather and himself. Although often out of work or working in intervals as harvesting day labourers, Don Denny's grandfather lived an active and circumspect life, and Don Denny himself experienced lots of event constellations of fun and adventure, of meeting remarkably gifted, understanding and helpful characters and of creative learning and imaginative new horizons. This might be comparable with long-term unemployed people living in often de-industrialized areas of East Germany: Many of them cooperate with their neighbours and help them to build their houses, they circumspectly repair broken cars and other equipment, they earn some black money from some of these cooperative activities and function as very reliable members of their local communities.

One has to realize the complex mixture of biographical processes of trajectory and metamorphosis and their social preconditions within the life situation on the San Carlos Apache Reservation:
- The life situation of social marginality and cultural hybridity and of being culturally and economically underprivileged under the structural conditions of poverty and cultural exclusion implies two very different biographical process structures: that one of metamorphosis

(Schütze 1994, 2001) in the course of permanently crossing the ethno-cultural demarcation line back and forth and that one of a trajectory of being restricted in one's biographical development.
- One part of the precondition for the unfolding of personal metamorphosis processes is learning to become a practically rational and resourceful actor under the living condition of a culture of poverty.
- Another part of the precondition for the unfolding of personal metamorphosis processes is learning to make use of the "prairie"[17] conditions for adventurous activities and experiences in a methodical and witty way.
- A third part of the precondition for the unfolding of personal metamorphosis processes is absorbing the impulses from visitors from the outside world: let it be the forest fire fighters with their money and their search for entertainment, the archaeology students from Tucson or the chorus teacher from Illinois.
- The structural conditions of poverty and cultural exclusion regarding the life on the reservation territory foster a collective trajectory of exhaustion and social demoralization (Shibutani 2000: chapter XI) for many of its inhabitants. Two features of it are collective alcoholism and cultural disloyalty. (An example remembered by the autobiographer is: Apache children identify with the powerful white men when watching movies about the fights between American Indians and the US Cavalry.)
- The collective trajectory of exhaustion and of social demoralization can condition individual trajectories of self-alienation and of being barred in one's biographical development. For example, one can feel racial prejudices in Globe High School with its majority of Anglo students. The experience of not being able or even allowed to date "white" girls can built up a trajectory attitude of total social retreat. The experience of social exclusion and systematic exhaustion can build up an attitude that academic learning is totally senseless and cannot be successful.
- Every child on the reservation territory must learn two totally different ways of culture: Apache language vs. English language, American

---

17 The Chicago Sociologists used this term in order to characterize adventurous territories, where the children and adolescents could play and act without much control by parents and official controlling instances (like teachers, social workers, police officers).

Indian religiosity vs. Pentecostal Protestant religiosity, agrarian life of poverty vs. urban Bohemian life style, life style of American Indian school boys on reservations vs. US American mainstream school culture. Children are expected to learn the two ways and to develop their personal approach to cultural hybridity. But the personal searching process is very difficult for them, and it is often misguided by wrong concepts and trap situations. Finding a personal intercultural counsellor, who himself had biographical experiences of transgressing back and forth over the ethno-cultural demarcation line would be extremely helpful in terms of biographical work in a life situation of underprivileged hybridity. (Don Denny is permanently searching for native Indian role models and native biographical care takers who became professionals and accomplished the process of ethno-cultural transgression already.)

6.2 The Life Constellation and Biographical Difficulties of Cultural Hybridity:

Embarking on a life course of cultural marginality or hybridity essentially means to change the cultural contexts and to part from the significant others who belong to these contexts. In addition, it becomes necessary to engage in intensive social networking in order to survey the new social and cultural landscape of the target culture and to get accepted by the members of the target community. This can cause a tendency to *extremely focussing* on social networking that absorbs almost all energies of attention, experiencing and managing. Finally, in many cases of a hybrid life courses there is an initial or temporary tendency to convert to the new culture, which de-emphasizes the experiences of having absorbed two cultures and having an inner life exactly in the complex mental space in-between them.—In hybrid life courses—like the one of Don Decker—one can therefore observe the following phenomena:

- The person who moves from one cultural group to another must part from her or his familiar significant others. Since this is emotionally and mentally very difficult, the person transgressing cultural borders might be inclined not to do the work of saying a real farewell to them and—even more—not to do the additional work of systematically and steadily keeping the relationship with the old significant others. This tendency of "not looking back" might amount to a par-

tial and/or temporary personal disloyalty towards the old significant others.
- In order to fulfil the unfamiliar tasks of the complex new life situation, the person transgressing cultural borders develops the habit of not looking back. Instead, he or she is always focussed on her or his future states of personal life. It is possible to observe that she or he shies away from an attitude of self-criticism with regard to possible faults in her or his own life history. Such a willingness to take a critical look at oneself requires retrospection—and this is a personal habit unfamiliar to the traveller into unfamiliar cultural worlds.

For at least a longer while of enculturation, the trans-cultural traveller tends to narrowly or even extremely focus on her or his work of social relating and networking, which is naturally very important within the life situation of an immigrant. She or he attempts to become "more than identical" with the target culture. Such a person follows the concept of conversion from one culture to the other and undergoes a categorical change of the self-definition of identity. Conversion implies the attempt to erase the features of one's former biographical identity, although in fact the converting immigrant actually cannot escape from her or his former life history and her or his "natural history" of biographical identity unfolding. Being oriented by the conversion formula of self-understanding, such a person doesn't understand that in most cases it is unrealistic to expect to become an ideal personal incarnation of the target culture, since the previous life history has shaped one's identity differently—and, in addition, hindered the emergence of personal learning conditions for a perfect valence (Antonina Klowskowska 1996/2001) and agency in the target culture. She or he partially and temporarily doesn't understand that it would be more realistic for oneself to expect turning into a culturally marginal or hybrid personality (in the sense of Robert Park 1967) with all its experiences of cultural shortcomings and suffering through self-alienation (and possibly stigmatization, too) on the one hand, and of open, creative learning processes and of rich potentials for building new inter-cultural bridges, on the other.
- Overwhelmed by the new opportunities of networking and encountering members of the new culture, the cultural immigrant neglects the onerous work of learning and developing the mundane tasks of the new life situation and of doing the pertinent daily chores. Instead, he or she attempts to run the fast track and to become an out-

standing performer in the target culture by using subcultures and arena structures for presenting and positioning oneself in the forefront of the cultural stages of the target cultural community: in the case of Don Decker, these are the urban-bohemian subcultures and arena structures of pop and folk music and alternative art production of Anglo-America.

- But this attempt to position oneself within the centres of the cultural arenas and at the forefront of their stages is essentially connected with the growth of the trajectory potential of losing a realistic stance towards oneself and of realistically working on one's difficulties within the hybrid life situation. After a while, especially when the failure of the conversion strategy becomes obvious on the stages of cultural performing, the primary trajectory of the perfectly encultured stranger and the concomitant self-alienation becomes more and more "palpable" for the cultural immigrant. (Of course, for a longer while it is only "seen, but unnoticed" by him.) Due to narrowly focusing on networking and staging oneself, the cultural convert is also characterized by a lack of achievement in daily learning work. In the case of Don Decker this results in a secondary trajectory of serious difficulties of his educational career; he flunks out of two academic programs. After a while it becomes even harder to make a living: the double trajectory course gets more and more disastrous.

- At the very end, the cultural immigrant and convert finds her- or himself in the trap of a treadmill trajectory phase of daily routines and exhaustion connected with an "inner life situation", i.e. a mental and emotional state, of a closed biographical future after having destroyed any opportunity of educational and occupational career and after having arrived at the dead end of her or his former cultural arena presentations in the social worlds of culture, science, music or art where he expected to excel as a stage performer. This can be precipitated by serious accidents and dramatic health problems. Only now the cultural immigrant as hybrid personality realizes the detrimental impact of the primary trajectory of the perfectly encultured stranger and the concomitant self-alienation that was furnished by the wrong concept of cultural and biographical conversion. Only now he or she is able to try to escape from it. In the case of Don Decker this firstly means that the concept of cultural conversion was wrong. He now understands that his biographical chance is to accept his hybrid personality, of accepting both his indigenous cultural background and his acquired Anglo-cultural competences and outlooks and to make use of his very personal experiences of suffering and learning connected to the life course of transgressing the cultural borders. In addition, he finally understands that he has to overcome his addiction to cultural arenas and cultural staging opportunities. Therefore he sells his still partially unpaid car as technical means to do networking in the cultural arenas of rock and folk music and to remove himself geographically from the centres of the still luring cultural arenas. In addition, he realizes that his biographical way will be to become a builder of bridges between the Anglo and Apache culture by becoming a teacher or counsellor for Apache adolescents.

- After such a realistic situational analysis as part of one's biographical work the person crossing the cultural borders is also able to focus on working through his or her secondary trajectory of serious difficulties in her or his educational and occupational career and of organizing his or her daily life with its necessary daily chores. She or he gets able to do a realistic and modest analysis of how it would be possible to do first down-to-earth steps for the attempt to find out about the way back to learning and achievement situations and about catching one's own biographical thread again.
- The person transgressing cultural borders is now able to biographically "walk back" to her or his former culture and cultural community. Now she or he can realistically exhaust the high potential of her or his own bi-valent (Klowskowska 1996/2001: chapter 6) cultural creativity within the structural life situation of the culturally hybrid person. This means to work on one's own concrete biographical-experiential materials. Being such a hybrid personality would mean not to hide oneself under the shield of abstract collective categories of the culture of origin or the target culture, but to do creative work through the medium of one's own unique and down-to-the-earth personal experiences and capacities. In the case of an artist this means not to schematically use superficial or just ornamental symbols of the target and/or original culture in paintings and music performances, but to work with very personal experiential material—

basically biographical recollections. This is the mature state of the person crossing cultural borders or the cultural learner as hybrid personality: the willingness and ability to abandon the tendency of abstract categorization on the base of only very limited empirical experience. In the case of Don Decker's becoming an artist this implies quitting the habit of permanently symbolizing his art production with American Indian ornaments and to arrive at the personal modesty of being just a normal type of artist who reaches his audience through his own, very individual art production.

- The hybrid or marginal personality finds it difficult to develop competencies of the culture of origin and the target culture at the same time. Therefore she or he tends to submit to an attempt of total conversion in the first phase of living between two cultures. This tendency is extremely powerful during the time of being a learner of the target culture and of living in the social environment of the target-cultural community.

In later stages of the biography of a hybrid personality there might be the attempt to go "full circle" and return to one's culture of origin and to practice the latter with a new, very high level of competency. This can even be connected with a temporary or enduring attempt to become the spokesman, the protector, the translator, the developer of one's culture of origin. Such a role and the connected work and biographical development will be successful, as long it is not connected with fading out of one's awareness the history of one's journeying to the shores of the other culture "abroad" and that one has developed into a truly hybrid or marginal personality which is partially rooted in the "culture abroad". In the case of Don Decker we can witness his partial artistic roots in white and black American pop (rock and folk) music and culture as well as in the political culture of the student' movement. (Of course the traditions of indigenous and Mexican music are also obvious in his folk music endeavours.) And in addition: he also returned as an estranged home comer (in the sense of Alfred Schütz 1964b) with all the tendencies and capacities of abstract categorization, analysis and explanation: As we know, this can also include failures of assessment of the present state of the cultural we-community of origin. But, on the other hand, the homecoming hybrid personality is very competent to do liaison, translating, interpreting, counselling work in the course of helping other, especially adolescent, hybrid and marginal personalities to form their own life courses and to do their related biographical work. They can help members of their own culture of origin to come to terms with the surrounding and dominant foreign culture and to do the pertinent biographical work. Almost all adolescent Apache Indians of today are forced to become hybrid personalities belonging to the Indian and Anglo culture to a certain degree. On the base of his rich biographical experiences of crossing cultural borders Don Decker can productively counsel them on their biographical way.

Conclusions: Biographical Work in Culturally Hybrid Life Situations

The chapter up to now is a single case study in form of (a) a biography-analytical portrait of the life and the biographical identity development of Don Decker / Don Denny (sections 3 and 4). It catches the essential biographical process structures of his life and their social and institutional conditions; this has been done on the analytical base of a structural description[18] of the sequence of all narrative units of the written autobiographical document. In addition, the chapter above also is (b) an analytical abstraction of systematic life constellations and their intrinsic difficulties connected with basic biographical process structures of the life history of Don Decker / Don Denny; the latter have been delineated on the empirical base of the supra-segmental text markers of narrative units (section 6). All these sections were mainly dealing with the reconstruction of the single case of the life history of Don Decker ; they attempted to show its basic principles of biographical unfolding. However, the delineation of analytical features of the single case of a biographical development under the condition of cultural hybridity transcended its singularity quite often.—Now it is necessary to do a last step of comparison with other cases and types of cultural hybridity and to deal with specific basic theoretical features of biographical work under the condition of Don Decker's type of life situation of cultural hybridity: that one of an attempt to accomplish total biographical alternation or conversion (in the understanding of Berger and Luckmann 1966: 144–150).

---

18 I am alluding here to the general work steps of qualitative social research and biography analysis as I see them. For more explicit reading see Schütze 2005 and 2008: 25–76.

In all types of hybrid life situations and life histories, the task for doing biographical work is urgent. One of two reasons for this is, that the hybrid or marginal personality must take into account the experienced expectations and imagined obligations of the two quite different cultural groups or even cultural we-communities (with their own collective identity work). The other reason is, that the hybrid or marginal personality by necessity must experience situations of biographical estrangement, stigmatization, prejudice, seclusion and self-alienation.

Of course, there are various life situations of hybridity to be witnessed. First there is the hybrid life situation of the globalized, cosmopolitan multi-culturalism (partially conditioned by post-colonial intersections and mutual influences of the cultures of the colonial powers and of the newly independent nations); it is mostly studied by scholars of literary studies (like Homi Bhabha 1994). Secondly and thirdly there are two very different types of hybrid life situations and hybrid life histories conditioned by *minority group* social figurations. One social figuration between minority and majority is a political and administrative constellation where one of the two involved cultural traditions and cultural groups is in a peripheral or minority position within the overall state constellation, although at the same time it normally is in the majority position within at least large parts of the local geographical and political scene. In this social figuration between minority and majority, the hybrid life situation and hybrid life history are embedded within a *stable* collective bi- or multi-cultural we-community. The other social figuration of hybridity between majority and minority is the *chaotic*, unprotected life constellation of hybridity, in which the biographical achievement of a bi-culturally and bi-linguistically fully competent hybrid personality is something extraordinary and has to be personally fought for.

In the figuration between minority and majority group of a stable collective bi-cultural and bi-lingual we-community, both cultural and linguistic traditions are lively and powerful and must be respected by everybody, even if one of the cultural traditions and the respective cultural group is much stronger in terms of economic and political power and is backed by a wider-state power elite of the majority group. It is collectively and generally expected, that, to a certain degree, the majority and minority members of the two different cultural groups of the stable bi-cultural we-community respect and even learn the language and the culture of both respective cultural groups. In Europe, such stable collective bi-cultural and bi-linguistic we-communities in a peripheral or in a minority position are to be found in Wales, Catalonia or in Western Friesland, in North America in Quebec and in South America for example in Peru and Bolivia. As said already, it is characteristic for such a stable collective bi- or multi-cultural we-community with a social figuration of minority and majority group that the members of the peripheral or minority cultural group are locally in a majority situation. Nevertheless, it is "naturally" expected from them, that all of them have to be bi-cultural and bi-lingual, and factually everybody is. In addition, even the members of the state-wide *majority* cultural group within such a stable figuration of a peripheral bi-cultural we- community are some bit expected to learn the minority culture and language, and if they don't do, they have to face disadvantages in their occupational and social life. Regarding the processes of primary and secondary socialization within the social figuration between minority and majority group embedded in such a stable collective bi-cultural we-communitiy, it is clear that the ideal product of socialization is the bi-cultural or hybrid personality, who is at ease with the required cultural and linguistic bi-valence and has learnt it swiftly.

Surely even such an enculturation into a stable bi-lingualism and bi-culturalism within a social figuration of minority and majority group conditions lots of biographical problems and suffering: Minority children are expected to learn the language of the state majority just automatically what factually is not the case; adolescents and young adults of the minority group are expected to have the same robust collective self-esteem as the adolescents and young adults of the majority group have, what factually is not the case; and members of the minority group are expected to identify with, and to master, the language and the stock of background knowledge (Schütz 1962) of the majority cultural group with the same depth and ease as the members of the majority group do it themselves, what, again, factually is not the case. In reverse, the "immigrated" members of the state-majority group and those members of the minority group grown up in distance from the teaching institutions of the minority group culture and their centres of language practice are expected to learn the language and the culture of the minority group as a second language and a second culture. And of course, after having done this, their finally acquired competence in the minority language and minority culture mostly is not perfect. Hence, they are often strongly criticised by the keepers of the holy grail of impeccable, "full" (linguistic and cultural) competence of the minority cultural group. In addition, since their cultural and linguistic competence is not perfect, they are socially categorized as not "pure" in terms of minority culture. This is why they have lots of difficulties to follow up occupational career patterns in the public sector (that in at least some parts of political entities like Wales, Catalonia or Western Friesland requires full competence in the language and the culture of the minority group). The tragedy of these second language and culture learners is, that their linguistic and cultural competence is always seen and assessed as less competent than the competence of the "born-into members" of the minority cultural group.

In sum: the system of a stable bi-lingualism and bi-culturalism within a social figuration of minority and majority conditions considerable biographical suffering, although it is quite transparent and even "caring" for both cultural groups. On the other hand, the system sets the conditions for amazing transcultural creativity as, for example, hundreds of years of cultural productivity of Welsh poets, artists, musicians, scholars and liaison-work politicians have shown (Humphreys 2000). In its aspects of biographical suffering and, at the same time, of biographical creativity the system of the stable collective bi-cultural we-community with its figuration between minority group and majority group in Wales was circumspectly scrutinized in Bärbel Treichel's study "Identity Work, Language Biographies and Multilingualism. Autobiographical-narrative Interviews with Welsh People on the Linguistic Figuration of Identity and Society". But such a system of a stable bi-cultural we-community with its social figuration between minority and majority group *does not require a categorical biographical identity change or even a conversion* of the members of this bi-cultural we-community. The members of the bi-cultural we-community are not forced to personal conversion or alternation in order to acquire the competence of bi-culturalism and bi-lingualism appropriate in life situations of cultural hybridity.—This, however, is very different in the life history of Don Decker as we have seen. The system of a stable bi-cultural we-community with a social figuration between minority and majority naturally requires an enlargement of the mental layer of imprints of collective identity on the personal development of the members of the bi-cultural we-community. This is because the members of the bi-cultural we-community from both cultural traditions and cultural groups permanently have to deal with two different collective we-communities they feel loyal to.

The mental enlargement of one's biographical identity is quite often difficult. It conditions personal suffering, and it requires lots of biographical identity work. However, *it doens't require any type of clear-cut conversion of one's collective and biographical identity.*

The chaotic, unprotected collective life situation of hybridity that Don Denny / Decker had to live in on the territory of San Carlos Apache Reservation is totally different. In the Fifties and Sixties of the last century, family and institutional education on the territory of the Indian reservations and its surroundings provided, at least to a certain degree, double competence in the culture and language of both, the Indian tradition and of the wider Anglo culture and society (as far as it was needed for living within the collective situation of the "culture of poverty" in the understanding of Oscar Lewis 1961). But it neither led to a highly sophisticated competence of the culture and language of the Anglo we-group and society, nor to a sophisticated scrutinizing of one's own Indian culture and language[19]. The latter would have required, for example, the existence, the permanently ongoing research and the strong educational influence of an autonomous university system of the indigenous ethnocultural minority groups as it is to be witnessed in Wales.

At least in the 1950s and 60s, the life situation of an unsheltered cultural hybridity on the U.S. Indian reservations and in their surroundings required that a native adolescent, who—more or less dimly—searched for a fuller bi-

---

19 For many years starting at the end of the 19th century, the basic educational attitude of the US "Bureau of Indian Affairs" (BIA) was as follows: "to educate native children in separate boarding schools, with an emphasis on assimilation that prohibited them from using their indigenous languages, practices and cultures". (Quoted from the English language version of Wikipedia, article on "Bureau of Indian Affairs", section of „History".) See also Banks, Dennis (2004): Ojibwa Warrior: Dennis Banks and the Rise of the American Indian Movement. University of Oklahoma Press, Chapter 3, 24-31. Dennis Banks was a protagonist of the American Indian Movement. Banks describes the federal governmental policy of school education. The Wikipedia article is grounded on his writings.—The assimilation tendencies of the BIA school education partially held true even in the 1950s and 60s. The Home Page of the Bureau of Indian Education, as an offspring of the BIA, adds: „The Indian Reorganization Act 1934 introduced the teaching of Indian history and culture." But a basic reorganization of the orientation of the BIA regarding school teaching only started in the Seventies according to the quoted articles.—Don Denny only attended the BIA *elementary* school on the reservation territory. After that he enrolled into the mainly white Junior High School and High School in Globe. The autobiographer gives credit to the caring attitude of his teachers at the BIA elementary school. But their education basically was an introduction into the US *Anglo* culture only and not a careful bi-cultural school education. (The autobiographer doesn't tell about topics of Indian culture in school, although we know, that he was very interested in it: for example, he tells about his being intrigued by the excavation of ancient Indian cultures as done by the University of Arizona in the surrounding of his summer camp—p. 78).

cultural and bi-lingual competence would leave the territory of the reservation, would transgress the cultural borders between the indigenous and the Anglo cultural we-communities as a cultural emigrant/immigrant and would undergo a categorical change of personal identity, which normally take the dramatic biographical shape of ethno-cultural conversion or alternation (in the understanding of Berger and Luckmann 1966: 144–150). The latter process was normally connected with the basically wrong self-theoretical concept of the cultural immigrant as someone starting biographically anew (or with "clean slate").

Having undergone this categorical alternation and having learnt all the new competences in foreign cultural lands, the cross-cultural traveller might then feel—or was then expected to feel— to be forced to listen to an inner voice (that one of biographical identity requirements), which would morally request him to return to his we-community of origin and to use her or his newly required cultural competences "at home". However, going home and doing this, she or he found her- or himself as the culturally and socially *estranged* home comer (in the understanding of Alfred Schütz 1964b), who was not embedded within the culture of her or his native homeland any more, but was just a detached onlooker of it. This meant, on the one hand, to be a very sharp-sighted and analytical observer, who would be theoretically interested and critical in her or his assessment of the cultural situation and social behaviour of her or his we-community of origin. (An example for this one can find on the last page of Don Decker's manuscript: *"Arizona, in 1974, still appeared primitve to me"*—p. 101). On the other hand and concomitantly, she or he could also observe herself making lots of mistakes in categorizing and assessing the behaviour and the life situation of the home-based members of her or his old we-community, since she or he hadn't grown older together with people at home and, hence, missed the background knowledge of everyday experiences within her or his old cultural we-community. Therefore, in a certain sense, the home comer had to *re-learn* the culture (and probably, in addition, the more recently evolved aspects of the language) of his cultural we-community of origin. Such a re-learning could certainly manifest itself to be remarkably creative: especially through comparing and matching both cultures having been experienced so diversely and through translating them into each other back and forth. But at the same time the re-learning was connected with lots of disorienting suffering reaching deeply into one's biographical identity.

In addition, some of the persons crossing the ethno-cultural border between two cultural we-communities and undergoing an almost total alternation or conversion (in the understanding of Berger and Luckmann 1966) never returned to her or his old indigenous we-community.

Therefore, travellers within the strange lands of unsheltered, chaotic cultural hybridity must do a tremendous load of biographical work. Amongst them, the task of biographical work is even more demanding than amongst the persons living under the conditions of the two other general life situations of hybridity: that one of the globalized, cosmopolitan multi-culturalism and that one of the stable collective bi-cultural and bi-linguistic we-community.—At the very end I will just jot down a list of most conspicuous features of the first type of cultural hybridity, that one of unsheltered, chaotic cultural hybridity, about which we have learnt so much from the difficult biographical experiences of Don Decker. With some aspects of biographical work (as listed below) Don Decker started early to deal with, with others only after much delay and still with others never up to the end of writing his autobiographical manuscript in 1997 (although the respective biographical situations would urgently point to it):

- Realizing and reflecting the trajectory traps of self-alienation within the life situation of standstill and arrest of biographical development under the structural condition of a culture of poverty. This would be followed by searching for an escape action scheme, and the result of such biographical work would be the emigration into the world of the other cultural we-community experienced as more prestigious and powerful;
- Trying to live as a cultural immigrant in a structurally marginal or hybrid life situation and to exhaust its potential of bi-cultural creativity. On the one hand, this would be fostered by the stance of being totally open to the impulses of the target culture and to be willing to change oneself. On the other hand, however, exhausting this potential of bi-cultural creativity would be also fostered by the attitude of keeping the red thread of one's life history and biography that evolved from former life. Exhausting the potential of bi-cultural creativity is also supported by a circumspect control of the typical abstraction tendency so characteristic for the point of view of the stranger. Last but not least it is supported by understanding the importance of working with one's own concrete experiential material;

- On the one hand, the cultural immigrant embarks on reflections how to manage networking and social relating work in order to inhale and learn the specific features, routines and mores of the target culture. On the other hand, she or he should also control and—after a while—even reduce the extent of social networking, in order not to forget to do the "daily chores", i.e. the universal learning work in school, university and vocational training as well as the work to fulfil the expectations of the significant others in one's everyday social surrounding;
- Living under the life situation of "being abroad" as a cultural immigrant who feels the obligation to undergo a partial biographical conversion, but who, at the same time, understands the dangers of the powerful lure to undergo a total identity alteration, total adaptation to the target culture and total identification with it. i.e., she or he realizes, understands and works-through the problem of the "inauthenticity trap" of conversion. This basically means: Dealing with one's own biographical history, underlining its continuity, keeping the relationship with one's former life as well as fighting the tendency to fade out of one's awareness the former life course, its cultural roots and one's own "identity past". In the case of Don Decker this meant: at first remembering his past on the reservation, later on going back to it as a teacher and finally writing up his autobiography;
- Understanding and controlling the essential disloyalty tendency of hybrid life courses; thinking about systematic attempts to keep the relationship with former significant others (in the case of Don Decker, for example, keeping the relationship with his step-grandmother Poison Ivy and with his adoptive parents; both he partially neglects quite conspicuously);
- Working-through structural mistakes in one's past: the general attitude of cutting the red thread of one's former life and forgetting the former dangerous willingness to accept the biographical costs of this oblivion; fading out of one's memory especially the tendency to disloyalty towards former significant others; super-focusing on networking and social relating in the target culture and in its social worlds; neglecting the necessity of strenuous daily learning work (in school, etc.);

- Fighting the lure of the promises and of the attempts to become an ideal cultural performer within the target we-community or becoming the ideal protector of the we-community of origin and its culture; controlling the abstraction processes of collective categorization and stereotyping (regarding the cultural we-community of origin and regarding the target culture and society); instead working-through one's own individualized mundane and biographical experiences and utilizing them as one's authentic personal "dough" for creative production and modelling;
- Writing-up one's own autobiography as an especially intensive form of biographical work. It takes lots of time and gives the possibility of circumspect reflection. One could even say that writing up one's autobiography crystallizes into an action scheme of biographical work with enormous relevance for one's own biography.

All these steps of biographical work as seen in the autobiographical document of Don Decker belong to the following general processes of biographical work: (a) searching for one's overall features of life history, (b) getting help of significant others as biographical counsellors, but emancipating oneself from them, too, (c) doing networking and entering social worlds and their arena structures in order to get new cultural incentives and to develop one's potential for creativity and to engage socially and culturally, (d) reflecting on collective orientation frames (frames of reference and mental spaces) and collective identities and getting engaged with them, as well as (e) re-individualizing one's life course and fighting against all the distractions involved in doing networking and engaging in arena structures and collective obligations. (Treichel 2004, Schütze 2008: 66–71; Schütze and Schröder-Wildhagen 2012). From Don Decker's autobiographical account we can receive lots of new insigths into the tremendously difficult biographical work in life situations of cultural hybridity. On the other hand, we can also learn from Don Decker's autobiographical manuscript, that a life course of cultural hybridity offers many new creative beginnings.

References

BERGER, PETER & LUCKMANN, THOMAS (1966). *The Social Construction of Reality. A Treatise in the Sociology of Knowledge*. Garden City, New York: Doubleday.

BHABHA, HOMI K. (1994/ 2004). *The Location of Culture*. Milton Park: Routledge.

GARFINKEL, H. (1967). "Passing and the Achievement of Sex Status in an Intersexed Person, part 1 and Appendix to Chapter 5". In: *Studies in Ethnomethodology*. Englewood Cliffs: Prentice Hall, pp. 116–185, 285–288.

HUMPHREYS, EMYR (2000). *The Taliesin Tradition*. Bridgend, U.K.: Seren.

JAHODA, MARIE, LAZARFSFELD, PAUL & ZEISEL, HANS (1933/1975). *Die Arbeitslosen von Marienthal. Ein soziographischer Versuch*. Frankfurt: Suhrkamp.

KLEIST, HEINRICH VON (1810/11 / 1962). "Über das Marionettentheater". In: *Sämtliche Werke*, ed. by PAUL STAPF. Berlin, Darmstadt, Wien: Deutsche Buch-Gemeinschaft, pp. 1088–1094. English Translation: *On Marionette Theatre*. Translated by Idris Parry. In: southerncrossreview.org/9/Kleist.htm. In addition, to be found in Google under the search-word cluster: "Kleist Marionettentheater English Translation".

KLOSKOWSKA, ANTONINA (1996/2001). *National Cultures at the Grass-Root Level*. Budapest: Central European University Press; original Polish language edition: Warszawa 1996.

LEWIS, OSCAR (1961). *The Children of Sánches. Autobiography of a Mexican Family*. New York: Random House.

MEAD, GEORGE HERBERT (1934). *Mind, Self and Society. From the standpoint of a social behaviorist*. Chicago: Chicago University Press.

MILLER, HERBERT ADOLF & PARK, ROBERT EZRA (1921/1969). *Old World Traits Transplanted*. New York: Henry Holt 1921 / London: Harper & Brothers Publishers 1969 (ursprünglicher Hauptautor: William I. Thomas).

MORITZ, KARL PHILLIP (1785–1790 / 1952). *Anton Reiser. Ein psychologischer Roman*. Berlin: Rütten und Loening.

MYRDAL, GUNNAR (1944). *An American Dilemma: The Negro Problem and Modern Democracy*. New York: Harper & Brothers.

OBAMA, BARACK (2004). *Dream from My Father. A Story of Race and Inheritance*. New York: Three Rivers Press.

PARK, ROBERT EZRA (1967). *On Social Control and Collective Behavior. Selected Papers*. Edited and with an Introduction by RALPH H. TURNER. Chicago and London: Phoenix Books.

PLESSNER, HELMUTH (1928/1975). *Die Stufen.des Organischen und der Mensch. Einleitung in die philosophische Anthropologie*. 3rd unchanged edtion. Berlin and New York: Walter de Gruyter.

POPE, LISTON (1942/1965). *Millhands and Preachers. A Study of Gastonia*. New Haven: Yale University Press.

RIEMANN, GERHARD & SCHÜTZE, FRITZ (1991). "'Trajectory' as a Basic Theoretical Concept for Analyzing Suffering and Disorderly Social Processes". In: MAINES, DAVID R. (Ed.) (1991). *Social Organization and Social Process. Essays In Honor of Anselm Strauss*. Hawthorne, N.Y.: Aldine de Gruyter, pp. 333–357.

SHAW, CLIFFORD (1930/1966). *The Jack-Roller. A Delinquent Boys Own Story*. Chicago and London: The University of Chicago Press.
SCHÜTZ, ALFRED (1962). "On Multiple Realities". In: *Collected Papers, Vol. I: The Problem of Social Reality*. The Hague: Martinus Nijhoff, pp. 207–259
SCHÜTZ, ALFRED (1964a). "The Stranger: An Essay in Social Psychology". In: SCHÜTZ, ALFRED (Ed.). *Collected Papers , Vol. II: Studies in Social Theory*. The Hague: Martinus Nijhoff, pp. 91–105.
SCHÜTZ, ALFRED (1964b). "The Homecomer". In: SCHÜTZ, ALFRED (Ed.). *Collected Papers , Vol. II: Studies in Social Theory*. The Hague: Martinus Nijhoff, pp. 106–119.
SCHÜTZE, FRITZ (1989). "Kollektive Verlaufskurve oder kollektiver Wandlungsprozeß. Dimensionen des Vergleichs von Kriegserfahrungen amerikanischer und deutscher Soldaten im zweiten Weltkrieg". In: *Bios* 2, pp. 31–111.
SCHÜTZE, FRITZ (1992). "Pressure and Guilt: War Experiences of a Young German Soldier and their Biographical Implications. Part 1 and 2". In: *International Sociology* 7, No. 2 and 3, pp. 187–208, 347–367.
SCHÜTZE, FRITZ (1994). "Das Paradoxe in Felix' Leben als Ausdruck eines 'wilden' Wandlungsprozesses". In: KOLLER, HANS-CHRISTOPH & KOKEMOHR, RAINER (Eds.). *Biographie als Text*. Weinheim: Deutscher Studien Verlag, pp.13–60.
SCHÜTZE, FRITZ (2001). "Ein biographieanalytischer Beitrag zum Verständnis von kreativen Veränderungprozessen". In: ROLAND BURKHOLZ, CHRISTEL GÄRTNER & FERDINAND ZEHENTREITER (Eds.). *Materialität des Geistes. Zur Sache Kultur – im Diskurs mit Ulrich Oevermann*. Weilerswist: Velbrück Wissenschaft, pp. 137–162.
SCHÜTZE, FRITZ (2002). "Das Konzept der sozialen Welt im symbolischen Interaktionismus und die Wissensorganisation in modernen Komplexgesellschaften". In: KEIM, INKEN & SCHÜTTE, WILFRIED (Eds.). *Soziale Welten und kommunikative Stile*. Tübingen: Narr, pp. 57–83.
SCHÜTZE, FRITZ, (2005). "Eine sehr persönlich generalisierte Sicht auf qualitative Forschung". In: *Zeitschrift für qualitative Bildungs-, Beratungs- und Sozialforschung. ZBBS* 6, Heft 2, pp. 211–248.
SCHÜTZE, FRITZ (2008). "Biography Analysis on the Empirical Base of Autobiographical Narratives: How to Analyze Autobiographical Narrative Interviews—Part one and two". In: *European Studies on Inequalities and Social Cohesion* No. 1/2, pp. 153–242 and No. 3/4, pp. 5–77.
SCHÜTZE, FRITZ & SCHRÖDER-WILDHAGEN, ANJA (2012). "European Mental Space and its Biographical Relevance". In: ROBERT MILLER (Ed.). *The Evolution of European Identities: Biographical Approaches*. London: Palgrave .
SHIBUTANI, TAMOTSU (2000). *Social Processes. An Inroduction to Sociology*. Lincoln, Nebrasca: iUniverse.com, Inc.
STONEQUIST, EVERETT V. (1937/1961). *The Marginal Man. A Study in Personality and Culture Conflict*. New York: Russell & Russel.
STÖTZEL, ANGELIKA (1998). *Dramatisches Spiel als biographische Arbeit: Interaktionsanalytische Studien über Rollen- und Phantasiespiele von Kindern in Frauenhäusern und zu den Potentialen der sie begleitenden pädagogischen Praxis*. Unveröffentlichte Dissertation. Otto-von-Guericke-Universität Magdeburg, FGSE.

STRAUSS, ANSELM L. (1993). *Continual Permutations of Action*. New York: Aldine – de Gruyter, especially pp. 215–219.

THOMAS, RONALD STUART (1997). *Autobiographies*. Translated from the Welsh With an introduction and notes by Jason Walford Davies. London: Phoenix Paperbacks.

THOMAS, WILLIAM, I. & ZNANIECKI, FLORIAN (1918/1927). *The Polish Peasant in Europe and America*, 2nd edition. New York

TREICHEL, BÄRBEL (2004). *Identitätsarbeit, Sprachbiographien und Mehrsprachigkeit. Autobiographisch-narrative Interviews mit Walisern zur sprachlichen Figuration von Identität und Gesellschaft* ["Identity Work, Language Biographies and Multilingualism. Autobiographical-Narrative Interviews with Welsh People on the Linguistic Figuration of Identity and Society"]. Frankfurt a.M.: Peter Lang.

TURNER, VICTOR (1964). "Betwixt and Between: The Liminal Period in Rites de Passage". In: *The Proceedings of the American Ethnological Society. Symposium on New Approaches to the Study of Religion*. University of Washington Press, pp. 4–20.

WANIEK, KATARZYNA (2006). *The Biographies and Identities of the Young Polish Immigrants in Germany after 1989*. Unpublished doctoral dissertation. Otto-von-Guericke-Universität Magdeburg.

WEBER, MAX (1920). "Die protestantische Ethik und der Geist des Kapitalismus". In: *Weber, Max. Gesammelte Aufsätze zur Religionssoziologie*, Vol. I, pp. 17–206.